Phoenix
The Decline and Rebirth of the Indian People

William E. Coffer
(Koi Hosh)

VAN NOSTRAND REINHOLD COMPANY
NEW YORK   CINCINNATI   ATLANTA   DALLAS   SAN FRANCISCO
LONDON   TORONTO   MELBOURNE

To

Judy
(*Nishkin Yukpa*)

Van Nostrand Reinhold Company Regional Offices:
New York Cincinnati Atlanta Dallas San Francisco

Van Nostrand Reinhold Company International Offices:
London Toronto Melbourne

Copyright © 1979 by Litton Educational Publishing, Inc.

Library of Congress Catalog Card Number: 79–4139
ISBN: 0–442–26131–4

Manufactured in the United States of America

Published by Van Nostrand Reinhold Company
135 West 50th Street, New York, N.Y. 10020

Published simultaneously in Canada by Van Nostrand Reinhold Ltd.

15 14 13 12 11 10 9 8 7 6 5 4 3 2 1

Library of Congress Cataloging in Publication Data

Coffer, William E.
  Phoenix: the decline and rebirth of the Indian people.

  Bibliography: p. 229
  Includes index.
  1. Indians of North America—History. 2. Indians of North America—Government relations.
I. Title.
E77.C68   970′.004′97   79–4139
ISBN 0–442–26131–4

Introduction

Once we were happy in our own country and we were seldom hungry for then the two-leggeds and the four-leggeds lived together like relatives, and there was plenty for them and for us. But the Wasichus (White men) came. . . .

Black Elk, Oglala Holy Man

And so it was when the first European "discovered" America. The Indian people were leading happy and contented lives within societies which had evolved over untold centuries. The Indian lifestyle was uncomplicated, yet completely functional. European invaders, with their aggressive, highly individualistic way of life, found the natives to be perfect specimens for their exploitation.

What happened when these two cultures met occurred because of their diametric philosophies of life and its values. The story is not a pleasant one, nor is it one which has been told in its entirety. Most historic manuscripts dealing with Indian/white relations have been written by the scribes of the conquering society in an effort to glorify the activities of their cultural group. Since there was little that was glorious in the treatment of the Indians, it became necessary to alter the accounts in some manner.

Historic facts had to be ignored or else presented in an incomplete form. As a consequence, most of our history texts tend to be historic novels presenting a one-sided view of what transpired.

When the Europeans arrived in this hemisphere, they found a civilization more varied than that in Europe. Throughout the Americas, Indians had developed a rich diversity of living styles, social structures, and government patterns. They had created hunting, fishing, and agricultural skills that enabled them to adapt to, and survive in, climates of extreme variety. More than 300 languages were spoken among the 1,000,000 people living in the area which is now the United States. Ignoring, denigrating, misrepresenting, and falsifying information concerning these people have been the weapons of conquest. Simplification of the complex Indian cultures provided and perpetuated the ignorant savage and barbarian stereotype. Attitudes toward the Indians were molded by the chroniclers until the general public felt no remorse or guilt over their fate, for they viewed them as little more than animals of the forest.

A few historians have attempted to present valid and accurate accounts of the chronology of Indian history. Angie Debo wrote *A History of the Indians of the United States* and other books which present an accurate, unbiased version. Edward Spicer, Virgil Vogel, John Collier, and D'Arcy McNickle have contributed to the dissemination of true history. Their publications, however, are not utilized traditionally by the academicians in the American educational system. Current textbook material, although somewhat improved in recent years, still falls far short of presenting accurate historic detail concerning the native people and their struggle for survival.

The intention of this author is to develop a personalized historic manuscript written in conversational language to assist in clarifying what happened when these divergent cultures met and confrontations developed. It is hoped that the reader will not feel overwhelmed by a heavy academic atmosphere, but instead will feel as if we are seated before an open campfire exchanging ideas.

William E. Coffer
(Koi Hosh)

Contents

One
The First Americans

Who are the American Indians? Where did they originate? How long have they been in the Western Hemisphere? These and other questions invariably are posed when an in-depth study of the native peoples of America is attempted.

Many theories have been presented as to the origin of the Indian, but since no one has discovered an acceptable, conclusive key to the mystery, the genesis remains speculative. Some reputable academicians postulate that people have inhabited North America for at least 100,000 years.[1] Their theories are strengthened by the discoveries of Dr. Louis Leakey, the famed African anthropologist, who dated archeological discoveries at Calico, California at from 75,000 to 100,000 years old. Needless to say, Dr. Leakey's position has caused controversy in the archeological community, for the oldest acceptable date used by most experts in the field is 20,000 to 35,000 years ago.

Another theory concerning the origin of the Indians which at best could be termed controversial is the Mormon story.[2] The Church of Jesus Christ of Latter-Day Saints (Mormon) promotes a story of refugees from Jerusalem coming to the shores of America about 600 B.C. and establishing a great civilization. Led by two brothers, Nephi and Laman, the membership began to factionalize and eventually became so diverse that the two groups became enemies. Civil war erupted, and the followers of Laman—the rebellious brother—wiped out the Nephites, the disciples of Nephi, the brother who had followed the proper spiritual guidance. According to the Book of Mormon, the Lamanites ruled the land and became a wicked and evil people. Cursed by God with a dark skin, they reverted to a primitive and savage society. They were called a "dark and loathsome" race but were given a promise of redemption: if they would renounce their evil ways and turn back to God, they would become "white and delightsome."

According to Mormon philosophy, the Indians of North, Central, and South America, along with the natives of the islands in the Pacific Ocean, are descendants of this cursed people and are called Lamanites, an extremely derogatory designation.

Other theories of the origin of the Indians are propounded by various groups. Most historical accounts at least allow credence to the Viking visitations in the New World around A.D. 1000 and their habitation of the areas of Greenland and Newfoundland. Most, however, do not allude to the inland treks of the Norsemen. These stalwart adventurers not only explored the Great Lakes area, but according to at least a few knowledgeable writers, were even present in Tennessee.[3] While the Norse were not involved in the genesis of Indians as a race of people, they could have had a profound effect on the physical appearance of many.

The Chinese also visited this hemisphere about A.D. 458, and they, too, could have changed the appearance of many western Indians.[4]

The oral tradition of the Indian people of most tribes indicates a recognition of how Indians happen to be in this particular portion of the world. Some of the origin stories have been recorded for posterity and they present interesting alternatives. Perhaps the best known is the Walum Olum, the detailed account of the Creation by the Delaware (Lenape) Nation.[5]

The Navajo people (Dine) have an extremely complex account of their beginning. It deals with the emergence from under the earth of strange masked spirits which prepared the world for the Navajos. When the Navajos finally came to the surface, they settled in their

present-day location.[6] Most tribal groups have similar stories of their origins.

In an article written by John Lear, a close similarity is noted in some of the Yuchi Indians' ceremonies and the Biblical account of the Hebrew Feast of the Booths (Leviticus, Chapter 23). This, according to Lear, would indicate the possibility of a common ancestry.[7] While Mr. Lear's theory does present an interesting analogy, he does not carry it as far as he should to make the story truly credible, especially since similar ceremonies and social activities exist among the Jicarilla Apaches and other tribes.

Attempts to correlate some of the ancient civilizations in the New World to those of Egypt, Mesopotamia, and other Middle East

cultures have been made for many years. One of the most persistent stories of this nature indicates that the American Indians are remnants of the "Lost Tribes of Israel." The Mexican writer, Miguel Covarrubias, hints at such a correlation in his description of the Olmec civilization of Mexico.[8]

There is a myriad of manuscripts which allude to the origin of the Indian or the mixture of the natives with visitors from Europe, Asia, Africa, or even outer space. Some publications go further and claim the beginning of man in the Western Hemisphere was a spontaneous evolution.[9] Who actually knows? They may all be partially correct or may all be totally wrong. Perhaps some day we may know the secret.

In the meantime, many controversies exist in the academic world concerning the origin of the Indian people and how long they have been in this part of the world. Actual dating of artifacts and documentaries of archeological discoveries restricts most of our evidence to 20,000 B.C. and later. Many finds have been made which pre-date this, but these can not be as conclusively proven. Therefore, here we shall only discuss the history of the American aboriginal inhabitants during the last 25,000 years.

Although there is much evidence to defend theories of earlier man and culture in this area, we will begin our history with the Llano culture from the Great Plains. The Llano was first called the "Clovis" after the original site near Clovis, New Mexico, but after other finds of the same general cultural make-up in diverse geographic areas were discovered, especially in the central portion of our country, the name was changed to Llano, a Spanish word meaning Plains.

This is not a well-defined culture, as are some later ones, but rather a group of people living in a large geographic area utilizing similar implements for hunting and subsisting on the same game animals. The similarities of game and climate over the wide area probably contributed more to establishing a general culture than did any social organization or interaction between groups. The great herd animals—mammoth, tapir, horse, and bison—that once roamed vast portions of the present-day United States provided meat for the families of early explorers. Bones with unique fluted projectile points imbedded in them have been found in many locations. These points are generally referred to as Clovis points and are

recognized by the groove on the side to provide for more thorough bleeding of the victim. It is generally accepted that many of the kills took place as these animals were bogged down in the swamps that were so plentiful during this period.

These early people were quite nomadic in their existence, following the animals as they moved from place to place. Particular water holes were favorite hunting grounds, as evidenced by the number of bones found there, indicating a certain schedule or pattern to their hunting.

As time passed, the game and hunting implements changed. Bows and arrows appeared, and the atlatl was invented to give greater killing power to the spear. In essence, this was an extension of the thrower's arm that increased the arc when the spear was hurled as well as increasing the speed and distance of the projectile. The mammoth began to disappear, and during the latter portion of this era, the bison became the dominant big-game animal hunted.

This animal was much larger than our present-day bison and must have presented an awesome sight to the early Indians. To even the odds a little in the hunt, the hunters initiated a new method of killing: trapping numbers of the animals in box canyons or gulches where they could not escape. The atlatl and the bow and arrow gave a small group of hunters the firepower to slay enough big game to supply their families with sufficient food.

As time moved on, the Llano culture gave way to a more refined one, the Folsom, which introduced a better type of point with better fluting. The point was so named because the original discovery was made near Folsom, New Mexico, and it is identified by its deeper and wider fluting, which allowed more profuse bleeding of the animal, thus hastening the kill. Mass kills by stampeding animals over cliffs apparently were introduced during this period and this practice continued through the centuries, up to the 1800's.

Climatic changes began to affect the hunting habits of the Indians as they entered the Plano culture era. The elephant and giant bison disappeared and were replaced by animals more similar to those found today. Grasslands took the place of swamps, and grazing animals dominated the landscape. Food gathering became more important to the people as new plants appeared; utensils for gathering and preparing vegetable foodstuffs were developed. Thus, 8,000 to

9,000 years ago, more sophisticated cultures came into existence. In the western part of the country, people began to use caves or rock shelters for more permanent homes. They used twine baskets and bark or grass beds, and made netting, matting, fur cloth, and sandals. They developed the atlatl, made small intricate projectile points, and utilized milling stones, scrapers, choppers, and digging sticks. For the first time in America, people started using sea-shell ornaments, rattles, medicine bags, and bird-bone whistles. This indicates there was enough time not needed for bare survival to begin the development of hobbies and entertainment. Some of the cultures more familiar to us began to evolve and become recognizable 7,000 or 8,000 years ago. We can by no means include all of these in our discussion, but some of these cultures which form a direct foundation to our current Indian tribes will be investigated.

The first cultural development we will examine is the Cochise culture of the Southwest, named after the famous Apache leader who lived in this part of southeast Arizona. This group of paleo-inhabitants of the desert developed into an identifiable unit about 7,000 years ago. They emphasized the use of vegetable foods growing wild in their area. During the tenure of this group, maize, the vegetable we call corn, was introduced from Mexico and became a staple item in the diets of the Cochise people, although they still depended to a large extent on hunting and gathering.

One of the contributions the Cochise made to their descendants was a basic form of horticulture. Toward the end of the Cochise culture, new crops began to appear in the area, and beans and squash supplemented the maize and gathering. These plants helped establish an agriculture-based society, typified by the Hohokam who later lived in this arid land. Metates and manos (grinding stones), scrapers, choppers, and mauls were fashioned from stone and made very utilitarian. These implements provided lasting evidence which we can view today. Bone tools were also used during this time, and some of them have been found in caves and other sheltered places.

The evolution of the Cochise and the origin of the later cultures took place over a period of many years. There was no sudden termination of one and immediate beginning of another. For this reason, it is virtually impossible to establish an accurate genesis for the succeeding groups.

About 300 B.C., the Mogollan culture (so named because the people lived along the Mogollon Rim in Arizona and New Mexico) became established as a separate identity from the declining Cochise. It remained identifiable for some 1,700 years, becoming extinct about A.D. 1400. Specific housing styles became evident during thi. period, as the Mogollan developed single-family pit houses architecture. No systematic village plan can be identified, however; houses were scattered along the summits of ridges, their placement conforming to no particular pattern. The villages were usually located adjacent to fields and evidently were continuously inhabited. Housing in the later Mogollan period began to be built above ground from masonry and to take on the appearance of Anasazi or Pueblo housing. Some of these "apartments" housed an entire village and contained as many as 800 or 900 rooms.

One development which sets the Mogollan apart from the Cochise is pottery. The earliest Mogollan pottery that has been found is of fine quality, which would indicate that they didn't develop pottery themselves, but learned the art, probably from Mexico. The earliest pottery was not colored, but in later work, ornate coloring and design are identifiable trademarks. The making of human and animal figurines from clay became popular, too, and the ground stone artifacts that are plentiful in the region indicate another popular form of art. Weaving was used in the manufacture of sandals, feather ornaments, girdles and belts, robes, nets, bags, and many other items.

One of the most interesting facts about the Mogollan is that after A.D. 500, their culture did not change drastically except to take on more and more characteristics of the Anasazi, whose peaceful invasion deteriorated the Mogollan as a separate cultural entity until about A.D. 1400, when they became Anasazi for all practical purposes. Remnants of the Mogollan moved eastward and can be identified today in the Zuni people. Their culture is not at all the original Mogollan, but is more the Anasazi as adopted by the Mogollan.

Another great culture which evolved from the Cochise was the Hohokam. When the Spanish first visited this area of the West, they were amazed at the artifacts they found. When they asked the local Pima Indians who had lived there and done the fine work in stone and pottery, the Pimas replied "Hohokam," meaning "those who are gone'' or ''the ancient ones.'' At first, the Hohokam was quite similar to the Mogollan, but as time passed more divergence developed, and the Hohokam became quite a well-developed society.

Both groups began pottery making about the same way and at generally the same time, but the Hohokam style differed from that of the Mogollan. In house types, there was a distinct difference, as the Hohokam built not pit-houses but houses within pits. The Hohokam houses became much larger as time passed, and before the end of their era, some were so huge they may have been used as meeting houses for the tribe.

The most impressive accomplishment of the Hohokam was the development of their extensive irrigation system. Canals branching from the Salt and the Gila Rivers watered the desert and made it bloom. Some of the major canals were over 30 miles long and extremely wide. One of these, found at Pueblo Grande in Phoenix, is 6 feet deep and 30 feet across. These feats of engineering are remarkable, for the canals were dug by hand with flat stone hoes or digging sticks, and skins or baskets were used to haul away the dirt. There were no transits or levels, no sophisticated engineering techniques or modern machinery, and yet twentieth century technology cannot improve on these ditches except to concrete the sides and bottom to prevent erosion. The pitch and grade were calculated only with the naked eye, by dead reckoning by the natives, and the canals are as accurately constructed as anything today's engineering could produce. The land irrigated by these people was farmed to as optimal a level as it is today. Crops such as maize and cotton were grown with excellent success. Cloth was woven from the cotton fibers and colored designs were worked into the cloth. Grain was grown so efficiently that storage bins were built to hold the surplus.

The construction of ball courts and stepped pyramids illustrates their architectural prowess and also hints at Mexican influences on their culture. Other Mexican items made were stone plates, pyrite mirrors, rings and bracelets, copper bells, and ornaments made from sea shells obtained in trade. The Hohokam developed a system of etching in shell using a mild acid made from the juice of cactus. Inlaying designs in this etching became a specialty, and the Hohokam far surpassed their European counterparts in this art. Their use of ground stone tools, paint palettes, and elaborate pottery indicates a strong artistic nature. Because cremation was the primary funerary arrangement, little is known about their physical characteristics.

By about A.D. 1100, the Anasazi (a Navajo word meaning the Ancient Ones) influence was beginning to be felt strongly in the Hohokam culture. It is displayed especially in the housing styles of this period. Multi-room dwellings, some extremely large, began to appear. Casa Grande, located near Collidge, Arizona, is a prime example of this style of architecture. Here, typical Hohokam houses were used alongside the large, typically Pueblo, four-storied apartment. The peaceful invasion by the Anasazi eliminated the Hohokam as a separate culture by about A.D. 1450 and little is known about them thereafter.

It is generally agreed that the present-day Papago and Pima Indians living in the same area are the remnants of the Hohokam people. Legends in both tribes tell of a migration because of too many new people moving into their country years ago. The tribe wandered south around the Gulf of California, into the central part of Mexico, and eventually back to their homeland. This migration could account for the blank space in their history between approximately A.D. 1450 and the time the white man arrived in the Southwest and began recording their history.

The Anasazi, the last of the Southwestern cultures we will look at, developed later than the Mogollan and the Hohokam, but it soon covered a very large area and acquired great richness. Located generally in the Four Corners area, with centers such as Mesa Verde, Aztec, and Chaco Canyon, the Anasazi is one ancient culture which can be positively linked to some of today's Indian tribes. The Pueblo Indians of New Mexico and Arizona are descendants of the Anasazi, and much of their culture directly corresponds to that of the Anasazi.

The first Anasazi housing—apartments with hundreds of rooms—does not resemble any other found in the United States. Their corn was not the same type grown by other Southwestern groups, but was the broad-dent type generally associated with the Southeastern portion of the country. Their early pottery was also different from that of their contemporaries, being much more ornate and flamboyant in design, resembling Southeastern or Mississippian pottery. Anasazi ornamentation was exquisite. Cooking and other household utensils were refined, the making of clothing evolved, and farming was developed. Turkeys and dogs were domesticated, and ceremonies were introduced to insure crop fertility, bring rain, and ward off storms and crop damage. The culture grew and expanded, and it was a time of plenty. Then disaster struck.

In 1276, the rain didn't come. The crops dried up in the fields, and there was no harvest. This caused some concern but no great dismay, for there had been dry years before. However, the next year was no better. Nor was the year after. Year after year passed and there was no rain. People starved and entire cities were abandoned as the inhabitants sought areas where they could raise their crops and feed their families. Food became extremely scarce and fighting broke out between groups as the quest for food became critical. It was about this time that a new peril appeared in Anasaziland. The Navajo and Apache moved in from the North and their raids made life even more trying. Mesa Verde was abandoned; then Aztec, Chaco Canyon, Wapatki, Walnut Canyon, and other places. Thousands of people died from starvation, and the refugees were no longer a large group. The few survivors resettled in the Rio Grande Valley and at Acoma. The descendants of the Anasazi still live at Acoma and at San Juan, Zia, Taos, Isleta, and the other modern Pueblo villages.[10]

Our discussion has been primarily restricted to the Great Plains and the Southwest. This is by no means intended to suggest that similar activity was not happening in other parts of the land. From the Arctic to Tierra del Fuego, Indian cultures were in the same general state of evolution. It would present too large a task to cover all of this progress in one volume of history, so we will limit our discussion to only a few selected groups in what is now the United States.

The evolution of cultures in the eastern portion of the country very closely paralleled that in the plains and the West. By about 2000 B.C., the Woodland stage, located in the eastern forested areas, made its appearance with several cultural distinctions: single-family housing began to appear as a patterned construction; refuse pits were used; firepits were built; flexed burials were the mode of disposal of the dead; and ground stone tools appeared. Pottery was used, but it was not developed to a great degree until later. This cultural group continued on its evolutionary movement and flowered from about 1000 B.C. to around A.D. 900, the Burial Mound Period. These Burial Mound groups were centered in the Ohio-Kentucky areas, but encompassed most of the area from the Mississippi to the Atlantic Coastal Plain and from the Great Lakes to the Gulf of Mexico. The Adena and Hopewell cultures (named for towns near archeological centers) were examples of this style of life and they existed for centuries. The two cultures differed to some extent, and so archeologists use separate classifications, but since we are not analyzing cultures to that degree, it is sufficient for us to combine them in one grouping, Adena-Hopewell.

From A.D. 500 to 900, this culture had evolved into a sophisticated society and many refinements are noted. Round, bark-covered houses were built, villages with geometric earthen walls appeared, and large conical burial mounds were constructed. Some of these mounds were quite large, with heights of from 10 to 70 feet. Pottery was developed for utilitarian as well as special uses. Many wild foods were gathered and stored, and animals of all kinds were hunted for food and skins. They used copper and shells in making ornaments and made effigy pipes of stone. The Adena-Hopewell developed high sociopolitical activity under a rather rigid system. This is evident because of the organization of labor which must have been necessary to build the huge burial mounds found in their area. Organized food gathering and hunting is also inferred, since a stable food supply for the large population centers of the city-states had to have been provided. We know, too, that these people participated in trade with regions all over the United States, as many foreign objects and materials from widely diverse geographic areas are found in their artifacts. This well-developed societal pattern set the stage for their successors, who, in turn, established the basis for the tribal units of Indians we recognize in historic times.

Before we can move to the contemporary Indian tribes, however, there are a few other cultures in the chain of evolution which should be considered. Some of these are still shrouded in mystery and only more time and examination will uncover the facts which remain buried.

One of these mysterious groups is the Effigy Mound culture of the upper Mississippi River Valley. Although it resembles the Adena-Hopewell culture in some ways, many facets of its structure are not known. No descendants have been found which can definitely be assigned to this group, and the time period of its existence is not known. The one thing that sets it apart from other cultures of its time is the presence of unique animal effigy mounds, in the forms of panthers, birds, bison, geese, bears, turtles, and lizards. No one knows the reason for the selection of these animals or the purpose of the mounds. The size of some of them is startling, though, when modes of construction are considered. Imagine the excavation of enough dirt by hand tools and human labor to construct an effigy of a bird with a wingspan of 624 feet. One panther is 575 feet long, and although most of the mounds are smaller, many are 100 feet or more in length or wingspread. This was an amazing feat for this comparatively primitive society to accomplish.

At this particular time, most of the cultural developments which had been evolving so rapidly began to slow down or stop. No one knows just what precipitated this phenomenon; perhaps the natives merely became contented with what they had. At any rate, a sort of stagnation process set in. However, this was not true of the Mississippi River Valley and the area drained by the river's major tributaries, where a culture developed which was one of the most impressive of the pre-Columbian era: the Temple Mound.

Archeologists are mystified by many facets of this Temple Mound culture and the origin presents a very controversial issue. Many theories abound, but concensus cannot be obtained for any of them. The size and number of the ruins, and the expense which would be incurred in extensive excavation and study of any of them, helps keep the Temple Mound an enigma.

The time accorded to the evolution of this extremely sophisticated people is as controversial as the culture's other attributes. Generally, the development is thought to have originated in the southeastern segment of the Mississippi (or Mound) culture in what is called the Caddo (eastern Texas) area around A.D. 500 to 600 and to have lasted in an evolutionary stage until about A.D. 1700. Although great technological innovations were introduced, the culture appeared to have had as its primary thrust the expansion of the ceremonial aspect of social life. The Indians were organized into cities which contained rectangular temple mounds built in a pyramid style. Many of these were constructed in tiers, as though they were added to several times to raise them to greater heights. The main cities were surrounded by smaller towns located in clusters throughout the territory. Each city had one or more of the temple mounds in a plaza, as well as temples, palaces, and housing for the ordinary citizenry. The temples and the houses of the leaders were built on top of the pyramids, which were sometimes huge. One, in Cahokia, Illinois, covered an area of 16 acres, was 1,080 feet in length, 710 feet wide, and 100 feet tall. The temples were enlarged versions of the domestic houses, and they were made of timbers, lath and plaster, and with a gabled roof. They were much like the temples located in Mexico and Central America.

The Temple Mound people were highly agricultural and supplemented their crops with hunting and gathering. Maize (corn), of course, was the principle domestic crop. Pottery of excellent quality was made and was utilitarian, durable, and ornamental—perhaps the best pottery found east of the Pueblos. Decorating pottery by painting was developed to a high degree by these people. They also made beautiful ornaments, especially funerary offerings, from copper. Burials were varied, and in addition to the mound burials, village cemetaries, private under-the-floor burials, and cremation were used. Bodies were placed in the grave in various positions. They were flexed, semiflexed, or extended, and were sometimes even buried in groups. Usually only the temple burials were accompanied by elaborate offerings of pottery, tools, and ornaments.

Since the discussion of the Mississippi culture includes an extensive geographic area, as well as a time element of about 1,000 years, comments in this chapter are intended only as an introduction to the study of this culture.[11] Any statement made about the Temple Mound people is subject to controversy, and the material presented here reflects the knowledge, opinions, and experience of the author. Combined with the previously noted limitations in the study of the Mississippians, this portion of the text could initiate extensive discussions.

In addition to the cultural developments discussed in this chapter, many others—far too numerous to attempt to itemize—added their part to the ever-widening jigsaw puzzle development which occurred in this hemisphere prior to the arrival of the permanent European settlers. No attempt has been made to include the extensive contributions to the evolution by the magnificent civilizations of Mexico, Central America, and South America. Their development in areas such as science, agriculture, politics, and social procedures are interwoven with the groups discussed here, along with countless others, in establishing the Indian cultures which greeted the non-Indian invaders after 1492.

Grand Canyon.

Grand Canyon.

Ruins of Tusayan at Grand Canyon. Early Hopi Village.

Kiva (Ceremonial House) at Tusayn.

Wapatki Ruins near Flagstaff, Arizona—4 stories high and over 100 rooms.

Kiva at Wapatki Ruins.

Ball Court at Wapotki similar to ones found in Hohokam areas in Mexico.

Walnut Canyon National Monument near Flagstaff, Arizona. Houses are built under ledges.

Walnut Canyon Housing.

Montezuma's Castle south of Flagstaff in the Verde River Area.

Montezuma's Castle.

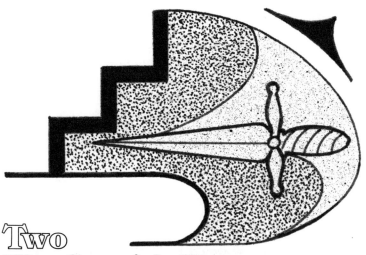

Two
The Spanish Rape
of the New World

The three major powers in Europe during the sixteenth century were Spain, France, and England. They each cast a greedy eye on the vast uncharted lands to the west, each with different desires and, as we see later, each using different tactics to attain these goals.

England needed land to establish colonies and expand her empire. The colonization and herding of the colonies under her protective wing established a pattern which was followed until well into the twentieth century, when these far-flung outposts throughout the world began to finally gain their independence. Of course, England was interested in the material wealth of the colonies as well, but the acquisition of the land itself was the driving force behind the expansion. Whatever methods necessary to bring the natives under this Imperial protection were used with little regard to the natives' lives or interests.

France was not as concerned with the land itself as with the products of the area. In most of the New World where French explorers traveled, it was the fur trade which seemed to attract them. Throughout the Canadian, Great Lakes, and western territories, the Frenchmen made their presence known. Unlike the English, these trappers did not attempt to change the Indian way of life. There was

21

no move to acculturate the natives. In fact, just the reverse was true. The Frenchmen moved into the Indian communities, married Indian women, and conformed to the Indian cultural mores. Because of their willingness to change to Indian lifestyles, the French generally were better liked than other Europeans. This reverse acculturation played a large part in the presence of fair-skinned natives found especially in the Great Lakes and Mississippi River Valley regions.

Since the Spanish were the "discoverers" of the New World, they had a slight jump on their Northern European counterparts. Their primary interest in this new land was to extract as much of the wealth as possible and ship it back to Spain. This was to be accomplished in the most expedient manner, and if it required killing the natives, so be it. Preferably, the Indians would be "Christianized" and kept alive to provide the labor force to work the mines and extract the wealth. If this was not possible, they were mercilessly put to death. Zealous churchmen were kept extremely busy attempting to baptise and rename the "Indios" before the military disposed of them. This cruel treatment, along with the introduction of new and deadly diseases, eventually exterminated large portions of the population of the Indies and reduced the mainland population drastically.

After Columbus returned to Spain in 1493, the Spanish crown was eager to claim all the New World in order to exclude the Portuguese and obtain what riches there were. Consequently, Columbus was sent back with seventeen ships and a large contingent of troops, artisans, nobles, and even five priests. No women were aboard and this caused problems later when the Spaniards insisted on the company of Indian women.

On his arrival, Columbus found that all the men he had left on his first visit had been killed. Their harsh treatment of the Indians and the taking of Indian women had brought about their demise.

The second group treated the natives the same way, and because of the greater number of Spanish, matters became even worse. The animosity of the Indians was increased with the introduction of syphillis, from which about a fourth of Columbus' men were suffering.

In all, Columbus made four trips to the New World and literally converted the Caribbean Sea into a Spanish lake. For about the first twenty years of the sixteenth century, the Spanish involvement was primarily in the islands of that body of water. Then, on February 10, 1519, a Spanish soldier named Hernan Cortez set sail from Cuba to lead an expedition to Mexico. It was at this point that the Indians of Mexico were started on the road to complete subjugation by the white invaders.

After establishing a beachhead and founding the city of Vera Cruz, Cortez began the actual conquest of Mexico. Accounts of this march to Tenochtitlan have been written in many books, and two such writings represent the extremes in descriptive accounts of this invasion. One, written by Bernal Diaz, a member of Cortez' army, glorifies the Spanish conquest and vilifies the defenders.[12] The other, a translation from the Aztec, provides a different perspective and indicates that the Spaniards did not all wear "white hats."[13] One of the most controversial accounts describes the massacre at Cholula. Diaz claims the Cholulan people were killed and their temple and idols destroyed because of their treachery and heathen human sacrifices. He does not go into great detail and passes it off as a minor incident in the march to Tenochtitlan. He even warns his readers to beware of the false report of great cruelties as described by the Bishop of Chiapas, Fray Bartolome de las Casas, who claimed the Spanish soldiers punished the Cholulans for no reason at all, or just to amuse themselves.[14]

Since the "benevolence" accorded the Indians by the Conquistadores is well known, it is likely that the good Father's story is valid. At least it corresponds with the account related by the Aztecs. They tell of the genocide perpetrated by the white strangers on several groups as they approached Cholula. They also relate what occurred when the Spanish and their Tlaxcalan allies arrived and then describe the actual slaughter:

When they arrived, the Tlaxcaltecas and the men of Cholula called to each other and shouted greetings. An assembly was held in the courtyard of the god, but when they had all gathered together, the entrances were closed, so that there was no way of escaping.

Then the sudden slaughter began: Knife strokes, and sword strokes, and death. The people of Cholula had not foreseen it, had not suspected it. They faced the Spaniards without weapons, without their swords or their shields. The cause of the slaughter was treachery. They died blindly, without knowing why, because of the lies of the Tlaxcaltecas.

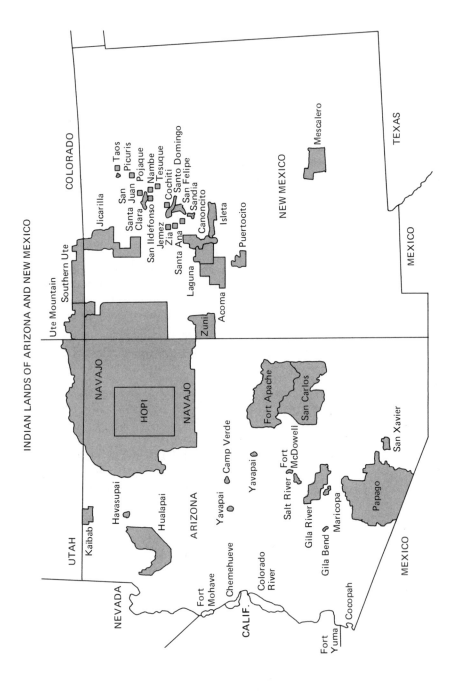

INDIAN LANDS OF ARIZONA AND NEW MEXICO

And when this had taken place, word of it was brought to Motecuhzoma. The messengers came and departed, journeying back and forth between Tenochtitlan and Cholula. The common people were terrified by the news; they could do nothing but tremble with fright. It was as if the earth trembled beneath them, or as if the world were spinning before their eyes, as it spins in a fit of vertigo.

When the massacre at Cholula was complete, the strangers set out again toward the City of Mexico.[15]

Other descriptions of events which took place during the attack and occupation of Tenochtitlan by the Spaniards are filled with gory and merciless killings. These occurred sometimes for retaliation, and sometimes for no apparent reason. One such story is of the surprise attack on a group of dancers during the fiesta of Toxcatl:

At this moment in the fiesta, when the dance was loveliest and when song was linked to song, the Spaniards were seized with an urge to kill the celebrants. They all ran forward, armed as if for battle. They closed the entrances and passageways, all the gates of the patio: The Eagle Gate in the lesser palace, the Gate of the Canestalk and the Gate of the Serpent of Mirrors. They posted guards so that no one could escape, and then rushed into the Sacred Patio to slaughter the celebrants. They came on foot, carrying their swords and their wooden or metal shields.

They ran among the dancers, forcing their way to the place where the drums were played. They attacked the man who was drumming and cut off his arms. Then they cut off his head, and it rolled across the floor.

They attacked all the celebrants, stabbing them, spearing them, striking them with their swords. They attacked some of them from behind, and these fell instantly to the ground with their entrails hanging out. Others they beheaded: They cut off their heads, or split their heads to pieces.

They struck others in the shoulders, and their arms were torn from their bodies. They wounded some in the thigh and some in the calf. They slashed others in the abdomen, and their entrails all spilled to the ground. Some attempted to run away, but their intestines dragged as they ran; they seemed to tangle their feet in their own entrails. No matter how they tried to save themselves, they could find no escape.

Some attempted to force their way out, but the Spaniards murdered them at the gates. Others climbed the walls, but they could not save themselves. Those who ran into the communal houses were safe there for a while; so were those who lay down among the victims and pretended to be dead. But if they stood up again, the Spaniards saw them and killed them.

The blood of the warriors flowed like water and gathered into pools. The pools widened, and the stench of blood and entrails filled the air. The Spaniards ran into the communal houses to kill those who were hiding. They ran everywhere and searched everywhere; they invaded every room, hunting and killing.[16]

According to the Aztec account, the siege of Tenochtitlan lasted eighty days, and the loss of native lives was tremendous. Of the more than 200,000 of the warriors from Tezcoco who were allied with the Spanish, about 30,000 died. More than 240,000 of the Aztec defenders lost their lives in the futile effort. Practically all of the Aztec nobility died, with only a few lords and knights and little children surviving. This siege and conquest of what was called the City of Mexico is one of the bloodiest accounts in world history. Perhaps the figures of the Aztecs are not correct, but it was an horrendous carnage by any calculation.

After the massacre at Mexico City, Cortez and the Conquistadores continued their march of conquest until all of Mexico, at least for practical purposes, was under Spanish rule. The pattern established by Cortez of enslavement of the natives and raping of the land continued throughout the Spanish period.

In 1529, Cortez returned to Spain with samples of life in the New World to show to Charles I. He took Indians, gold, silver, animals and plants, and specimens of Mexican handicrafts. He was accorded much honor by the Spanish royalty and was granted absolute control over a large area of Mexico, which assured him immense wealth. He returned to Mexico, but he was too restless to remain idle very long.

The lands of the Pacific with their unconquered natives called to him, so he organized four expeditions to the area. One of these he commanded himself, and while on the voyage, discovered the coast of California. This restless life kept him occupied for a while, but finally he returned to Spain, where he died in 1547 at the age of sixty-two.

Cortez was not the only Spaniard who was engaged in exploration during this time. Others were busy investigating different parts of this new hemisphere to ascertain the riches it might hold. Panfilo de Narvaez began the exploration of Florida but did not have the luck of Cortez. He and most of his men were killed by fever and Indians before very extensive explorations could be accomplished. Four survivors of this group, led by Alva Nunez Cabeza de Vaca (Head of a Cow), made an unbelievable eight-year journey across Texas and eventually to Mexico City. Their experiences stirred the curiosity and greed of the Spanish enough for them to form the famous Coronado expedition, of which more is discussed later.

In 1539, Hernando de Soto landed in Florida and led his men on a tour of rape, pillage, and murder across the southeastern part of what is now the United States. He, like Cortez, very quickly established his pattern of dealing with the Indians he met. When he arrived at a town, usually welcomed by the natives who didn't know the fate which awaited them, he would seize their stored food and anything else of value, demand carriers and women, and force their leaders to serve as guides to the next village. He used this same "modus operandi" throughout Creek country. One of his stops was at Cufitachiqui (Cusseta) on the Savannah River, where a woman chief dressed in all her finery came out to meet De Soto and welcomed him to her village.[17] The Spaniards were accorded the usual Indian hospitality and responded in their usual brutal manner. They kidnaped the "queen" and forced her to lead them to other villages. She led them into Cherokee country and acted as their guide for seven days. She then disappeared along with her attendant and the pearls she had with her, and no account discloses information indicating she was ever seen again.

De Soto turned south again, and, following his practice of raping the villages as he came to them, finally arrived at Choctaw country, where he encountered his first real resistance.[18] He was welcomed by one of the Choctaws, Tuskaloosa, who was an important leader over many towns. De Soto demanded the usual carriers and women, and Tuskaloosa promised to gather them and turn them over to him at Mabila (for which the city of Mobile, Alabama is named). Now, Tuskaloosa did not become a powerful leader by being stupid, so he gathered his warriors and presented *them* to De Soto. The Spanish discovered that these Choctaws, and later the Chickasaws, were no easy match when they became angered. The invaders were nearly annihilated in the battle that followed. Finally, they rallied their forces, and, through superior weaponry, defeated the Choctaws. They fired the town, trapping the Indians inside, and most of them were burned or killed as they attempted to escape the holocaust. De Soto was forced to remain in the area for a month to bury his dead and give the wounded time to heal. There are no other accounts of his trying the Choctaws; he evidently learned his lesson at Mabila.

When his troops were sufficiently recovered, De Soto moved northwest to Chickasaw country, where he spent the winter. He was received warmly and everything was peaceful until spring arrived and De Soto prepared to continue his explorations. Evidently, he did not realize the Choctaw and Chickasaw were closely related peoples, for he made his usual demands for carriers and women. The Chickasaw became angry and attacked, killing most of De Soto's horses and eleven of his soldiers. As soon as he could, De Soto headed northwest, for he wanted no more to do with the fighting Chickasaw or Choctaw people.

In the spring of 1541, De Soto and his men crossed the Mississippi River and marched into northern Arkansas. They continued their harsh treatment of the Indians; this time the Quapaws drew their fire. The invaders found it fairly easy to capture the scattered villages of this tribe and they collected a large number of men and women. The Spaniards probably came close to Oklahoma in their travels, and, unknown to them, were only about 300 miles from Coronado's group, which was concurrently moving eastward through Indian lands.

De Soto spent an unhappy, unprosperous winter in Arkansas, and in the spring he gave up and set out for home. He followed the Arkansas River to the Mississippi, where he became very ill. His men had evidently forgotten how independent the Choctaw and Chickasaw were, for when they sent word across the river to the tribes, demanding carriers and provisions for the "Child of the Sun," the chief sent word back that the "Child of the Sun" should be able to dry up the river and walk across. De Soto was too weak by this time to attempt punishment for such disrespect, so he took his frustration out on a small group of friendly Arkansas Indians. The surprise attack was so sudden and fierce that no resistance was possible. Many were killed, but many more were wounded and allowed to escape to strike fear into the hearts of others.

This was De Soto's last brutal treatment of the Indians, for soon after that, he died. He was secretly buried by his men so his body would not be found, and the natives were told he ascended to the sun. This ruse failed to properly impress the Indians and they constantly harassed De Soto's men until 1543, when the Spaniards gave up and sailed down the Mississippi. They finally reached the Gulf of Mexico and sailed to Vera Cruz, ending this expedition of terror.

Concurrent with De Soto's rampage through the southeastern part of the country, other Spanish activity was taking place which would drastically affect the lives of American Indian people. As indicated earlier, Cabeza de Vaca spent eight years wandering across the vast uncharted areas of the Southwest. The stories he told in Mexico City, real or imaginary, stirred the curiosity and greed of the Spaniards and triggered one of the most famous of all the exploratory campaigns in early American history: the Coronado expedition.

Because of the enormity of the task, it took three years of planning and political maneuvering before the exploration could begin. The expedition was placed under the command of Francisco Vasquez de Coronado. Before he started with the main body of the expedition, Coronado sent a reconnaissance party out under the direction of Fray Marcos de Niza, a Franciscan. The padre had been in the New World for a number of years and had had much contact with the native people of Guatemala and Peru. He should have been well-versed in dealing with any Indians encountered on his journey northward.

The reconnaissance party was guided by the only member of de Vaca's group remaining in America, a giant Negro slave called Estevanico. He was quite a character, and his antics were viewed as somewhat irrational by the very stilted Spanish of the time. He was always preceded by a group of "domesticated" Indians, one of whom carried his rattle trimmed with feathers and little bells. His "servants" were treated as slaves, and Estevanico passed himself off as some sort of a deity. The natives he encountered along the way were understandably impressed, for they had never seen a black man and the pomp and ceremony of his cortege kept many in awe. Estevanico's job was to guide the de Niza group and go ahead to establish routes and friendly relationships. As they progressed farther north, he began sending accounts of approaching the fabulous "Golden Cities of Cibola" which the natives were supposedly telling him about.

Eventually, the Indian servants reached Hawikuh, the westernmost pueblo of the Zunis. This was one of the fabled "Cities of Cibola," but instead of being gold, as the Spanish thought it would be, it was merely stone and adobe. When the runners presented the head man of Hawikuh with the fancy rattle and demands for preparation for greeting the giant Negro, the chief became angry and was not at all impressed. Perhaps the bells reminded him of the bells of the slave traders who had preceded this group. More likely, word had reached him of Estevanico's arrogance and insatiable appetite for the women of previously occupied villages.[19] Whatever the cause, when Estevanico came swaggering in, he was attacked and killed by the Zunis. The legends of the Zuni people still speak of the death of the "Black Mexican with chili lips." Evidently, Estevanico liked the southwestern chili about as well as he liked the women, and the excessive consuming of the extremely spicy vegetable will literally burn the lips and make them swell.[20] "Chili Lips" was quite a character and is the subject of several interesting books.

When Estevanico was killed, his Indian companions were terrified and hastily retreated to the main caravan and Fray de Niza. There they told of the problems encountered at Hawikuh and of the death of Estevanico. History is not clear as to what was reported or what Fray Marcos thought of their report, but when he returned to Mexico City, he told of finding a huge settlement with riches greater than in any land yet discovered by the Spanish. Naturally, this whetted the appetites of the gold-hungry Spaniards, and Coronado rushed to prepare his expedition for its journey to this new land.

Fray Marcos evidently was caught up in the fever he created by his descriptions of Cibola, for his stories got wilder each time he told them. Bishop Zumarraga, writing to a friend in Spain, said: "There are partridges and cows which the father says he saw, and he heard stories of camels and dromedaries and of other cities larger than this one of Mexico." Another priest, in a letter to a friend in Burgos, wrote: "The people the friar saw in Cibola wore shoes and buskings of leather and many wear silk clothing down to their feet. Of the richness of this country I do not write you because it is said to be so great that it does not seem possible. The friar himself told me this, that he saw a temple of their idols the walls of which, inside and outside, were covered with precious stones; I think he said they were emeralds. They say that in the country beyond there are camels and elephants."[21]

The good padre intimated to all who would listen that he had found the road to Cathay. The thought of a route to India and the

Hopi corn field. Hopies have farmed this way for untold centuries.

Enchanted Mesa—sacred ground to the Zuni Indians in New Mexico.

Laguna Pueblo in New Mexico.

riches of the Orient spurred the Spaniards to even more dedicated preparation for their campaign.

Finally, in February 1540, Coronado was ready to explore this new land and gain the riches of the "Seven Cities of Cibola" for Spain. He left Compestela with 200 horsemen, 100 foot soldiers, 1,000 Indian carriers, and 1,000 extra horses. Besides huge supplies of food and other provisions borne by Indian porters, the natives drove large herds of cattle, sheep, and swine.

After seventy-seven days of miserable travel over extremely rugged terrain, with adverse weather and shortages of food and water, the vanguard finally reached its destination. But instead of the Golden Cities of Cibola, Coronado and his group found the crude mud and stone huts of the Zuni village of Hawikuh. About 200 of these houses lay before the Spaniards, and the Zunis were prepared to defend them. Coronado ordered an attack; there was a fierce battle, and the Spanish took the town. Coronado was seriously injured in the fight and remained in the pueblo for about two months, recovering his strength.

Father Marcos returned to Mexico followed by the curses of Coronado's men. Completely humiliated by his own actions, he suffered a paralyzing stroke and soon died in obscurity.

Coronado continued his exploration and exploitation of the Southwest for two more years. During this time, he sent expeditions to scattered areas in search of riches which would put him in better standing with the crowned heads of Spain. Since his entire excursion had been rather costly and there seemed to be nothing to add to the credit side of the ledger, he was getting desperate. These side trips were no more profitable than the main journey, but they did provide contact with some new country and new groups of Indians.

One trip, headed by Cardenas, one of Coronado's lieutenants, was into the land of the Hopi, where the Spaniards became the first white men to view the Grand Canyon of the Colorado River. Coronado had also heard of a great river to the east—the Rio Grande—and he decided to investigate it, too. He sent a detail of about twenty Spaniards, under Hernando de Alvarado, to explore this area and contact the Pueblo people. Coronado decided to winter in this beautiful area, and while there, he heard stories of the great plains to the east and their huge herds of buffalo. Expeditions into that country bore out the stories: the shaggy animals were so plentiful, they could only be compared to the fish in the sea.

Following the Indian guides, who tantalized Coronado with stories of gold deposits, the Spaniards traveled as far as central Kansas before they gave up and started the long trek back to Mexico. The had traversed a tremendous portion of the Southwest and had discovered new lands and new people. They had not, however, found the thing that had initiated the expedition: gold.

In their sojourn, the Spaniards left behind them a legacy of pillage, torture, murder, and destruction. Thousands of natives were tortured and killed as the Spaniards tried to force from them information of nonexisting gold mines. Many more lost their lives trying to protect their homes. What little material possessions they had were confiscated by the bearded invaders. Entire villages were depopulated and burned, some never to be rebuilt. Whole groups were exterminated, sometimes with but a few escapees moving in with neighboring tribes. The entire ethnologic make-up of the Southwest was changed by the ruthless Spaniards. So cruel and heartless were their atrocities that the Spanish government, which was not noted for its benevolence in the treatment of Indians, prosecuted Coronado and Cardenas for their inhumane activities. Coronado was acquitted for his part of the cruelty, but Cardenas was fined and sentenced to a year of rigorous army service. Since the army was his vocation, that part of the sentence was actually no punishment, for he would have served the time anyway.

The Spanish not only made contact with the Indian people by land expeditions, but also by sea. On June 27, 1542, Juan Rodriguez Cabrillo sailed from Mexico and made his way north to the shores of California. He put in at several harbors and established peaceful relations with the Indians. They exchanged gifts and were on most friendly terms, since the Spanish were not interested in initiating colonies at this time. Cabrillo's party traveled as far north as the Rogue River in Oregon before returning to Mexico.

When Spain received the disappointing reports from the three exploratory groups, the leaders decided the establishment of colonies, or expansion of ones already established, was just too much trouble at this particular time. Thus, Spanish colonization was fairly dormant until the end of the sixteenth century.

From 1581 to 1595, the Spanish frontier pressed northward from Mexico. Explorers and missionaries harassed the Indians, leaving trails of blood across the great Southwest. The Indians attempted to defend their homeland with crude weaponry which proved no match for the armor and firearms of the invaders. The natives either fled, were killed, were taken as slaves, or were subdued and used as chattel servants by the Spanish aristocracy. Seldom were other alternatives available to the Indians.

Finally, in 1595, the Spanish governor placed Juan Oñate in charge and instructed him to begin serious colonization efforts. Oñate, with his nephew, Vincente de Zaldivar, as second in command, finally got started in 1598. They left Chihuahua with 130 soldier-colonists and their families, a band of Franciscans, a large group of Negro and Indian slaves, 7,000 head of cattle, and 83 wagons. They traveled north into Pueblo country, where, for the most part, they found no Indians. Having heard the Spanish were coming, most of the Pueblo people moved into the hills until the invaders were gone. The vivid memory of some of the Coronado expedition's escapades still burned in the minds of the Indians after nearly fifty years.

Oñate set up his headquarters at San Juan Pueblo and continued the same pattern of conversion and exploitation his predecessors had established. Angie Debo gives a very clear description of this in her book, *A History of the Indians of the United States.*[22]

In October 1598, Oñate extracted an oath of allegiance to the crown of Spain from the head men of Acoma. He accepted their "gifts" and took his party of officials to the Zuni and Hopi to allow these tribes the honor of becoming vassals to the Spanish Empire. About six weeks later, Juan de Zaldivar, with a party of approximately thirty men, arrived at Acoma and demanded food and supplies. At first, the Acoma natives were friendly and attempted to supply the Spaniards' desires. On December 4, however, something happened to anger the Indians and they attacked the intruders. Most of the Spaniards were killed, including Zaldivar, and only a few escaped to carry the news to Oñate.

When accounts of the battle reached him in San Juan, Oñate was infuriated. He organized an avenging party of seventy of his best fighters and sent them to Acoma to wage war without quarter. He assigned Vincente de Zaldivar, Juan's brother, as the leader of the group, thus assuring that severe restitution would be meted out to the Acomans.

Vincente reached his destination on January 21, 1599, and set out to avenge his brother's death. The battle lasted for three days, with severe losses on both sides. Between 600 and 800 Indians were killed; 70 or 80 men were taken captive, along with about 500 women and children. Zaldivar marched these prisoners to Santo Domingo Pueblo, where Oñate presided over a hearing to ascertain the seriousness of the Indians' crimes and assign appropriate punishment. After hearing testimony from both sides, according to Spanish chroniclers, he pronounced the following sentence:

In the criminal case between the royal court and the Indians of the pueblo and fortress of Acoma, represented by Captain Alonso Gomez Montesinos, their defender, accused of having wantonly killed don Juan de Zaldivar Oñate, Maese de Campo general of this expedition, and Captains Felipe de Escalante and Diego Nuñez, eight soldiers, and two servants, and of other crimes; and in addition to this, after Vincente de Zaldivar Mendoza, my sargento mayor, whom I sent for this purpose in my place, had repeatedly called upon them to accept peace, not only did they refuse to do so, but actually received him with hostility. Wherefore, taking into account the merits of the case and the guilt resulting therefrom, I must and do sentence all of the Indian men and women from the said pueblo under arrest as follows:

The males who are over twenty-five years of age I sentence to have one foot cut off and to twenty years of personal servitude.

The males between the ages of twelve and twenty-five I sentence likewise to twenty years of personal servitude.

The women over twelve years of age I sentence likewise to twenty years of personal servitude.

Two Indians from the province of Moqui (Hopi) who were present at the pueblo of Acoma and who fought and were apprehended, I sentence to have the right hand cut off and to be set free in order that they may convey to their land the news of this punishment.

All of the children under twelve years of age I declare free and innocent of the grave offense for which I punish their parents. And because of my duty to aid, support, and protect both the boys and girls under twelve years of age, I place the girls under the care of the father commissary, Fray Alonso Martinez, in order that he, as a Christian and qualified person, may distribute them in the kingdom or elsewhere in monasteries or other places where he thinks that they may attain the knowledge of God and the salvation of their souls.

The boys under twelve years of age I entrust to Vincente de Zaldivar Mendoza, my sargento mayor, in order that they may attain the same goal.

The old men and women, disabled in the war, I order freed and entrusted to the Indians of the Province of Querechos that they may support them and may not allow them to leave their pueblos.

I order that all the Indian men and women who have been sentenced to personal servitude shall be distributed among my captains and soldiers in the manner which I will prescribe and who may hold and keep them as their slaves for the said term of twenty years and no more.

This being a definite and final sentence, I so decree and order, Don Juan de Oñate.

Murder and cruelty were the methods most of the Spaniards used to extract payment from the Indians throughout the Southwest. In 1609, Oñate was replaced as governor by Pedro de Peralta, who was ordered to find a better site for the capital. In 1610, he founded Santa Fe. He built the ornate governor's palace, the Church of San Miguel, and other beautiful buildings. Many of these examples of architecture of this period still stand, at least in part, for tourists to view today. Oñate and Zaldivar, when they were recalled to Spain, were tried and convicted for their barbarous acts toward the Indians. However, the convictions and sentences were a farce, reminiscent of the trials of Coronado and Alvarado. Their type of oppression continued until 1680, when the Pueblo people finally had enough and revolted.

By the time of the Pueblo Revolt of 1680, the Spanish and Indian population along the Rio Grande made this one of the most heavily populated areas in the western New World. Edward Spicer, in his *Cycles of Conquest,* estimates the Spanish population at 2,350 and the Indian at between 25,000 and 30,000.[23] Most of the Spaniards lived in Santa Fe, but there were some living in groups both north and south of the capital.

Two of the Indian leaders of the rebellion were Popé of San Juan and Catiti of Santo Domingo. Both were religious leaders of their people, and Popé had even been flogged for his overt opposition of Catholicism. Under their direction, Santa Fe was besieged and most of the missionaries in all the villages were killed, as were any other Spaniards the Indians could catch.

Santa Fe capitulated after five or six days of siege, and Spanish resistance ceased. The survivors were allowed to leave the Pueblo country and make their way southward toward Mexico. Within a few days, the Indians destroyed all the missions, killed 21 of the 33 friars, slew 375 colonists, and drove the remaining Spaniards out of their country. Allowing most of the colonists to escape indicated that these peaceful Pueblos were not interested in retaliating against the Spanish by wholesale slaughter, but merely wanted to eliminate the mission system and drive the invaders from their land. They were not interested in waging war, but wanted only to be left alone to practice their religion and live in peace.

The Spanish—being of noble ancestry and not about to lower themselves to menial labor—hired, bribed, forced, or in some way persuaded some of the Indian people to accompany them on their exodus and act as carriers of their possessions. When they reached El Paso del Norte (Juarez), they were unable to continue into Mexico because of political unrest, and had to remain in the El Paso area for about twelve years. The Indian slaves formed their own community and were the ancestors of the present-day Tigua Indians. The Tiguas were finally recognized by the United States government for benefits in 1973, after almost 300 years of isolation, and given their tiny community as a reservation. Over 400 of these fiercely independent Tiguas now inhabit the town of Ysleta, Texas.

For about thirteen years, the Pueblo land was free of Spanish conquerors. The Conquistadores made sporadic raids—burning, killing, and carrying on with their usual treatment of Indians. They were unable, however, to re-establish their colonies during this period.

In 1692, Diego de Vargas, the newly appointed governor, made a trip to the Pueblos in an attempt to make peace. His overtures fell on deaf ears, for the Indians remembered all too well the treatment they had received from these "doves of peace" before. Since he couldn't connive or coerce his way to power, Vargas returned to Mexico and gathered his forces for the typical Spanish takeover. Returning, he captured Santa Fe and once again established the seat of Spanish government in Indian country. From this center, he began the systematic invasion of the pueblos. If one gave in without battle, officials and priests were sent in to control the economic and secular life. If the natives resisted, the town was forcibly taken, the women and children made slaves, and the men who surrendered were executed. This treatment soon forced abandonment of many of the pueblos, and the people fled to the Navajo and Apache tribes, or to pueblos that still were resisting. Even with superior armament and training, it took the Spaniards about five years of hard fighting to crush the resistance. The Hopi people, in spite of the tremendous pressure, never capitulated; they remained free through the rest of the Spanish occupancy. They were isolated in their villages atop the high mesas and maintained themselves in their traditional manner.

Pressures applied or influenced by the Spanish forced the Apaches into the predatory existence for which they became so well known. No credit is given by most historians to the contributions by the Apache people to the peaceful coexistance of the various Indian nations in the area prior to the coming of the white man.

From about A.D. 1300 to 1400 the Western Apache, Navajo, Hopi, and other Pueblo groups lived together in comparative harmony in northeastern Arizona. These groups continued their trade and cohabitation until this Spanish interference caused the hostility which still exists.[24]

Activities similar to those in the Southwest were also taking place in Florida during the same period of time. Spain had established herself in the West Indies and attempted to colonize the Florida Peninsula. Those tribes were little more receptive than the Pueblos had been. By 1634, the Catholic Church had made some progress and claimed some 30,000 converts. There were thirty missionaries directing the activities and regulating the lives of the neophites. The Christian influence, or the Spanish example of Christianity, was not as powerful as the number of converts might suggest, for in 1656, the natives revolted against their white conquerors. As in Spanish New Mexico, the revolution was brief, and the Spanish atrocities kept Florida under iron-fisted rule for many years.

Three
England and France
in the New World

Since the Spanish were the "discoverers" of the New World, they had a slight head start in the exploration. England and France were the other two leading powers in Europe at the end of the fifteenth century and were close behind Spain in the investigation of this hemisphere.

In 1577, Francis Drake began his "around the world" trip. He followed Magellan's route around the southern tip of South America and sailed northward along the Pacific Coast, past Central America and Mexico, until he reached the northern coast of California. He landed at Drake's Bay, just north of San Francisco, on June 17, 1579.

Drake's party was warmly received by the natives and treated with the utmost hospitality. The visitors were showered with gifts of food and herbs and were considered deities by their Indian hosts. The Englishmen's response was typical of the response the aboriginal people would receive many times in future contacts. Drake claimed the entire country for his queen and her successors, accepting it as a gift from the Indians. To commemorate the occasion, he erected a brass plate which read: ". . . . whose king and people freely resigne their right and title in the whole land unto Her Magesties keeping."[25]

The "generosity" of the Indians, illustrated by the ignorant dona-tion of their land and the acquiescence to unstated demands of sub-jugation to a foreign ruler, was typical of the strategy of conquest used by many Europeans during the exploration and colonization period. Most of the time, these "peaceful agreements" were totally unilateral and the Indians surrendered their rights and possessions without even knowing it.

Sir Walter Raleigh, one of the early English colonizers, established a colony on the North Carolina coast in 1584. The Indians were friendly and did not make trouble, but the settlers met discourage-ment from several sources. Supply ships from home did not arrive, and since the group had not planted crops, they suffered from hunger and lack of clothing and other necessary imports. The hospitality of the natives soon became strained and the colonists decided it was time to leave. They hitched a ride to England with Sir Francis Drake, when he dropped in from one of his raids on the Spanish in the Indies.

Raleigh established several other colonies along the Atlantic coast in America and had similar results. One such endeavor is a part of an intriguing mystery which remains unsolved even today.

After its founding, a colony was cut off from home while the English were engaged in defeating the Spanish and their Armada. When supply ships finally reached the area, they found the colony had vanished. Instead of a thriving community, there was *nothing;* 117 men, women, and children had vanished. Search parties met with no success, and, after Jamestown was established in 1607, some of the men from that colony attempted to establish what had hap-pened. Captain John Smith recorded in "True Relation," which he wrote in 1608, that friendly Indians told of men in the Chowan-Roanoke River area of North Carolina who dressed like Englishmen. Other stories provided evidence the colony was still intact but had moved inland. However, no contact was ever made between the English and the "lost colony."

In 1730, when white settlers came to what is now Robeson County, North Carolina, they found fair-skinned Indians speaking broken English living there. The houses of the natives were patterned after English architecture, and agricultural methods were the same as those found in England. Even the names of the tribesmen were the same as those of the vanished colonists. The assumption was that these natives were descendants of Raleigh's group who had mixed with the local Indians. Even now, there is no conclusive evidence which substantiates or disproves this theory. Even among the Lumbees (as they are now called) there is controversy. While birth records or other documents are not likely to ever be found, the circumstantial evidence, when joined with logic, does support the theory of a connection with the Raleigh colony.

One of the earliest French colonizers was Jean Ribaut. In 1562, he began a search for a suitable place to found a colony of French Huguenots. He sailed along the east coast of Florida until he came to the mouth of the St. John's River, where he found a lovely land with friendly natives who welcomed him and replenished his ship's stores with fresh water and food. He claimed the territory for France but sailed on, looking for even a better place. He finally arrived at the tip of what is now South Carolina and established a colony he called Port Royal. Ribaut returned to France for supplies, and when he was detained because of religious wars, the colonists became discouraged and left.

In 1564, one of Ribaut's lieutenants, Rene de Laudonniere, led a group of French settlers to the St. Johns River location visited two years earlier by Ribaut. The Indians were overjoyed to see more of their French friends, but after a while, when the supply ships again failed to appear, friction developed. Some Frenchmen were killed and an uneasy peace prevailed.

Supplies finally arrived at St. Johns, but soon afterward came Menendez and the Spaniards. They killed the settlers and converted the French settlement into a Spanish military fort. By the time the French began again to colonize, the Spanish were so strongly established in the southern areas that French colonization was restricted to the north Atlantic area.

Samuel de Champlain founded Port Royal, Nova Scotia in 1605 and Quebec in 1608. Trois Rivieres started in 1634 and Montreal in 1642. Soon the French were pursuing the fur trade in the Great Lakes, the Illinois country, down the Mississippi River, and westward into the Rocky Mountains.

The French and the Indians generally got along quite well. The philosophy used by these fur traders was different from that of the other Europeans. France was more interested in the New World products that could be converted into cash or used to decorate themselves for the extremely ostentatious lifestyle of the seventeenth century French. While the Spanish and English were taking land and gold, the French were making friends with the natives. They accepted the Indians' hospitality by moving into the wigwams. They learned the Indian languages, married Indian women, and adopted the ways of the tribes. There was little imposed to acculturate the Indian and, in fact, it was the French who were the ones to change their culture. This made them more acceptable than other Europeans.

Although the English-Indian conflicts are not well publicized, and the general public is not aware of British depredations, they did occur and the relationship between the groups was far from peaceful. The treatment of the natives by English colonists was as inhumane as that afforded by the Spanish. Christianity and civilization were the rationale used to justify whatever action was taken in the conquest of the Indians. The first charter given by King James for the colonizing of Virginia stressed not only bringing the natives to "the true knowledge and Worship of God," but "to human Civility, and to a settled and quiet Government." He also recognized the expedience in providing educational facilities to speed the civilization or acculturation process. In 1617, he called on the Anglican clergy to provide funds for educating "children of these Barbarians in Virginia." The clergy responded and founded the College of William and Mary, "a college for the children of the infidels."

The first permanent English settlement in the New World was established on April 20, 1607, at Jamestown. This colony was saved from disaster by the Indians and their contributions of food. The pattern of demanding sustenance from the natives was continued by most of the European invaders and inevitably led to confrontations. Captain John Smith and other leaders spent so much time chasing the Indians and demanding corn that they neglected to plant any of their own. If it were not for the generosity of Powhatan, the chief of a confederacy of Tidewater tribes, life would have been extremely tenuous for the newcomers. This great leader was also able to keep peace between the groups in spite of extreme pressure by his younger warriors. If he had not contained this element of the tribes, they would surely have wiped out the puny settlement. In typical English gratitude, John Smith urged the enslavement of the "viperous brood" whom he admitted saved Jamestown from starvation.[26]

Before the Powhatan Confederacy realized it, the English had become too powerful to dislodge. They had taken over Indian farmland, driven off the game, and settled in large areas along the James River.

Powhatan died in 1618 and was succeeded by Opechancanough, his brother. The new leader was not interested in peaceful coexistence, for he recognized the peace would only last until the settlers needed more land. On March 22, 1622, the Indians instituted a well-organized surprise attack. They killed over one-fourth of the settlers and would have undoubtedly destroyed Jamestown had it not been for a Christianized Indian who warned the settlement. The colonists rallied their forces and defeated the Powhatans in a fierce struggle.

Far from being conquered, Opechancanough—now nearly 100 years old—led another uprising against the English in 1644. Again he struck with a surprise maneuver that caught the colonists completely unprepared. Nearly 300 whites were killed, but the cause of the Indians was now hopeless. The colonial population was nearly 8,000 by this time and they quickly quelled the rebellion. Opechancanough was captured and executed, and the great Powhatan Confederacy died with him.

After the fall of the Powhatans, events happened very rapidly which would drastically affect the lives of the Indians in America. As more Europeans arrived, they brought new diseases for which the Indians had no resistance. Measles, smallpox, and syphilis ravaged the tribes and many became extinct even before English guns could accomplish the deed.

The Pilgrims landed at Plymouth in 1620 in late fall and began to build their settlement. Since they arrived too late for planting, the first winter was a horror for the group. The Indians were not much help, as they would make only sporadic appearances and even then would not approach very closely. For the most part, they remained in the woods and curiously watched these strange, bearded foreigners.

When spring arrived and the worst was over, the twenty-one surviving Pilgrims set to work. Assisted by the chief of the Wampanoags, Massasoit, who had become friendly with the settlers, they attempted to plant crops. The Indians instructed them on how to set their corn, where to fish and hunt, and how to utilize the natural foods of the woods and fields.

The first year proved to be a bounteous one, for the corn did exceptionally well. The seeds which had been brought from England did not do very well, but because of their Indian friends, the Pilgrims harvested enough to sustain them through the next winter. It was thus appropriate that they and the Wampanoags celebrate a thanksgiving feast. Without the aid of the natives, survival for this small band of Englishmen would have been impossible.

Relations between the Pilgrims and the various Indian groups in the area remained peaceful for a time. In letters sent back to England, the colonists wrote of the faithful and loving nature of the natives and how they felt perfectly safe in the New World. Then, for some unknown reason, they built a fort and launched an unprovoked attack on the Massachusetts. Captain Miles Standish led a small group that killed seven of the tribe and beheaded their leader, mounting his head on the blockhouse as a warning to the others. Occasionally, a quarrel or skirmish would take place with the Narragansetts, but no serious encounters occurred. For the most part, the Pilgrims did not encroach further on Indian land and peace was maintained.

The great Puritan immigration to Massachusetts Bay took place in 1630 and the area began to be dotted with settlements. Roger Williams was exiled and found refuge with the Narragansetts. He allied himself with some Quakers and other refugees and founded Rhode Island. Williams performed invaluable service in his role of mediator between the Indians and the English. He was able to successfully calm the fears of the tribes and at the same time influence the colonists to deal fairly with them. He was instrumental in promoting payment for land taken from the Indians and in providing bills of sale and deeds. Because of his advocacy for fair treatment and equality for the Indians, legal protection was provided by the Massachusetts Bay colonies and peace prevailed.

Another of Williams' activities which did little to enhance his position with colonists was urging the Christian leadership to relax their missionary work with the tribes. He was against "forced conversion'' and prophesied that if the colonists did not control their ''missionary zeal,'' Indian war might result. His advice was again heeded and for a while New England was quiet.

As more colonists arrived from England and the Indians began to realize they were being crowded out of their homelands, difficulties arose. The powerful Pequot Nation resisted colonizing efforts in the Connecticut Valley, and in 1636, they killed two English traders. A punitive expedition embarked from the Massachusetts Bay colony to retaliate. The militia surrounded the Pequot village and set it afire. Most of the inhabitants were incinerated or shot as they attempted to escape the flames. The few who escaped death were hunted down, shipped to the West Indies, and sold as slaves. A small number managed to evade the colonists and hide in the forests. Their descendants still live in Connecticut, but have lost much of their tribal identity.[27] The Puritan religious leader, Cotton Mather, is reported as giving thanks that ''on this day we have sent 600 heathen souls to Hell.''[28] Forty years later, as the remnant Indian groups were attempting their last efforts to free their lands, Mather was still gloating over their sorrow and hardships. Mather's attitude typifies the rationalizations of many European leaders as they performed barbaric acts which were diametric to their stated religious doctrines. Mather wrote: ''We may guess that probably the devil decoyed those miserable savages hither, in hopes that the gospel of the Lord Jesus Christ would never come here to destroy or disturb his absolute empire over them.''[29] Statements such as these removed any moral restraints in dealing with the Indians.

Settlements continued to be established in New England and Indian land continued to diminish. By 1674, the English outnumbered the Indians by a two-to-one margin. Massasoit had died and his young son, Philip, was the Wampanoag leader. Realizing what was happening to his people, Philip began to make plans to wage an all-out war and free his homeland. He formed a confederacy from the remnants of about twenty tribes, and in 1675, they struck the villages in New England with a well-organized and coordinated attack. Of the ninety towns in the area, fifty-two were assaulted and twelve were completely destroyed.

The Indians fought with desperate bravery and ferocity and would have probably annihilated the English if it were not for internal treachery. Due to the discord among the tribes, Philip's forces were decisively defeated on August 12, 1676. Philip was killed and his wife and children were captured. The heads of Philip and some of the other leaders were displayed on the Plymouth blockhouse as a warning to all Indians. Philip's family was sold into slavery in Bermuda. The cruel mentality of the religious leadership was again displayed when Mather wrote of the few survivors: "When they came to see the ashes of their friends mingled with the ashes of their fort. . . .where the English had been doing a good day's work, they Howl'd, they Roar'd, they Stamp'd, they tore their hair. . . .and were the pictures of so many Devils in Desperation."

Even if Philip had succeeded in freeing New England, his efforts would have been temporary. The English had a stable line of settlements from Maine to the Carolinas which in Virginia reached to the foothills of the Appalachian Mountains. The fate of the Indians had been sealed. Philip had come too late.

William Penn founded Philadelphia in 1682 and made his treaty between the Quakers and the powerful Delaware (Lenape) Nation. This agreement established treaties as a means of peaceful invasion, and they were used by the Americans as tools of conquest until 1871. The inexorable march of civilization had begun and it would not cease until the philosophy of Manifest Destiny had been fulfilled.

With Spain firmly established in Florida and the Southwest, with England in complete control of the Atlantic seaboard, and with France solidly entrenched in Canada and along the Mississippi River, the Indians in the eastern half of what is now the United States found themselves surrounded by white men. This situation brought on the "manipulation period" in Indian/white relations. For the next century or so, the various European powers were busy expanding their empires at the expense of the natives. Not only did they lose much of their land, but the tribes were decimated by warfare promoted by England, France, and Spain. Tribal warriors were engaged in fighting one European power as allies of another or battling other tribes in alliance with one of the white groups. Many Indians died for the glory of France, England, or Spain, but few died for the benefit of their own nation.

In the Southwest, Spain agitated and promoted animosity against the warlike, independent Apaches and Navajos, until constant fighting among the tribes made it easy for Spanish colonizers to take control of the entire area.

These same tactics were used by France and England with the great nations of Indians in the Southeast. The closely related Choctaws and Chickasaws became enemies and did the fighting for their European allies. The great Natchez Nation was destroyed by a few Frenchmen and a large Choctaw army. Choctaw civil war erupted between the English and French factions. Warfare was incited between the Cherokees and the Creeks, the Cherokees and the Tuscaroras, the Creeks and the Choctaws, and other tribes. A constant state of conflict existed, and during the entire process, the Europeans expanded their land holdings and the Indians contracted theirs. The final conflict, which grew out of the English-French rivalry over the land north of the Ohio River, was the French and Indian War.

The Iroquois, although they didn't particularly like the English but did value their trade, made war on the Ohio Indians in order to break up their trade with the French. The French then built a series of forts to protect their Indian allies and stepped up their warfare against the English. By 1753, they had advanced to western Pennsylvania and posed a threat to the colonies there. George Washington was sent to drive the French away but was defeated. This was the first of many defeats this young Virginian would have in colonial warfare.

Governor Dinwiddie of Virginia incited the Cherokees to send a war party against the Shawnees in Ohio, allies of the French. The Shawnees thoroughly defeated the Cherokees and persuaded them against their alliance with the English. All-out war was declared by these resentful Cherokees against Dinwiddie and the Virginians. Settlements were attacked and the inhabitants killed. This raiding lasted until 1761, when the Virginians, with superior numbers, finally forced the Cherokees to surrender.

The war ended in 1763, and in the Treaty of Paris, the French lost their holdings in the New World. The Indians became subjects of the crown of England. They were not happy with being passed from one empire to another and some revolted. Peace finally was established in 1768, and boundaries were created for the white and Indian lands in a treaty negotiated by Sir William Johnson for the British and representatives from the Iroquois Confederacy. The treaty was signed at Fort Stanwix and was designed to give the Indians permanent possession of their heartlands.

With the cessation of the French and Indian War and the existence of definite boundaries, it would seem that a period of quiet might at last be in order. Such, however, was not the case. With the removal of the French menace, the English began to encroach on Indian land at every border. As pressures mounted, warfare broke out in many areas. Colonists applied concerted efforts to acquire land from some tribes and occasionally succeeded. In 1773, the Creeks ceded a large portion of land in Georgia, and settlements began to appear all over the frontier. In the midst of the turmoil, another threat loomed on the horizon for the Indian people. The United States declared its independence from England and the Revolutionary War was under way.

Four
The Revolution
and the United States

Although generally ignored or, at best, treated lightly by historians, the American Indians drastically affected the Revolutionary War. Both the English and the rebellious colonial government courted the various tribes in attempts to win them over. England wanted them to join in the fight to defeat the rebellious colonies, while the rebel diplomats encouraged the Indians to remain neutral. As the war progressed, the Americans changed their tactics and attempted to enlist the Indians' aid in warfare against the "mother country." These recruitment attempts were studied very closely by the tribal leaders, and the history of Indian-white relations played an important role in their decisions. Another factor examined closely before decisions were made by the Indians was the consequence if the wrong side was chosen.

As armed rebellion was being planned and the colonial leaders were preaching freedom and equality, they were offering the tribes new treaties which would open more Indian land for white settlement. In direct contrast, England was introducing its new Indian policy of reserving for the tribes exclusively the land they then occupied. Considering this, and also realizing through years of experience that the colonists' cupidity would soon overcome any agreement or alliance, the Indian nations generally joined the British. Since the colonists were directly involved in the usurpation of Indian land, and the English government provided contact only through skillful agents, it was more desirable to have England as a friend. The tribes knew the policy of extermination most colonists propounded and considered the "Great Father Across the Water" as their protector.

English agents in the South easily engaged the Cherokees in the conflict and they provided 3,000 warriors to the crown. Their purpose was to join with the Chickasaws, who were also loyal to the King, in ravaging the southern colonies. Although the Choctaws, Creeks, and Seminoles would not enter formal alliances with the British, it was evident that they would definitely not assist the colonies and that many of their warriors would lend their hand if they had the opportunity. Before the end of the war, most of the Creeks had joined their Indian peers, and by 1778, were dealing much misery to the American colonies in the South. They were not effective as far as taking over large amounts of land—in fact, the reverse was true—but they disrupted the colonial army enough so that special militia had to be kept free to cope with them. This relieved the pressure on the British at other, more strategic locations.

Indians in the Old Northwest were also applying pressure on the colonials. Shawnees, Iroquois, Delawares, Ottawas, and Chickasaws kept the entire western frontier active. George Rogers Clark and a large force of Kentucky militiamen defeated the British and the Indians in two campaigns (1778 to 1779). The Shawnees were driven west into Indiana, and about 400 families even crossed the Mississippi River, settling just north of Cape Girardeau, Missouri.

On September 17, 1778 at Fort Pitt, the United States signed a treaty with the powerful Delaware Nation. This was the first such agreement between the new American government and the Indians, but it established a precedent in dealing with the tribes.[30] This treaty permitted American troops to pass through Delaware country to attack British troops in the West. Promised in the treaty was an "Indian state," but this, of course, was never formed. In 1782, Americans massacred a group of friendly Christian Delawares and this alienated the entire tribe. Some of the Delawares became leaders of the hostile tribes in the Ohio country. A number of the tribe moved across the Mississippi and joined the Shawnees at Cape Girardeau.

George Washington sent General John Sullivan against the Six Nations (Iroquois) in 1779. He defeated the Indians in a fierce battle near Elmira, New York and then marched through their country devastating everything in sight. The Iroquois Confederacy, once a great power in the politics of North America, was completely broken by the Revolution.

The Cherokee Nation suffered the same fate as the Iroquois and had to accept defeat as their reward. In 1785, two years after the close of the war, American commissioners made the first treaty with the Cherokees at Hopewell, South Carolina, on November 28. The Indians were forced to recognize the new republic and gave up a large portion of their land. The new boundaries were strictly defined and the United States promised to force its citizens to respect them. They also offered the Cherokees the equivalent of statehood, but this was never realized.

The new government was too weak to keep its promises to the Cherokees even if it wanted to. Settlers began to occupy Indian land and drive the natives away. One group of Cherokees, the Chickamaugans, moved across the Mississippi River in 1785 and established settlements in Spanish-owned Arkansas.

The Choctaw and Chickasaw Nations had been invited to the treaty council at Hopewell but were undecided about accepting. They finally arrived in January 1786 and signed treaties similar to the Cherokee treaty but with no provision for statehood. The Nations were reduced and boundaries firmly established. Promises of lasting friendship and protection were made and mutually acknowledged. Little did the three groups realize that this was the beginning of the end for them.

The Indian people had for nearly 300 years dealt with the great powers of Europe—England, France, Spain, Portugal, and Holland. Now they were forced to negotiate with a new power which would affect their lives to a much greater extent than all the Europeans combined. The United States had won its independence from England and had taken its place as one of the world's great powers. George Washington was inaugurated as the first president in 1789 and, with his Secretary of War, Henry Knox, he began an earnest effort to settle the warfare between the settlers and the Indians.

Washington's Indian policy was one of humane treatment and he considered himself a friend to the tribes. In referring to the Cherokee, he called them "My beloved Cherokee." He wanted to expand the frontier and at the same time protect it. His solution to the pressures applied to the natives was to attempt to make farmers from the hunting groups. Those who were already farmers were to be taught to exist on smaller tracts of land, thus opening up vast areas for white settlement.

Indian-white relations in the Ohio territory had deteriorated and frontier warfare ravaged the area. Although Washington worked diligently to keep peace, all-out war erupted on September 19, 1790. The Shawnees, Ottawas, Potowatomis, Delawares, Wyandots, Miamis, Mingos, and Chippewas, acting as the United Indian Nations, began their last attempt to secure a homeland.

Colonel Josiah Harmer, a veteran soldier with an outstanding reputation, marched with a force of 1,500 men on the principal Miami village near the present Fort Wayne, Indiana, where the Miamis had assembled under the leadership of Mishickinikwa, or Little Turtle.

As the American troops drew near, Little Turtle set all his villages on fire and deployed his warriors for the attack. His superior battle skills were soon evident as he soundly defeated a large detachment under the command of Major Fontaine. Harmer, realizing his raw recruits were no match for the hardened Miami warriors, ordered a general retreat during which many of his men lost their lives.

The Indians, jubilant at the ease with which they defeated Harmer, invited the Six Nations to join them. The Iroquois were having trouble with the United States government and were on the verge of joining forces with the Confederacy. Realizing he was in a precarious situation with the tribes, Washington ordered Governor St. Clair to assume command of a new strike against the Indians. St. Clair assembled 2,000 men and, after building Fort Hamilton and Fort Jefferson on the Miami River, marched north from Cincinnati. He made camp on the Wabash River a few miles west of Greenville, Indiana, and prepared to engage the Indian forces.

The Shawnees, Wyandots, Delawares, and other tribes had joined the Miamis and had an army of about 1,000 warriors under the leadership of Little Turtle. On the morning of November 4, the Indians attacked in all their fury. Blue Jacket of the Shawnees,

Buckangahelas of the Delaware, and Blackfish of the Miamis carried out Little Turtle's attack plans with great skill. The battle was short and decisive, with the Americans fleeing in panic in the face of such a furious onslaught. Fort Jefferson fell immediately, and before the fight was over, St. Clair had lost over 900 men and suffered the worst defeat in the history of the country. It was in this battle that Tecumseh distinguished himself as a warrior and leader.

After a number of lesser skirmishes between the Americans and the Indians, Washington placed Major General Anthony (Mad Anthony) Wayne in charge of the forces in the Ohio country. In the fall of 1793, Wayne marched his 3,000-man army north from Cincinnati in an effort to destroy the Confederacy. He spent the winter at Greenville, resuming his march in late spring. His army finally met Blue Jacket and about 1,400 warriors in a place called Fallen Timbers on August 20, 1794. The Indians were finally defeated and the great United Indian Nations Confederacy came to an end. Wayne destroyed the villages of the Indians and in the spring of 1795 called a council. Leaders from twelve Indian tribes were present and signed a treaty, giving up land in Indiana and Ohio. In the meantime, the United States had concluded a treaty with the Iroquois, so the Northwest Territory was quiet at last. Settlers flocked to the area and Ohio became a state in 1802.

While these activities were taking place in the Ohio country, the southern Indians were also receiving their share of oppression. In a message to George Washington, Henry Knox observed that the violations of the Treaty of Hopewell were disgraceful. He also recognized that if local citizens in the East could get away with flagrant contempt for federal law, there would be no way to enforce the statutes on the frontier. Because of the urgent situation, Washington called another treaty council with the Cherokee. They met in 1791 on the Holston River near Knoxville and signed a new agreement. The Cherokees lost the land which settlers had occupied since the Treaty of Hopewell, but once again they were promised protection against future encroachments by white settlers. The new treaty also provided for assistance in converting the tribe to an agricultural people and promised assistance in technology and tools to accomplish this.

Although white settlers ignored the treaty and crossed into

Cherokee land, and in spite of retaliatory raids by the Chickamaugans—the more hostile of the Cherokee bands—an uneasy peace was established and the Cherokees made considerable progress in "civilization." They developed large plantations, raised cattle and hogs, plowed their fields, and built comfortable dwellings. They took on many facets of European culture and became quite successful by the end of the eighteenth century.

The Creek Confederacy presented a problem to the government of the new United States. In spite of George Washington's attempts to enter into treaties with them, Creek warriors continued to raid the Cumberland area on their northern border and refused to acknowledge themselves within the jurisdiction of the state or federal government. Bribes, threats, and diplomacy could not seem to sway their desire for freedom. It was not until 1790 that they gave in, and on August 7, they entered into an agreement. Alexander McGillivray and about thirty of the head men of the confederacy journeyed to New York, where they agreed to the boundaries of Creek country and to other particulars of the treaty. They also became subject to the laws of the United States and agreed to relinquish land claimed by the state of Georgia. This was the first of a series of treaties that greatly reduced their land and gave the states more and more control over their lives. Treaties were signed in 1796, 1802, 1805, 1814, 1818, 1821, 1825, 1826, and 1827. Finally, on March 24, 1832, the Creek Confederacy came to an ignominious end when they agreed to give up all their land east of the Mississippi River and migrate to Oklahoma. The removal of these people is discussed at greater length in a later chapter.

Five
The Frontier Advances

When Thomas Jefferson became the third president in 1801, Indian-white relations were at an all-time low. His predecessor, John Adams, had done nothing to alleviate the problems during his tenure. The frontier had progressively moved westward to the Mississippi River, and land acquisition was the need most expressed by the settlers. Even though the Indians held aboriginal title—guaranteed by treaty, the supreme law of the land—the American frontiersmen flagrantly ignored the legality and took over. Tennessee and Kentucky became states and the Florida boundary was defined. Georgia, Alabama, and Mississippi settlers were applying pressure on the government to move the Indians and open up tribal land for settlement. Such was the state of affairs inherited by the new president.

Even though Jefferson had been a removal advocate for years, he was reluctant to chase the Indians across the Mississippi River. In 1803, he was presented an opportunity to solve the Indian "problem." France sold the huge Louisiana Territory to the United States for a paltry fifteen million dollars. The purchase was rather a "pig in a poke," for no one actually knew the size of the area, the topography, the inhabitants, or the potential. Jefferson commissioned Captain Meriwether Lewis and Captain William Clark to survey the country with the stated purpose of "extending the internal commerce of the United States." His ulterior motive for the exploration was evidently to ascertain the feasibility of transferring the eastern Indians into the territory. He gave the two explorers specific instructions to make careful observations of the tribes they might encounter and report in detail information concerning all facets of their cultures.

On May 4, 1804, Lewis and Clark left St. Louis with a party of forty-five persons and headed up the Missouri River to begin their famous exploration of the Louisiana Territory. They arrived at the Mandan villages in October and spent the first winter with the Yankton Sioux. The progress of the expedition was not impeded by any of the native groups, which were extremely friendly and hospitable to the white visitors. Until this time, they had escaped the harsh colonization and cruelty of the European and colonial forces and had had only the peaceful exposure to fur traders. Little did they realize what forces of destruction would follow these apparently harmless visitations of Lewis and Clark.

Setting out in the spring, the explorers hired a guide and interpreter, Toussaint Charbonneau, to assist them in their journey. With Charbonneau came his young Indian wife, Sacajawea, who would prove indispensable to the party. Her exploits have been well publicized and are the subject of numerous publications and dramatizations.

Sighting the Rocky Mountains in May, the group passed over them in September and entered the Nez Perce country. This tribe was aware of the coming of the expedition and welcomed the explorers with food and offers of assistance. A Nez Perce guide took them down the Snake River to the confluence with the Columbia and westward to The Dalles. Through their guide, the group made friends with the many tribes of Indians they met.

The expedition continued down the river to its mouth, where the group found the coastal tribes who had been contacted by traders. They spent the winter on the Pacific shore, and in the spring, they began their return journey. While following the tributaries back to the Missouri, Lewis, along with three men, decided to leave the main party and explore the Marias River in Montana. It was on this side trip that they encountered a band of Blackfeet. The Blackfeet were an extremely independent and volatile group that was totally unimpressed by the Americans and their peace message from Jefferson. A confrontation developed and two of the Indian party were killed. After this incident with Lewis, they became unrelenting enemies of the Americans.

Except for this event, Lewis and Clark found the Indians eager for trade with the whites. The white traders, both American and European, soon descended on this virgin territory in swarms. Fur trade was the primary motivation for this invasion and, as the traders began their campaigns, the decline of the Indian cultures was started. Whiskey was introduced and this became one of the most popular trade goods for the whites. New diseases, such as smallpox, were brought to the natives, who had no immunity and suffered unmercifully. The Mandans were eliminated as a tribe by smallpox in 1837 and only a few individuals survived. They fled in terror and sought refuge with the neighboring Arikaras, where their descendants still live on the Fort Berthold Reservation in North Dakota.

When Lewis and Clark reported to President Jefferson of this great expanse of land and its resources and potential, he was delighted. This new territory, aside from the economic effect it could have for the country, provided a possibility for relieving the pressure on him in dealing with the Indian "problem."

During his first administration, Jefferson seemed callously indifferent to the precarious conditions of the Indians in the East. By this non-action, it could be said that he condoned flagrant violations of the various treaties and the depredations perpetrated against the Indians within the borders of the United States. However, by the time he was inaugurated for a second term, he became very active in Indian affairs and an advocate of altering the culture and geographic location of the eastern tribes.

In his second inaugural address, Jefferson said:

The aboriginal inhabitants of this country I have regarded with the commiseration their history inspires. Endowed with the faculties and the rights of men, breathing an ardent love of liberty and independence, and occupying a country which left them no desire but to be undisturbed, the stream of overflowing population from other regions directed itself on these shores; without power to divert or habits to contend against it, they have been overwhelmed by the current or driven before it; now reduced within limits too narrow for the hunter's state, humanity enjoins us to teach them agriculture and the domestic arts; to encourage them to that industry which alone can enable them to maintain their place in existence and to prepare them in time for that state of society which to bodily comforts adds the improvement of the mind and morals. We have therefore liberally furnished them with implements of husbandry and household use; we have placed among them instructors in the arts of first necessity, and they are covered with aegis of the law against aggressors from among ourselves.

But the endeavors to enlighten them on the fate which awaits their present course of life, to induce them to exercise their reason, follow its dictates, and change their pursuits with the change of circumstances have powerful obstacles to encounter; they are combatted by the habits of their bodies, prejudices of their minds, ignorance, pride and the influence of interested and crafty individuals among them who feel themselves in the present order of things and fear to become nothing in any other. These persons inculcate a sanctimonious reverance for the customs of their ancestors; that whatsoever they did must be done for all time; that reason is a false guide and to advance under its counsel in their physical, moral, or political condition is perilous innovation; that their duty is to remain as their Creator made them; ignorance being safety and knowledge full of danger; in short, among them also is seen the action and counter action of good sense and of bigotry. . . .

This Jeffersonian philosophy, which advocated the tribes becoming farmers and living on smaller tracts, was not very logical. First, the eastern tribes were mostly farmers originally and were utilizing their land for agriculture, rather than hunting, so the president's suggestion did not really affect them. Second, if the tribes had been hunters and had converted to farmers, this would have been only a temporary solution, and it would not have taken very long for the Americans to absorb the Indian land. Indeed, that is exactly what happened in the area only a few years after Jefferson retired from office.

Although it seemed the northwestern tribes were disorganized and apparently would not cause the government much of a problem, such was not the case. While the Madison administration was bickering with England and reducing southeastern Indian land holdings with new treaties, the great Tecumseh of the Shawnee Nation was diligently working to consolidate the Indians throughout the country. He propounded the philosophy that the earth belonged to all the Indians and no tribe had the right to sell any part of it. He felt the Indians had surrendered enough land and they should unite to prevent the whites from forcing them to give up any more. At first, he did not feel it would take a war to stop the displacement of the natives, but it was not long before he concluded that war was inevitable.

In 1808, Tecumseh and his brother built a town in Indiana to be used as a refuge for their followers. There they lived in the "old ways" and revived some of the lost rituals. The two leaders circulated among the northwestern tribes, recruiting many to join their group. Tecumseh even journeyed to distant tribes in the South and across the Mississippi, where he won many converts. It was while he was on one of these trips that a disastrous event took place.

Some of his Potowatami warriors killed some whites in Illinois in July of 1811. This gave Governor William Henry Harrison the excuse he needed to move against Tecumseh's stronghold. He raised a force of about 1,000 men and marched to battle. Although Tecumseh had told them to keep the peace, about 450 Indians attacked Harrison's force. The Americans drove off the Indians and burned their village. This started an Indian war which proved to be an extremely bloody confrontation.

On June 18, 1812, the United States declared war against Great Britain and the Indians in the Northwest joined with the British. They assisted their allies in the capture of Detroit and General William Hull's entire army of American troops. The Indian forces under Tecumseh's command were instrumental in keeping the territory a British-controlled section until the latter part of 1813, when Tecumseh was killed in battle.

Meanwhile, some of the southern Indians were also at war with the Americans. The Creek followers of the great Shawnee had been named "Red Sticks" and were busily engaged in dealing misery to the white settlers. On August 30, 1813, they attacked Fort Mims in Alabama. The commander had not even bothered to close the gates and the Indians were able to kill most of the inhabitants. This brought the wrath of the government forces and many Indian groups down on the "hostiles."

With the northwestern Indians defeated and the English in retreat, it was now possible for the white armies to turn their attention to the South. The "Red Sticks" fought desperately but were unable to stop the army of Andrew Jackson and his Choctaw, Cherokee, and northern Creek allies. At the final battle on March 27 at Horseshoe

Bend on the Tallapoosa River, the rebellious Creek forces were finally defeated.

Jackson and his Choctaws, under the command of Chief Pushmataha, went on to capture Pensacola and then marched to New Orleans. It was here that Jackson gained the fame which later would help propel him into the presidency.[32]

In 1818, Jackson invaded Florida, where British subjects had been inciting the Seminoles to raid settlements in the United States. Although this was an invasion of Spanish territory, no Spanish troops opposed Jackson. He ousted the officials, captured and executed the English agitators, and killed a few Creek "Red Sticks." When Spain protested, the American government demanded that she adequately police the territory or sell it. Since the Spanish military force was depleted and the crown needed money, Spain agreed to sell Florida. The transfer was completed in 1821 and the last vestige of foreign land east of the Mississippi River was gone. Settlers soon invaded the area and the Seminoles felt the force of American land-grabbers. They were pushed back into the swamps, where they would be harassed for many years.

After Jackson's campaign in Florida, he turned his attention to the rest of the southeastern area. Mississippi, Alabama, and Louisiana had been admitted to the Union, and it was time to clear the land of Indians in order to make way for white settlement.

Governmental philosophy concerning the disposition of the Indian "problem" had been fairly consistent since Washington's day. Each of the chief executives seemed to realize the impossibility of cohabitation between Indians and whites in the eastern part of the country. The manner in which to alleviate the situation was the only point of difference. Now James Monroe was faced with this same situation, and with an extremely humanitarian view of the indigenous people, he advocated removal to the West. In his message to Congress on March 30, 1824, he said:

My impression is equally strong that it would promote essentially the security and happiness of the tribes within our limits if they could be prevailed on to retire west and north of our states and Territories on lands to be procured for them by the United States in exchange for those on which they now reside. Surrounded as they are, and pressed as they will be, on every side, by the white population, it will be difficult, if not impossible for them, with their kind of government, to sustain order among them. Their interior will be exposed to frequent disturbances, to remedy which the interposition of the United States will be indispensable, and thus their government will gradually lose its authority until it is annihilated. In this process the moral character of the tribes will also be lost, since the change will be too rapid to admit their improvement in civilization to enable them to institute and sustain a government founded on our principles . . . or to become members of a state, should any state be willing to adopt them in such numbers, regarding the good order of peace and tranquility of such State. But all these evils may be avoided, if these tribes will consent to remove beyond the limits of our present States and Territories. Land equally good and perhaps more fertile, may be procured for them in those quarters. The relations between the United States and such Indians would still be the same.

Considerations of humanity and benevolence, which would now have great weight, would operate in that event with an augmented force, since we should feel sensibly the obligation imposed on us by the accommodation which they thereby afforded us. Placed at ease, as the limited states would then be the improvement of those tribes in civilization and in all arts and usages of civilized life would become a part of a general system which might be adopted on great consideration and in which every portion of our Union would then take an equal interest. . . .

I submit this subject to the considerations of Congress under a high sense of its importance and of the propriety of an early decision on it.

Monroe realized that regardless of the morality of the issue, in order for the Indian nations to survive and retain their autonomy and identity, they would necessarily have to move away from the avaricious dominant society.

In order to expedite the handling of the affairs of the tribes and with the concept of protecting them, in 1824, Monroe initiated the formation of a fiscal bureau in the War Department called the Bureau of Indian Affairs. This bureaucratic arm of the government has not always fulfilled its role of advocate and protector of the Indians, as we shall see in later chapters. At times, it appears that the Bureau of Indian Affairs' goals were to destroy those it was mandated to protect.

Monroe's last message to Congress was delivered on January 27, 1825, and he again foretold disaster for the Indians if the federal government refused to act in a protectorate role. He said,

. . . It has been demonstrated with equal certainty that without a timely anticipation of and provision against dangers to which they are exposed, under causes which it will be difficult, if not impossible, to control, their degradation and extermination will be inevitable.

His warnings were unheeded, and the government continued with its pattern of constricting the Indians in their eastern homeland.

With the election of John Quincy Adams, any benevolence in the presidency ceased. Adams set his sights on the removal of the Indians from the East by whatever means it took to accomplish it. Under his administration, the proliferation of treaties began, with the removal of Indians and the concentration of Indian land base as the means of dealing with the "problem." Many tribes west of the Mississippi found themselves existing on a much smaller land area than they had lived on before, and some—the Shawnees, for example—were moved further west. This was the beginning of the era of political manipulation of the Indian people: providing "legal" means to free the East from the occupation of the natives.

Andrew Jackson was elected president in 1828 and it was clear that whatever his profession of benevolence, he would remove the Indians to the West—by force, if necessary. Georgia, Mississippi, and Alabama passed laws extending their jurisdiction over tribal lands, and Indians were prohibited from testifying in court. This opened the tribal land for plunder and settlement, with no fear of recourse by the owners. To the tribes' pleas for protection, Jackson responded: "Remove." In the spring session of Congress, he recommended removal legislation—and on May 28, 1830, it was enacted into law.

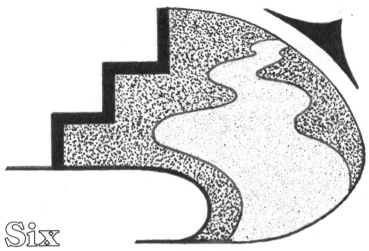

Six

The Trail of Tears,
The Trail of Death

One of the most insidious acts ever perpetrated by the United States government against any group of Indian people was the enforcement of the infamous Removal Act of 1830. This legislative move by Andrew Jackson and his disciples made it possible to remove 125,000 to 150,000 human beings from their homes, confining many in stockades, and finally marching them hundreds of miles, under conditions that should not be used to transport cattle, to a hostile environment in the Indian Territory. Over one-fourth of the total emigrees lost their lives because of the inhumane circumstances surrounding the removal. By the ineptness of the logistics of the removal, it would seem that it was a plan hurriedly conceived and put into operation. Such was not the case, however. As early as 1801, during the administration of Thomas Jefferson, the erosion of the Choctaw land base was initiated. The Treaty of Fort Adams on December 17, 1801 provided a cession of 2,641,920 acres of land. Jefferson had already indicated that he considered the removal of the Indians to the West the ultimate solution to the land acquisition problem. This diplomatic action established the pattern to be followed until the total Choctaw land base in Mississippi was lost on September 27, 1830, with the Treaty of Dancing Rabbit Creek. The agreement ceded the remaining 10,423,180 acres of land to the rapidly expanding United States. Each administration from Jefferson to Jackson had advocated removal as the solution to the Indian problem, but it took Andrew Jackson to implement the mass exodus.

The Choctaws expressed both anger and dissatisfaction over their great loss, and began to prepare for the ordeal ahead with a sense of extreme sadness. They were unhappy over leaving their native land and pessimistic concerning the relocation to new homes in the West.

The largest and most powerful of the southeastern Indian Nations, the Choctaw was the first to recognize the futility of opposing the United States government's Removal Act. Fully understanding the necessity of arbitration, the tribe negotiated with the government and was the first southeastern tribe to agree to remove, they received comparatively favorable terms. They also received the best and the largest amounts of land. However, even with these advantages, their removal was an horrendous experience.

Sacred cave at the old burial mound close to Nanih Waiya, Sacred Mound of the Choctaws in Mississippi.

Nanih Waiya, Sacred Mound of the Choctaw Indians near Philadelphia, Mississippi.

The migratory route began on the Mississippi River, usually at Vicksburg. The Choctaws proceeded northward by wagon train or were ferried across the river to begin their trek on the western shore. Those who had transportation used it, but those who were on foot had to keep up as well as they could. Many of the boats were overloaded and either broke down and couldn't cross or had to deposit their passengers at the nearest point of land instead of the agreed terminal. Overloaded by the migrating Choctaw, some of the rickety old tubs overturned, and many of the people perished in the swift, cold water. A few of the natives were transported by steamboat up the Mississippi and deposited at the mouth of the Red or Arkansas Rivers. From there, they traveled on foot across the unfriendly country to Fort Smith. Many departed overland from their homes and arrived at Memphis. They were then transported to Arkansas and left to find their own way to Indian Territory. Several of the refugees never did go on to Oklahoma, but instead settled with the whites in Missouri, Arkansas, Illinois, Kentucky, and Tennessee. Descendants of these settlers are found today in these states, generally assimilated into the white culture with only oral tradition to keep alive their Indianness.[33]

Several factors added to the natural misery felt by the Choctaws as they left their homes. The federal government had contracted with private businessmen to transport and support the Indians during the marches. These men were more mercenary than humane and reaped tremendous profits by overcharging, lengthening the march time, and using other unscrupulous methods of obtaining money. Many Choctaws died from starvation and exposure; many others were saved from this fate by sympathetic whites along the route.

The first winter on the trail was one of the coldest ever known. To a people accustomed to the mild weather of their homeland, it was unbearable. Insufficient clothing, bedding, and shelter caused many deaths en route.

The second winter was equally as bad because of the wetness. The interior of the Arkansas territory became a quagmire, prolonging the march and exposing the Choctaws to more time in this sickening dampness. Large numbers died from pneumonia and other pulmonary illnesses.

Travel during the intervening summer was no less treacherous. A major cholera epidemic broke out, and hundreds of defenseless Choctaws in their transiency died from the dread disease.

Even after reaching the territory of Oklahoma (Choctaw words meaning Red People), the hardships were not over. Infertile land, unfriendly neighbors (both white and Indian), and the toll of the trip made it extremely difficult for the Choctaws to re-establish themselves as they were in Mississippi. Through determined effort and hard work, they tackled the task, and in a comparatively short time, they had hewn out of this inhospitable territory a nation which rivaled that of any of their contemporaries. In fact, in many cases, Choctaws were far ahead of their white counterparts in conquering the frontier.

By 1834, approximately 13,000 Choctaws had been moved to the Oklahoma territory, and some 6,000 remained in Mississippi in hopes of being able to continue as citizens of the state. Registration as Mississippians would theoretically have allowed them to remain in their homeland.[34] This action proved to be very difficult to initiate, for the registration rolls were constantly disappearing, or the registrar would be too ill to function, or the Indians were directed to the wrong places. This made it virtually impossible for the Choctaws to live in the state. Today, even with the rapid growth in Indian population, there are only about 3,500 Choctaws living on the tiny reservation located near Philadelphia, Mississippi. Although the loss of life was great and the hardships many, the Choctaw suffered less than some of the other southeastern tribes.

After the Choctaws were removed from the frontier, the government began a concerted effort to relocate the Creek Confederacy. These affiliated tribes utilized a different philosophy than the Choctaw in dealing with the federal representatives. Since they were offered the prerogative of leaving or remaining, the full council of the Confederacy met in 1829 and voted to remain in their homeland and submit to state jurisdiction.

Within two years, even though the United States government had promised protection, the Lower Creeks furnished the government a list of over 1,500 names of settlers who had illegally moved into their territory and established farms. No assistance was provided by Washington, and the only alternative suggested was to remove to Oklahoma.

In the spring of 1832, the Lower Creeks succumbed to the white pressure and signed a treaty similar to the one agreed to by the Choctaw. In exchange for all their land in Alabama, they were to receive land in the West where they could establish their nation with the guarantee of no outside interference. Provision was made for individual allotments of land and state citizenship should anyone choose to remain. The tactics employed to prevent the implementation of this provision were a little different than those used against the Choctaw.

The methods used by whites for "legal" purchases of land from the Creek established a precedent for future transactions. Because of the illiteracy among the tribesmen, many signed away their homes without even knowing it. The Indian would awaken one morning and find he had legally sold his home with no monetary exchange. Numerous allotted holdings were "sold" while the Creek owner was intoxicated and incapable of discerning the importance of the transfer of ownership. Another tactic used with great success was to have the Indian sign blank forms before a notary which would be

SOUTHEASTERN TRIBES

completed at a later date to subscribe to the "buyer's" favor. Documentation of certain instances indicate the use of a proxy for the Indian in signing away title to land. Of course, the actual owner did not know he was represented by the proxy. If all other methods failed to gain the transfer of ownership, the land-grabbers could always resort to using the corrupt judicial system by having the land made available by the probate procedure—the act of transferring title of Indian lands of a "deceased" Indian to a white man. Sometimes the Indian had died, sometimes he had been murdered, and sometimes there was no death at all. Coercive tactics such as the threat or actual use of armed forces also hastened the decision of many Creeks to part with their property and move westward.

On March 24, 1832, Creek delegates—disheartened, disillusioned, and exhausted—signed the Treaty of Washington, which ceded all the remaining Creek land east of the Mississippi River to the United States. Under this treaty, certain leading Creek politicians were to receive 2,000,000 acres in large portions from the 5,000,000 acres ceded. These parcels were to be developed by the owners as plantations, but, as noted earlier, non-Indian land-robbers had methods to relieve the natives from the burden of land-ownership. Within a few months after the signing of the treaty, thousands of Creeks were wandering around in the forests and swamps of the area, attempting to survive under the most adverse circumstances.

About 2,500 of these refugees moved to Cherokee country only to be removed with these people shortly thereafter. Some of the Upper Creek towns, driven by desperation, revolted and committed "hostile" acts toward the white settlers. The Secretary of War ordered the complete removal of all Creeks to Oklahoma as a military act, and the Governor of Alabama proclaimed that any Creek who would not aid in the suppression of the revolt would be considered an enemy. Thus, the Creek Confederacy was forced into a civil war. Opothle Yahola and nearly 2,000 Creek warriors finally broke the resistance by the summer of 1836. The entire contingent of "hostiles" was deported in irons to Oklahoma, where they were dumped—naked, and with no implements or weapons, to live or die in this strange land.

In 1837, over 500 Creeks were hunted down from among the Cherokee and forced to move. Those who hid out were rounded up with their Cherokee benefactors when that tribe was removed. About 800 Creeks moved in with the Chickasaws, and when that tribe was moved, they joined the rest of their people in Oklahoma. The fate of the ones who were left in Alabama was abominable; many were hanged for their part in the rebellion, and others were forced into slavery.

Through the hardships placed on these people by harassment, cruel punishment, and the forced march to the West, the Creek Confederacy lost forty-five percent of its population. This fact stands as one of the blackest marks in the pages of American history.

As though the depredations on the Creeks were not enough, the United States then turned to the Cherokee Nation. These people, well versed in white tactics, used every resource at their command to avoid leaving their beloved homeland. The diplomacy of Chief John Ross, Major Ridge (whose real name was Walking-on-the-mountain-tops), and his brother Oowatie held the Americans at bay for a time. The brilliant editorials of Buck Oowatie (renamed Elias Boudinot) in the tribal newspaper encouraged the people to remain united in their efforts to hold their land. The Cherokees felt they could coexist with the white man and become a functional part of American society.

If there was ever any possibility of this happening, it disappeared when gold was discovered on the Cherokee land in Georgia. Almost overnight, the area was flooded with over 10,000 intruders hastily laying out claims on land owned by the Cherokee people. Since the Indians were not allowed to testify in court against white men, there was no choice except to pack up what they could carry and abandon their farms.

The implementing of extreme state laws by Georgia, supplementing Jackson's Removal Act, placed additional obstacles in the attempts of the Cherokees to avoid removal. These Georgia anti-Indian laws made it illegal for the Cherokee Council to meet; forbade the tribal officials to hold court; and refused to allow the Indians to mine gold on their own land. Authorization was also provided for the surveying of the Cherokee land and its disposal by lottery to white Georgians. A very strong regulating force was formed by the state when it created the Georgia Guard to enforce the new laws. These mercenaries went far beyond the necessary steps needed for law enforcement and set out on a well planned reign of terror. They systematically physically abused and incarcerated Cherokees without even fig-leaf legality. Even the missionaries came under attack by the Georgia laws when white men living among the Indians were forced to swear allegiance to the state under the threat of four years of imprisonment for non-compliance.

The Cherokee Nation resisted these savage laws by appealing to the judicial system of the United States. In many cases, decisions rendered by the courts were sympathetic to the Indians, but nevertheless, they generally favored the white man because of the ambiguity of most of the laws. While these enforced rulings were technically legal, their morality left many questions in the minds of Indian and non-Indian alike. In the Cherokee Nation v Georgia decision of March 5, 1831, the court expressed sympathy for the Cherokee people but refused to assume any jurisdiction on the matter at hand because the Cherokee Nation would have to be recognized as a foreign state before jurisdiction could be legal. One of the more positive results of this court decision was the definition of the Cherokee status. It established a precedent which influenced subsequent rulings concerning Indian tribes. In essence, the court described the nation as a distinct political society capable of managing its own affairs and of governing itself. It further indicated that these Indian societies were "domestic dependent nations" and suggested that their relationship to the United States was that of a ward to his guardian.

Even when court decisions favored the Cherokee, lack of executive power to enforce the rulings made the whole affair a farce. Such was the famous Supreme Court decision in the Worcester v Georgia case in February 1832. Worcester was a missionary to the Cherokees and refused to take the oath of allegiance to Georgia. Consequently, the Georgia Guard roughly arrested and jailed him. The ruling of the court in his case stated:

> The Cherokee Nation, then, is a distinct community, occupying its own territory, with boundaries accurately described, and which the citizens of Georgia have no right to enter, but with the assent of the Cherokees themselves, or in conformity with treaties and with the acts of congress. The whole intercourse between the United States and this nation is, by our constitution and laws, vested in the government of the United States.

This made the law under which Worcester was convicted unconstitutional and therefore unenforceable. The state was forced to free him.

This momentous decision could have had very favorable ramifications for the Cherokee people, except for one obstacle: Andrew Jackson. He is reported to have said, "John Marshall (Chief Justice of the Supreme Court) has made his decision; now let him enforce it." Whether he actually made this statement or not is irrelevant. What matters is that he totally ignored the ruling of the court and encouraged the Georgians to continue their harassment of the Cherokees.

Jackson himself promoted removal activities at every opportunity. On April 17, 1832, he proposed a removal treaty and a land exchange with the Cherokee. The terms were so unacceptable and the Nation was so distrustful of the president, the council unanimously rejected the offer.

The next move was to place the Cherokee land in a lottery as a method of establishing white ownership. Sponsored by the state of

Georgia and sanctioned by the federal government, this game of chance changed ownership of many of the elegant homes, large plantations, and other facilities from Indian to white. Many of the wealthy mixed-bloods saw their entire holdings taken from them. John Ross' extensive plantation was one of those lost, and he moved his family across the border into Tennessee. It was quite a change, living in a one-room log cabin instead of the mansion which had been their previous home.

The federal government utilized an ancient military tactic against the Cherokee, as they had with other tribes in the East. Since the Cherokee had for years displayed a unity in opposing the removal, the government attempted to create division and separation among the people. Although they only represented a small minority of the tribesmen, a few of the Indian leaders were "bought." This was initiated in part by outright gifts of money, but more often the land of these pro-removal tribal members would be excluded from the lottery and would remain in their ownership. Loyal contemporaries, seeing their own lands taken from them, became extremely angry at these "sell-outs," and this feeling eventually caused a major division within the tribe. This contention of the wealthy minority against the poorer majority tended to drastically weaken the tribe's effectiveness in the confrontation with the white man.

By 1834, the situation had reached a critical state, and the Nation retreated from its adamant stand of non-removal. The Cherokees began to utilize all the diplomacy in their power to negotiate a favorable treaty. Even John Ross conceded there was no hope for remaining in the homeland and proposed selling the Cherokee land to the government for $20,000,000. He even made overtures to the Mexican government for the purchase of land; however, nothing came of these negotiations. The United States knew the Cherokees would eventually be evicted, and the Mexican government did not appear too anxious to have the Cherokees move to their country.

The United States officials formulated a treaty with members of the Removal Party, but the Cherokee council unanimously rejected it and directed John Ross to attempt to negotiate one which would provide more reasonable benefits for their people. While Ross was in Washington arbitrating with the government, federal officials in New Echota, the Cherokee capital, called for another council meeting to again consider the original treaty. Only a small contingent of the Removal Party attended, and they signed as authorized representatives of the Cherokee people. Although Cherokees and non-Cherokees alike objected bitterly to the government that the treaty was illegal, the Senate ratified it, and removal became an inevitable fact of life. The general terms of the agreement were that the Cherokees would receive $5,000,000 for their nation and would remove themselves by the end of three years. Even the money provided was categorized and was to be used only on educational endowments and other public purposes.

A few of the Cherokee, generally members of the treaty group, left immediately for Oklahoma, but most of the tribe refused to move and continued in their efforts to escape removal. Their unfair treatment by the United States government had caused so much furor, they attempted to negotiate a new treaty which would allow them to remain in Tennessee. These efforts were also to no avail, for Jackson had determined that all Indians would be removed, and his successor, Martin Van Buren, followed his mandates as religiously as if he had originated them.

In the summer of 1838, federal troops were sent to the Cherokee territory to force the migration. Although he was sickened by his assignment, General Winfield Scott began the removal as efficiently as possible. Following Jackson's orders, he began rounding up the Cherokees, driving them into stockades as if they were cattle, and sending detachments to Oklahoma. The logistics of the operation were as poorly implemented as the Choctaw's and Creek's, and many people suffered and died. Finally, appalled by the loss of life of his people, John Ross obtained permission to manage the removal of the rest. Even with this personal attention, many people perished, including Ross' wife, Quatie. It is estimated that about 4,000—nearly one-fourth of the total emigree force—failed to complete the journey. Personal testimony of some of the soldiers assigned to escort the travelers attested to the deplorable conditions of the march. Things were so bad that some of these military escorts did not survive. With the horrendous conditions, the physical suffering, and the appalling death rate, it is no wonder the Cherokees called the march "The Trail of Tears."

A number of the Cherokee managed to escape removal and hid

out in the hills of their former territory. Their survival depended on their ability to live off the land, and they maintained themselves in this manner until a white friend purchased some land in western North Carolina for them to live on.[35] The 5,500 descendants of these few stalwart people constitute the inhabitants of the present-day reservation at Cherokee, North Carolina. The federal government finally took over the land on March 3, 1875 and extended recognition to the group, making them eligible for Bureau of Indian Affairs' benefits.

Physically, the Chickasaw Nation suffered less than did any of their neighbors. They had been relinquishing their land by a series of treaties beginning with a sale of their land north of the Tennessee River in 1805, so the final cession in January 1837 was not as great a shock as it was to the Choctaw.

The Chickasaws embarked on a self-governed migration. Because of their astute bargaining and affluency, they left when they wanted to and by routes of their own choosing. Arrangements had been made for stockpiles of supplies to be waiting at advantageous points along the way.

Realizing the Chickasaws were more prosperous than the other Indian nations, greedy contractors took advantage of them in providing these supplies. They shortweighted the grain and beef and stockpiled such huge quantities of food that much of it spoiled before it could be eaten. These same benevolent procurers also charged outrageous prices for any other services they provided and drained the treasury as much as possible during the migration.

Smallpox broke out among the Chickasaw on the trail, and after their arrival in their new homes, it reached epidemic proportions. Arriving too late in the year to get a crop in 1838, the Chickasaws found that they were broke, hungry, and in a strange land. Although they had started out in much better condition than their neighbors, they ended up in the same dismal shape as the rest. Their only solace was their friendly cousins who had sold them the land in Oklahoma. The Choctaw people had become established by the time the Chickasaw arrived and were able to assist in getting them started in this new home. The two groups were so closely allied that for many years they were identified as a composite nation.

Those members of the Creek Confederacy living in the Florida

Territory were called Seminole. This Muskogean word meaning "those camped away" was used because of the separation of the people by the political boundary of Spanish Florida. By about 1800, the division was so acute that the Seminoles were assigned a separate tribal status.

Tricked into agreeing to removal, the Seminoles suffered more than any other group of southeastern Indians. In the early 1830s, about one-half of the total tribal population was rounded up by various means and loaded naked and hungry onto ships. Leaving Florida, the Seminoles were subjected to abuses as they made port in New Orleans and other stops on the Mississippi. Because of their practice of granting asylum and tribal membership to escaped slaves, many Seminoles were black or black-Indian mixture. This gave slave owners and traders excuses to initiate claims on the lives of many of these people. Since the authenticity of such claims was virtually impossible to refute, much arbitration was required to enable the Seminoles to continue their journey.

Meanwhile, the United States continued to harass the Florida Seminoles. Led by Osceola, these Indians were leading the Army a merry chase through the swamplands they knew so well. By ruse, under a supposed peace flag, Osceola was finally captured and confined to a damp prison, where he died on January 30, 1838. This loss did not stop the resistance of his people, however, and remnants of these determined Indians are still living in the Florida homeland. On May 4, 1858, the Army officially declared that the operation of attemped removal was over. Most of the Florida Seminoles eventually moved to reservations, and today's Seminoles are still there. One group of Indians closely affiliated with the Seminoles only officially made peace with the United States government in 1962. This small tribe, the Miccosukees, is extremely independent, and after only a few years of federal assistance were attempting to revert back to their self-reliance. They have assumed the responsibility for educating their own children and are conducting as many of their own affairs as possible.

Although the removal of the "Five Civilized Tribes" from the Southeast is one of the most dramatic of the events involved in ridding the East of Indians, it is by no means the only "removal." The Shawnee, Delaware, Sauk and Fox, Seneca, Sioux, Potawatami, Ottawa, Chippewa, Winnebago, Kickapoo, and many other tribes felt the inexorable march of civilization forcing them farther and farther west. Even when they located west of the Mississippi, many tribes were forced to move again, even farther west, to the confines of Oklahoma. As Iowa, Missouri, Arkansas, Kansas, Nebraska, and Texas felt the pangs of growth, the Indians within their boundaries suddenly became obstacles that had to be removed. Coercion, fraudulent treaties, purchase of land, and outright force was used to convince the Indians that it would be most expedient to move to Indian Territory. The Frenchman, Alexis de Tocqueville, stated it quite plainly as he observed the removal of the Indians: "They kindly take the Indian by the hand and lead them to a grave far from the lands of their fathers. It is accomplished with felicity, tranquility, legality, philanthropy and all without the shedding of blood. It is impossible to destroy mankind with more respect for the laws of humanity." He also predicted the Indians would not be undisturbed in their new home, but would be driven from the one "final" location to another "until their only refuge is the grave." His prophesy was accurate, for, as history documents, the Indian people were given no rest and even today are using government land for their reservation homes, and these land bases are constantly shifting boundaries. Many reservations have been converted to public domain via the "termination process," and the Indian people are still given no rest.[36]

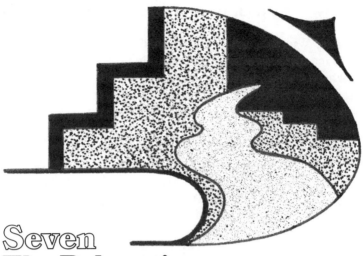

Seven
The Relocation Period: 1830–1860

Beginning with the Norsemen in 1004, the European invaders brought with them the philosophy of "might makes right" in dealing with the indigenous peoples of the New World. Columbus in the West Indies, Cortez in Mexico, and the Puritans in the New England area perpetuated this course of action. After the formation of the United States, the same strategy prevailed as the Iroquois were subdued or driven to Canada; the Northwest Territory was cleared of Shawnees, Miamis, and Sauk and Foxes; and the five great southeastern Nations were driven out of their homeland. During the next half century or so, the Americans in their fervor to follow the concept of Manifest Destiny not only repeated the earlier inhumanities, but for the most part, outdid them.

When the Americans began their War of Independence in Texas, they first extended the hand of friendship to, the various Indian groups. It was not long, however, before the Texans changed their attitude and began the unrelenting pressure against the Indian inhabitants. Chief Bowl and a group of Cherokees had settled in northeastern Texas and were living contented and prosperous lives. However, in 1839, the old chief was killed and his followers were driven across the Red River into Oklahoma. The Caddos, of eastern

Texas, although always peaceful, were soon crowded out of their homeland by the ever-expanding frontier. Peace treaties were written to protect the Indians as well as the whites, but these quickly proved to be impotent. The Caddos, Tonkawas, Comanches, Kiowas, Wichitas, and related tribes were all driven from their homelands by the Texans.

The only bright spot in Texas-Indian relations was the creation of a reservation area in eastern Texas by Sam Houston for immigrants of the Alabama and the Coushatta tribes.[37] Houston had always been sympathetic to the Indian cause as he'd been raised by Tennessee Cherokees and was married to Talahina, daughter of a Cherokee mother and an American father. The small plot of land secured by Houston was the only reservation in the huge state of Texas until 1973, when President Richard Nixon established the tiny Isleta Reservation for the Tigua Indians at El Paso.[38]

The southeastern Indians, after reaching Oklahoma, began to re-establish their nations. This was not an easy task, for many obstacles soon became apparent. Changes in agricultural methods and crops, adaptation of new architectural concepts, and political pressures from the expanding United States posed difficulties for the people. To expedite solving these and other problems, the tribes initiated council meetings and developed agreements among themselves, which presented a united Indian front to the outside world and facillitated solutions to many internal difficulties.[39]

The Choctaw and Cherokee had developed comprehensive public school systems in their eastern homeland, and as soon as they were re-established as nations in Oklahoma, one of the first interests expressed by these people was the education of their youth.

The Cherokee National Council enacted legislation on December 16, 1841 which established a common school system for the Nation. By 1843, 500 children were enrolled in the tribal schools. The schools continued to progress, and in 1859, there were 1,500 children attending 32 schools in the Cherokee Nation. Many of the teachers were local Cherokees who had gone to the "States" to receive higher education and had returned to assist in the tribal system. In 1859, all but two of the teachers were Cherokees.

The Choctaws were also very active in educating their children, and a friendly rivalry developed between the two nations in educational innovations. Because the Choctaw language could be so readily indicated by the Roman alphabet, the people had little difficulty learning to read. Before a generation had passed, the Choctaw, as a whole, became a literate people.

Both of these nations, not content with merely providing rudimentary education on an elementary or secondary level, established "Normal" schools to provide training for Choctaw and Cherokee teachers.[40]

The Choctaw, Chickasaw, and Cherokee nations in Oklahoma began to prosper as soon as the shock of removal wore off. Trails were established and communities began to appear. Post offices were set up and the urban areas thrived as gold-seekers headed for California and land-seekers crossed Indian Territory on their way west. Newspapers, hotels, blacksmith shops, and markets did a booming business with the travelers.

Most of the southeastern Indians were agriculturists and immediately on arrival established farms and plantations. Many of these displaced Indians had been slave holders and had brought their black servants and laborers with them. Prosperous farms were soon begun along the rivers and fine orchards, and extensive fields of grain appeared. Poorer Indians farmed the smaller hillside locations, raising abundant vegetable crops for their consumption and turning much livestock onto the "free ranges" of the vast wooded areas. Large quantities of cotton and farm products were exported in exchange for manufactured goods from the "States."

Elections were held in the Nations and tribal governments began to form. Chiefs and council members were selected and constitutions were drawn up which established a well-regulated government for each tribe. Taxes were levied and collected to finance the operation of the governments and for a time some Indians enjoyed peace and prosperity.[41]

As indicated earlier, the Creeks and Seminoles suffered more than did the Choctaw, Chickasaw, and Cherokee during removal. This same situation was perpetuated during the relocation period. Since they arrived later than the others and were even more decimated, they were assigned the poorest of the land. Crops failed, diseases ravaged the people, and their lot was a sorry one. Many of the Creeks made their way back to their eastern homeland and the conditions there became critical. They were literally people with no country and many ended up as slave labor to the white farmers who now owned the former Creek land.

The Seminoles, because of their fierce resistance to removal from their homeland, incurred the wrath of the United States government. This involved the imposition of punitive and humiliating measures on these once indomitable people. One of the most harmful of these was the absurd policy of relocating them with the Creeks and assigning them to the worst sections of that area. The Seminoles, destitute and broken-hearted, had no desire or initiative left, and most preferred to collect welfare rather than face beginning again in a cold and hostile land.

Those Seminoles who did attempt to re-establish their traditions were met with almost insurmountable obstacles. Needing axes and saws to clear the land, the Seminoles received hoes to till the soil. Tools needed to sustain themselves were constantly late in arriving from the governmental supply offices. Climatic conditions also hindered their transition. Accustomed to the mild Florida weather, they were ravaged by extreme cold in the winter and unbearable heat in the summer. Diseases also devastated the Seminole and they were a most miserable group. Only their resolute spirits enabled them to survive. By 1849, the condition of the Seminole had changed very little and they were still for the most part a dejected and dispirited people.

While the Indians were living fairly well, isolated and protected in Oklahoma, Americans were looking for new areas to settle and were sweeping over the balance of the western frontier like a tidal wave. So great were the numbers of settlers following established trails that even today it is possible to trace some of the migration by the ruts cut deep into the prairie sod by the thousands of wagons. These immigrants not only left their mark on the earth, but also on the lives of the Indian people.

As early as 1825, the Nez Perce, Flatheads, Spokane, and Kutenais expressed an interest in learning more about the white man's religion. These were the friendly northwestern Indians who had welcomed and assisted the Lewis and Clark expedition. Emissaries were sent from the tribes to St. Louis in an effort to obtain teachers and religious missionaries to bring their instructions to the Indians. Finally, two representatives from the American Board of Commissioners for Foreign Missions, Samuel Parker and Marcus Whitman, began missionary activity in the area of the Nez Perce and the Cayuse tribes. Soon, more of the northwestern tribes were contacted by the expanding missionary force and most were converted readily to Christianity.

By 1840, the Oregon Trail had been established and thousands of settlers filed through the homeland of these Indians on their way west. The villages of the Nez Perce and the Cayuse became centers of trade and commerce and the Indians prospered by selling horses, food, and other supplies to the travelers. It was not long, however, before the usual confrontations began. Whites killed the game, overgrazed the pastures, stole from the natives, and introduced smallpox, measles, and scarlet fever. Indians, especially the Cayuse, rebelled and warfare developed. Warriors from the Cayuse tribe attacked one of the missions established in their territory. Whitman and most of the men were killed and the women and children were taken captive. One of the wounded men made it to Lapwai in Nez Perce territory and spread the alarm. The head chief of the Nez Perce was able to prevent any hostile acts against the other missions, but the missionary efforts were brought to a standstill for many years because of the Whitman killing.

Since the area was a part of the United States, and England had relinquished her claim, the military forces, both regular army and volunteers, launched a retaliatory campaign against the Cayuse, devastating the tribe. The public denigrated the Indians and glorified the missionaries and the military. This resulted in the villification of the Cayuse Nation in historical accounts, a procedure which was typical in Indian-white encounters and one which culminates a few decades later at the Battle of the Little Big Horn.[42] The Indians are depicted as the instigators of trouble and the ones who waged savage warfare, while the whites are usually described as the victimized party.

The Cayuse uprising, coupled with the growing concept of "Manifest Destiny," quickly brought things to a head in the Northwest. In 1849, the Oregon Territory was officially formed; in 1853, it was divided into two segments, Oregon and Washington. The government made treaties with the small Pacific coast tribes and assigned them to tiny reservations. This provided much land for the hordes of new settlers that flocked to the area. Soon it became apparent that, in order to fulfill the desires of the white frontiersmen, the interior tribes in the western part of the Washington and Oregon Territories would require attention. These tribal units had been relatively undisturbed as far as land reduction was concerned, for the Americans had been only passing through on their way to the Pacific. By the 1850s, however, the situation had changed, and settlers were casting covetous eyes toward the homeland of the Nez Perce, Yakima, Cayuse, and other tribes in the vicinity.

Coercion, force, fraud, and bribery were used to negotiate treaties with minority groups within these tribes, and the Americans began moving in. The tribal members were disturbed because of the invasion and resistance developed. Before long, the entire frontier was aflame in what is known as the Yakima War. Tribe after tribe joined the conflict and bitter fighting ensued. Many battles were won by the Indian forces, but little by little, the superior numbers and armament of the Americans brought the inevitable results. The Indians were broken and defeated and assigned to small reservation areas to live as animals in cages. Peace was then secured and the entire Northwest Territory was open for white settlement.

As this great westward expansion of the United States continued, it brought another group of people who would have a drastic effect on the lives of the Indians. On February 15, 1846, Brigham Young and a group of his disciples set out from Nauvoo, Illinois, in search of a "promised land" where they could establish their Mormon empire. The Church of Jesus Christ of Latter-Day Saints, which is the correct name for the organization, had been under fire from local residents—first in Ohio, then in Missouri, and finally, in Illinois. The founder, Joseph Smith, had been killed and Young was elected President. He led his people westward to Utah in hopes of finding a place where they could live without the religious persecution they had experienced elsewhere.

Since the Mormons believed Indians were descendants of refugees from Jerusalem who had been cursed with a dark skin because of their sinfulness, they had a special interest in them. According to the Mormon teachings, the Lamanites, as Indians were called, received a promise that if they repented and turned back to God, their skins would become "white and delightsome." This stirred the missionary zeal among the Mormon people to "save" these "dark and loathsome" wretches and bring them into the fold.[43] Consequently, when Brigham Young and his colonists established the Nation of Deseret in 1847, they were vitally involved in improving the lot of the natives. Since Deseret was in fact a theocracy, Young's orders were followed scrupulously, and the Indians were exposed to many facets of "civilization." Although the Mormons did not make many converts, they did establish peace in the area and started some of the tribes in agriculture.

Young, who was appointed Governor when Utah came under the United States at the end of the Mexican War, was very hesitant to relinquish authority to outside administrators appointed by President Buchanan. The situation became so tense that federal troops were dispatched to bring the Mormon empire under control. Nothing developed as far as warfare was concerned, but the Mormon missionaries taught their Paiute pupils to hate the "Mericats" (Americans). Feelings ran high in Utah and a large wagon train headed for California received the force of these feelings. When members of an immigrant party boasted of helping run the Mormons out of Illinois and Missouri, they were attacked by the local militia and their Indian friends at Mountain Meadows in southern Utah. All the travelers were killed in the raid except eighteen children, who were considered to be too young to remember the incident. Young issued orders which prevented a reoccurrence of this type of action, but the Mormons found the Indians were easier to incite than to stop, so they continued their attacks on wagon trains until brought under control in the 1860s.

In 1848, the United States defeated Mexico in a "war" and acquired the vast area which included the present states of Arizona, New Mexico, Nevada, California, Utah, and part of Colorado. Along with the huge land area came jurisdiction over the natives. The treatment of the Indians in California is one of the blackest pages in American history.

Beginning in 1769, when the Franciscan Padre Junipero Serra established the first California mission on June 16, the Roman Catholic Church and the Spanish government, through its military forces in Alta, California, instituted a new system of genocide. As these two units sent their representatives northward from Mission San Diego de Alcala, they developed a mission chain which reached north of San Francisco to Mission San Francisco de Solano. The method of operation never changed as mission after mission was built.

The soldiers would round up all the natives and herd them into a central area where the padres would baptize and rename the "converts." As soon as this ritual was completed, the physical labor began for the Indians. Construction would begin on an edifice which would include a church, living quarters for the clergy and military, and a storehouse for produce raised by the Indians and taken from them. All activities centered around the mission and the natives were forced to live in a condition of feudalism and semi-slavery. If they attempted to escape the control imposed by the mission, they were hunted down by the military and either killed or dragged back. Generally, if their lives were spared, they were publicly punished for their actions.

Since California in the pre-white era was a land of plenty with mild weather, plentiful vegetable foods, and an abundance of game, there was an aura of peace and contentment. The natives were non-aggressive and lived in small, autonomous groups with no large tribal structures. This condition made it very easy for the Spanish to pick them off one at a time with little or no resistance. Being forced to live in the conglomerate society of the mission, the Indians began to lose their tribal identity, and their languages gradually disappeared. Today it is virtually impossible to reconstruct these tribal units and they are gone forever. The Southern California Indians are referred to as Mission Indians or by some repugnant, erroneous Spanish terminology such as Diegeno, Luiseno, or Gabrieleno.

The basic impetus behind this missionizing endeavor was twofold. The Spanish Crown was vitally interested in adding more land to the Empire, and at the same time, in Christianizing the Indians who would supply the labor to the colonies. Spain also hastened the expansion into California in an effort to halt the southern march of the Russian otter hunters who were moving down the Pacific coast from Alaska. If it were not for this threat, it is doubtful if Spain would have made her move northward until later.

Northern California Indians were accorded a different treatment and the pattern was one of removal or extermination. The lowland natives were fairly passive in their resistance to the white intruders and generally were herded into isolated reservations where there would be a minimum of contact with the white settlers. The removal was implemented with much more cruelty than was necessary and many emigrees were killed during the move; others slowly starved after relocation. The entire operation was reminiscent of the infamous removal of the southeastern tribes discussed previously.

The mountain tribes presented a much greater problem to the early settlers and gold miners, as their natures were more aggressive than those of their lowland neighbors. These mountain Indians resisted removal and retaliated when pressure was applied by the military. This action brought on destruction, for they were hunted down as if they were animals and nearly annihilated. All-out war was instituted and the tactics of the invaders were awesome. Not only were Army regulars used, but civilians and local militia were supplied with weapons at state expense and encouraged to wipe out the rebellious Indians. Newspapers carried advertisements for Indian scalps and massacres became commonplace. Newspapers also capitalized on the bizarre situation and presented glowing accounts of valor displayed by the various vigilante groups.

On April 15, 1857, the *Petaluma Journal* reported that within the past three weeks, three or four hundred "bucks, squaws, and children" had been killed by whites for running off stock. Most of the remaining women and children were removed to the Round Valley Reservation, but the "bucks were safely disposed of."[44] The *Redding Courier* in the September 17, 1859 edition describes in detail the forming of a company of nineteen whites and their hunting down Pitt River Indians, killing twenty-two warriors and forty "squaws" and children. Two hundred Indians were massacred at Eureka in April, 1860 by thugs and settlers who attacked at night and cut the throats of all men, women, and children. One man who had sat on the previous grand jury at Eureka boasted of killing sixty infants with his hatchet at the different "slaughter grounds."

Even when they were placed on reservations, the Indians were not safe from massacre, as the Nome Cult Valley example shows. Upon investigation of the incident, the military gave the following account of what happened after a few cattle had been lost by some settlers:

Armed parties went into rancherias in open day . . . and shot the Indians down—weak, harmless and defenseless as they were, without distinction of age or sex; shot down women with sucking babes at their breasts; killed or crippled the naked children that were running about. . . .[45]

Casualties from massacres, although numbering in the thousands, were relatively low compared to deaths due to disease in California from 1848 to 1867. Secretary of Interior Ickes stated before the 76th Congress:

. . . . Thousands have died from these diseases—the sanitary and other conditions are such that death usually followed closely upon the attack of the disease.[46]

Sometimes friendly tribes were called together on the pretense of food distribution and shot as they enjoyed the gifts from their white benefactors. Women were raped—even many who were pregnant. Cruel and vicious actions were common.[47]

Other groups of Indians vanished as white slave traders decimated the tribes. Indian men were killed and women were raped and driven with the children in caravans to the South, where they were sold into slavery. This activity was partially legalized by the state of California through its indenture statute of 1850, which allowed any person to obtain a minor on the approval of his parents and friends for the purpose of work in return for food, shelter, and clothing, even beyond the subject's majority.[48] In October 1862, George Hanson, United States Agent, reported he had captured three men with nine Indian children. The men said they were taking the children as an act of charity because the parents had been killed. When Hanson inquired how they knew the Indian parents had been killed, one man replied, "Because I killed some of them myself."[49]

Many Indians died from poisoned food left by whites. The reduction of population was more appalling because of the senseless manner of the deaths. Exact figures are not available, but reliable estimates fix the number of California Indians in 1850 at a figure of 100,000 to 250,000. Fifty years later, the estimate ranges from 13,000 to 17,000. This represents a decrease in population of from eighty-three to ninty-five percent.[50]

Understandably, not all whites were insensitive to the harsh treatment accorded the California Indians, and many cried out in opposition. Their cries, however, were not heeded. John Collier, Commissioner of Indian Affairs in the Roosevelt administration, said, in his report to the 74th Congress:

> They were actually murdered. They were outlawed and treated as wild animals, shot on sight . . . They were enslaved and worked to death. They were treated as predatory animals. They were driven back to the totally barren vastness, and out into the desert, and they died of starvation. Their life was outlawed and their whole existence was condemned and their hearts were broken—and they died.[51]

And thus, Manifest Destiny became a reality. The new United States stretched from the Atlantic Ocean to the Pacific, and from the Great Lakes to the Rio Grande. The area east of the Mississippi was generally cleared of Indians and the Far West had eliminated most of the problems with the natives by either slaughtering them or confining them to concentration camp types of reservations. This left the great central portion as the next area to be opened for settlement. Until the 1850s, it had been considered a vast wasteland which had to be crossed in order to reach the wealth of the coastal area. The Indians were generally left to their own devices and, aside from a comparatively few incidents, the Plains Indians had not caused much of a problem to the Americans. Settlers had crossed their hunting grounds in huge numbers, even dividing the great buffalo herd, but had continued their westward trek without displacing the natives. Soon, however, this changed and the battle for land again raged.

An event which moderated the movement into the Plains by the white settlers and seriously affected the lives of many Indians was developing. On April 12, 1861, the Civil War began.

Eight
The Civil War

As the shelling of Fort Sumpter affected the lives of the United States and Confederate States inhabitants, so it affected the Indian nations west of the Mississippi River. In spite of their isolated locations and their desire to ignore the conflict for the most part, the Indians were inextricably involved. Even those who took no part in the actual fighting found themselves responding to the circumstances brought on by the war. This response varied from actual participation in military actions by some of the "Five Civilized Tribes" to being recipients of pent-up anger by settlers, as represented by the "Sand Creek Massacre"—the flagrant murderous attack on peaceful Cheyenne and Arapaho Indians.

The southeastern tribes had been in Oklahoma for only one generation and were getting their nations re-established when the Civil War interrupted their progress. Some of the tribesmen were plantation owners and slaveholders. Their sentiments naturally were with the South. Some felt an empathy with the northern cause but found themselves in a precarious geographic location. Others felt they had been abandoned by the Union and turned to the South for survival. A few of the people stubbornly held a neutral position throughout the war and suffered tremendously for their efforts.

The Choctaw, located adjacent to the strong Confederate states of Arkansas and Texas and with a strong pro-southern element, joined the South and never wavered in their support. The Chickasaws, although they did not border strong Confederate states, also remained with the southern forces. The Cherokee, Creek, and Seminole Tribes were divided in their loyalty and all three had civil wars of their own.

On May 17, 1861, the Congress of the Confederacy passed an act annexing the Indian Territory and placing all tribes under the jurisdiction of the new southern government. Albert Pike was appointed as Indian Commissioner and given the responsibility of negotiating new treaties with the tribes. He was also instructed to obtain their aid in fighting the Union troops. Pike waged a successful campaign among the tribes and secured treaties with many. The Choctaw-Chickasaw alliance furnished three regiments of troops to the Confederate Army and they saw action in Missouri, Arkansas, and eastern Oklahoma.[52] The Creeks and Seminoles supplied one regiment, and the Cherokees provided two more regiments for the South.

Thousands of Cherokees, Creeks, and Seminoles, maintaining their loyalty to the United States, were forced from their homes. The refugees gathered around Fort Gibson in northern Oklahoma, where they suffered terrible hardships. Congress gave them inadequate support and some of this went into the pockets of corrupt officials. Since the territory was a hotbed of Confederate guerrillas, the Indians were unable to leave the protection of the fort to provide for themselves. Deprivation, disease, and death decimated the loyal Indians and they were victims of much more suffering than those who joined the Confederacy. At the end of the Civil War, there were still some 19,000 Indian refugees scattered throughout the territory.

At the close of hostilities, the United States government began a series of ''peace treaties'' with the defeated Indian nations. These agreements of 1866 varied in severity according to the bargaining strength of the tribes. Since the government officials were unable to fragment the united Choctaw and Chickasaw people, these two nations received better terms than did their divided neighbors. The two southern sympathizers did not have to surrender their tribal rights, but they did have to cede the western portion of their country, already under lease to the United States, for settlement of other Indian tribes. They also gave concessions for railways to be built on their land.

The other three members of the Five Civilized Tribes, although generally more loyal to the Union, received far less generous treatment. The Cherokees, divided throughout the war, had John Ross, and he was able to obtain better terms. The Creeks and Seminoles, who had suffered so much for their Union loyalty, were even required to subscribe to a confession of war guilt. The Creeks lost part of their land and the Seminoles had to give up all their holdings and relocate once again on a smaller, less desirable tract.

The Cherokees, Creeks, and Seminoles were forced to give their freed slaves citizenship and property rights. The Choctaws and Chickasaws were allowed to adopt their freedmen and receive money for the ceded land.

Although the treaties were rather harsh, they did allow the Indian nations to re-establish themselves under their own institutions. The Indians in the Oklahoma Territory began a rebuilding process reminiscent to that of the 1830s and 1840s, when they rebuilt their nations after removal. They exhibited once again the remarkable resilience and recuperative power of the Indian people. By the end of a decade, the nations were functioning much in the same manner as in pre-war years.

Meanwhile, other Indian groups, generally on the frontier, were drastically affected by the Civil War. Some of the most affected were the various bands of Sioux, and, in particular, the Santees who remained in Wisconsin and Minnesota when their relatives migrated to the Great Plains.

Although some unrest existed and minor differences between the Santees and the white settlers had occurred, the situation had never become tense enough for concern by either party. It was a minor incident which changed the comparatively quiet scene to one of all-out warfare.

About twenty young Sioux went on the warpath in an attempt to "prove" themselves and killed three men and two women. They then rode to their reservation and informed the tribe of what had happened. The leaders assembled the tribal council and debated whether to commit themselves to war or seek peaceful settlement for the acts of the young warriors. Probably encouraged by the absence of many of the settlers who were fighting in the Civil War, the decision of the council was to launch full-scale attacks on the whites.

Warfare began in August 1861 and the settlers were caught completely unprepared. Sioux warriors left their tiny reservation along the Minnesota River and attacked every white settlement they found in the area. Men, women, and children were killed or taken hostage as the Indians gave vent to their pent-up emotions. They fought with such ferocity that the southwestern portion of Minnesota was depopulated and, after the Indians were defeated and removed, it took many years to resettle the region.

The Indians won several battles with the military, but the final disposition was inevitable. The military might of the United States forced capitulation in only a couple of months and the government began a retaliatory campaign of "war trials" and sentences. Over 300 Sioux were tried, convicted, and sentenced to hang for their part in the uprising. President Lincoln commuted the sentences of those who were only guilty of warfare, stating they should be treated as prisoners of war. Thirty-eight Sioux were convicted of murder and rape and were hanged for their crimes. The balance of the Santee Sioux were removed from Minnesota and relocated in the northeastern corner of Nebraska where their reservation is today,

Although sporadic fighting continued in the northern Plains until the "Wounded Knee Massacre" of 1890, the savage retaliation and retribution accorded the Santee is considered by some historians as the "fatal blow."

In Colorado, extreme malevolence was the common practice toward the Cheyenne, Arapaho, and other indigenous natives. Unprovoked attacks on these peaceful tribes were carried out to provide practice for troops stationed in the West, to provide publicity for some ego-maniacal leaders, or in some cases simply for entertainment.

One of the worst offenders and one of the advocates of "Indian genocide" was Colonel John Chivington. He was an itinerant preacher with political aspirations and was placed in command of the District of Colorado. In April 1864, after a false report that Cheyennes had stolen some cattle, Chivington and his Colorado Volunteers took the field with orders to kill every Cheyenne they found and to take no prisoners.

The Volunteers raided friendly Cheyenne camps and murdered the unsuspecting Indians. This cruel slaughter soon stirred up warfare, not only with the Cheyenne and Arapaho, but also with the Kiowa, Comanche, and Sioux, who received refugees from the Colorado tribes. It was not long, however, before the Cheyenne peace chiefs tired of the warfare and requested the protection of Federal troops. They moved to a place on Sand Creek, about 40 miles from Fort Lyon, and established a friendly camp of approximately 700 Cheyenne and 75 Arapaho, mostly women, children, and old men. There, on November 29, 1864, one of the most horrendous events in Indian-white relations took place.

Chivington, with 750 armed and mounted soldiers, attacked at dawn. A few Cheyenne men reached their weapons and attempted to defend their families, but were quickly cut down. Women and children were brutally murdered and their bodies horribly mutilated. It was as if the soldiers had become possessed by demons, and no action was too cruel or debased for them to perform. Major Scott J. Anthony, commander at Fort Lyon, later wrote, "We, of course, took no prisoners," and Chivington's heroic display of over 100 scalps gave mute testimony that Anthony was correct.

As facts began to come out concerning the raid, even the tough Colorado Territory became concerned and investigations were conducted. The testimony by participants of the massacre revealed the true character of Chivington, but he had resigned from the service and could not be court-martialed. What happened at Sand Creek not only ruined Chivington's political ambitions, but it did much more. As word of the murders reached the Sioux, Arapaho, and other Cheyenne groups, they began a campaign of retaliation which turned the northern Plains red with blood. These tribes combined their fighters and declared war on the whites with about 1,600 of the greatest mounted fighting men the world has ever known. They emulated the white soldiers in battle and proved they were apt pupils. The warfare was cruel and waged without quarter. Men, women, and children were killed as outpost after outpost fell. Chivington's murderous activity was returned by the allied Indian forces before they withdrew to the Powder River country, their revenge completed. The whites had been taught that Indian retaliation was swift and merciless. Perhaps peace would have been possible, at least for a while, if it were not for one thing—the railroad.

To those in America with broad vision, it was apparent that California and the Pacific Coast regions existed in a different philosophical and geographical realm from the East. If this new nation was to flourish, the situation had to be remedied and the tool to bring about the cohesion of East and West was the railroad. In binding the two geographic extremes, it was necessary to people the vast midcontinent area to provide services and continuity to the welding of these two empires. To meet these needs, in 1862, President Lincoln signed the Morrell Act, creating land grant colleges in each state; the Homestead Act, providing free land to settlers; and the Railroad Act, which assured a coast-to-coast railway. These acts had a drastic effect on the Indian people in the central portion of the United States.

When Lincoln signed the Act authorizing the construction of the transcontinental railway, an army of laborers poured into the West. Towns appeared almost overnight along the rights of way to house and support the construction crews. Homesteaders flooded into the area in such numbers that they were like a great tidal wave. To feed this mushrooming population, meat was required and buffalo contractors were employed to meet the demand. Scouring the plains with no regard for the Indians' needs, these contractors slaughtered the animals promiscuously, and as the thin line of whites stretched the iron rails farther west, the great buffalo herd was divided into two parts. This division separated more than the herd; it also divided the northern and southern Plains tribes and destroyed much of the unity which was established following "Sand Creek."

Since the rights of way were patrolled and protected by military and "friendly" Indian units, homesteaders were free to squat, gradually pushing farther and farther into Indian territory.

Although Mr. Lincoln expressed a sincere empathy with the Indians' problems, his actions did not necessarily follow his articulation. In ten years, he had pre-empted Indian ownership of 71,000,000 acres for land grant colleges, 85,000,000 acres to homesteaders, and 155,000,000 acres to railroad companies in rights of ways and alternate sections of land. With this land depletion and the division and decimation of the buffalo herd, the Plains Indians teetered on the brink of total destruction. As if this were not enough, the cessation of hostilities in the Civil War brought a new mass of invaders to the Plains.

Union soldiers, having been discharged from military service, flocked to the area looking for land and wealth. Some, oriented in wartime pursuits, merely were looking for adventure. Many of the Confederate warriors, finding only destruction and desolation in the South, turned westward to get a new start. And so, wave after wave of whites rolled over the Indian country and the Plains Nations prepared for their final stand in defense of their homes.

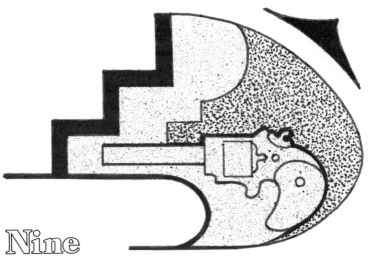

Nine
Reconstruction and the Indian Wars

The effects of the Civil War were felt in the Southwest as well as in other portions of Indian country. During the conflict, General James H. Carleton, military commander of the New Mexico Territory, launched an active campaign against the Indians under his jurisdiction. He rounded up over 400 Mescalero Apaches, confined them at Bosque Redondo in New Mexico, and built Fort Sumner to guard them. He then turned his attention to the Navajo and sent Kit Carson to round them up and move them to join the Mescaleros at the Bosque.

The story of this campaign is well known and presents another black mark in American history. When Carson attacked the Navajos, they retreated to Canyon de Chelly and hid in the almost inaccessible cliffs. It was immediately apparent to Carson that the only tactic to dislodge the Indians was to starve them out. He instituted a "scorched earth" policy, burning their crops, destroying their orchards, and killing or capturing their herds. The Navajos eventually surrendered and were marched across the desert to Bosque Redondo on their infamous "Long Walk." By the end of the war, over 8,000 Navajos had moved in with the unfriendly Mescaleros. This situation was untenable for both tribes, and in November 1865, the entire group of Mescaleros vanished. Even to this day, no white man knows where they went or how they lived. Finally, on May 29, 1873, a reservation was established for them in their homeland, where they still live.

The Navajos continued to live at the compound, constantly pleading to be allowed to return to their homes. They entered into a treaty with the United States government on July 25, 1868 and were assigned a huge area of their homeland which no one else really wanted. There, they re-established their culture and began the process of rebuilding their nation.[53] Other tribes would soon follow this process as reservations were established over the United States.

Ulysses S. Grant was elected President of the United States in 1868 and introduced a new concept in dealing with Indians. He stopped negotiating with the Indian tribes as independent, sovereign nations of people and began assigning them to reservations where they could be protected and treated as wards of the government. This policy was generally humanitarian, but while it eliminated warfare and

Canyon de Chelly, Navajo sacred ground.

Navajo hogan—traditional house style still used by the Navajo people.

physical extinction, it inadvertently instituted cultural genocide on the Indian people.

President Grant's concepts of private ownership of the land and dissolution of communal life would become one of the most effective genocidal tools yet devised. Indians would cease to exist in their natural form and would be remade to conform to the cultural patterns introduced by European invaders. In changing the Indians into white emulators, Grant envisioned economic stability for the individual Indian without realizing the price of the conversion. Grant's reconstruction process had a drastic effect on the lives of Indian people, and ramifications of his Indian policies were apparent for many years.

The Five Civilized Tribes faced a physical rebuilding process during this period. The Creeks, Seminoles, and Cherokees suffered great losses of population during the war and their homeland was ravaged. They therefore were faced with physical restoration. The Choctaws and Chickasaws were not so drastically affected and were soon on the road to recovery. Schools were reopened, education was again started, and the war was soon pushed into the background. It took the rest of Indian Territory longer to recover and some had not even regained their former status when Oklahoma became a state in 1907.

While the tribes in Indian Territory were faced with many troubles, they were generally allowed to seek solutions and rebuild without the presence of any warfare. Such was not the case, however, for the Plains Indians. The release of thousands of soldiers from military service and the wide-open, unspoiled hunting grounds in the southern Plains created a situation which had to conclude in physical confrontation. As though the atmosphere were not tense enough, another element entered the picture and assured that the Plains would erupt into general warfare. Major General Winfield Scott Hancock was appointed commander over the region and his Indian policy was extremely harsh. He concluded the Plains Indians needed a lesson in discipline and selected the Cheyenne as the ones to provide the example for the rest. Hancock is attributed to advocating killing enough Cheyenne to inspire fear and then moving the balance to reservations where they could be controlled. He used every opportunity to provoke the Cheyennes into armed confrontation. Peace conferences arranged with the Indians were disrupted by Hancock's threats and his arrogance in dealing with the tribesmen. The Cheyennes, with the memory of Sand Creek still fresh in their minds, did not trust Hancock, and his attitude strengthened this mistrust.

General Hancock finally pushed the Cheyenne far enough that they rebelled and he had his war. Hancock found, however, that fighting the central and southern Plains Indians was no easier than battling the Sioux. These warriors were equal to or better than any fighters on earth and they led the Army on a merry chase. Stage stations, farms, supply wagons, and towns were ravaged by these warring Indians. They even learned how to wreck trains and looted them pretty much at will. Hancock had started something the military was not prepared to handle.

The Cheyennes were joined in their efforts by the Kiowas and the Comanches of the southern Plains, and these combined forces were awesome in battle. It took five years of concerted military effort to confine the Cheyennes to a reservation, but once they did settle down, they remained peaceful until a general war broke out in 1874. One by one, the other combatants also made peace and moved to reservations.

The tribes kept the peace except for isolated incidents which could not actually be blamed on the Indians. From time to time, settlers would encroach on Indian territory or some young military officer would attempt to establish a name by attacking hunting parties, and small-scale wars would ensue. Generally, though, it was quiet in the area until 1874, when fighting broke out between the Comanches and the Army. The Kiowas, Arapahos, and Cheyennes joined in, and once again the Plains were afire with Indian war.

The hostilities continued for a while, but the Indians were worn out from the years of relentless pressure and fighting. The winter campaign of 1874 and 1875 ended warfare in the central and southern Plains. The tribes settled down for good on their reservations and began the process of converting from hunting to ranching. This released many of the army troops from the area and allowed them to concentrate on the Sioux, northern Cheyenne, and Arapahos in the northern Plains.

These tribes had been enjoying a peaceful existence in the Powder River country since the 1865 victories over the cavalry. The discovery of gold in Montana and later in the Black Hills would ignite the rapacious greed of the whites and cause the eventual collapse of the native lifestyles of the Plains Indians.

As the miners and settlers poured into Sioux country, all-out war developed. The brash young Army officers, fresh from successful battles during the Civil War, seemed to feel they were invincible. They soon found they had grossly underestimated the Indian forces and their very capable leadership. The Plains were soon engulfed in bloodshed and, in 1868, the United States entered into a treaty with the Sioux, with the Indians dictating the terms. This Fort Laramie Treaty gave the Sioux a huge area of land, including western South Dakota, part of North Dakota, and the Powder River country. The United States agreed to close the Bozeman Trail that crossed the area, evacuate all military forts, and keep all whites out of the territory. This treaty was generally observed and respected by both parties for about six years, until an incident in 1874 ended the peace and precipitated another war, the final struggle in the northern Plains.

In the spring of 1874, an exploration expedition under the command of Colonel George Armstrong Custer was sent into the sacred Black Hills. The military was accompanied by a large party of scientists, reporters, and gold prospectors, and although the government never admitted it, the party was unquestionably seeking gold. Soon the area was over-run by miners and settlers and the treaty was forgotten.

When the Indians refused the government's offer to purchase their land, war was begun by the Army. Brigadier General George Crook, Major General Alfred Terry, Custer, and other noted Indian fighters were sent to subdue the northern Plains tribes. The combined forces of the U.S. Army were under the command of General Terry and he vowed that this time the Indians would not escape. He sent Custer to the Little Big Horn River, where a camp of Sioux had been discovered, and he planned to join forces with Custer on June 26, 1876.

Pushing his command to the limit, Custer arrived at the rendezvous point one day early, on June 25. Spurred by his egotism and political ambitions, he made some extremely poor decisions. He divided his troops, sending Major Marcus Reno with three troops to the south, Captain Fred Benteen with about 125 men to scout the western edge of the camp, and he led six troops in from the north. These divided groups, not waiting for Terry's forces, attacked the Indians without realizing the force they were meeting.

Gathered on the rolling hills were Sioux warriors under the leadership of Gall and Crazy Horse; Cheyennes under their great war chief, Two Moons; and a large number of Arapaho warriors. These groups, with their families, constituted the greatest concentration of Indians ever assembled at one place. They were led by the great spiritual leader, Sitting Bull, who had received a vision of their victory over the whites. Encouraged by the prophesy and directed by the greatly respected war leaders, the Indians attacked Custer in a highly organized manner. First, they isolated Reno and Benteen and inflicted heavy losses on their troops. While part of the Indians kept these two groups of cavalry pinned down, Crazy Horse led the major portion of the warriors in an onslaught against Custer. The result was a staggering defeat for the Seventh Cavalry. All of Custer's men were killed, along with a large number of Reno's and Benteen's. The entire group would have been annihilated if Sitting Bull had not intervened. He had seen enough killing and it was now time for other things. The Indians, had they utilized the white man's method of warfare, could have also wiped out Terry and Crook at the same time, but chose instead to break camp and disperse.

The Army attempted to retaliate for Custer's defeat, but without success. The Sioux were tired of war and did not want to lose their women and children. Sitting Bull and Gall, with many of their followers, moved to Canada and lived in peace for many years. The other Sioux groups surrendered and settled around the agencies on their reservations.

The Arapahos surrendered and were kept at Camp Robinson for a while. This location was not appropriate for these mountain people and they soon began to die. After about a year, they were transferred to the Wind River Reservation, which they shared with the Shoshoni tribe.

The Cheyenne were removed to Indian Territory to live with their southern relatives, and this proved disastrous for these northern people. They could not adjust to the climate and large numbers died from disease. After being refused permission to return to their homeland, they walked out of camp and began an exodus that was one of the saddest in history. Led by their chief, Dull Knife, and their war leader, Little Wolf, they made their way through adverse weather and hostile white territory, evading or defeating U.S. troops all the way, until they reached their homes. So much public sympathy had been aroused by their heroism and sufferings that the federal government established a reservation for them and they were allowed to remain.

The fear of another "Little Big Horn" incident had drastic effects on other Indian tribes. One of the saddest and most poignant stories of all time is the account of Chief Joseph and the Nez Perce and their flight.

The Nez Perce resisted selling their land and settling on a reservation. Theirs was not a militant resistance but one of logical argument with the government agents. Located in the mountainous area of present-day eastern Oregon and Idaho, this tribe had long been friendly with the white settlers.[54] Their religious attitudes of keeping the land where their ancestors' bones were buried and their refusal to tear their "earth mother's skin" with plows did not make sense to the American arbitrators. They construed this argument as a militant gesture, and to prevent Chief Joseph from forming a confederacy of northwestern tribes, the government ordered all Nez Perce bands to the reservation at Lapwai. Although most of the peaceful Nez Perce moved, a few young hot-heads resisted and the war was on.

Joseph and the other Nez Perce leaders attempted to avoid warfare and tried to move their people to Canada. The United States military forces, under the command of General Oliver Otis Howard, the "Christian General," tried to prevent the exodus. The Nez Perce outfought, out-maneuvered, and outsmarted the army forces. They had travelled over 1,300 miles in their journey before being stopped just 30 miles from the Canadian border by the combined forces of General Howard and Colonel Miles. After several days of fighting in a cold gale, Chief Joseph delivered his famous surrender speech to General Howard.[55]

Tell General Howard I know his heart. What he told me before, I have in my heart. I am tired of fighting. Our chiefs are killed. Looking Glass is dead. The old men are all killed. It is cold and we have no blankets. The little children are freezing to death. My people, some of them, have run away to the hills and have no blankets, no food; no one knows where they are, perhaps freezing to death. I want time to look for my children and see how many of them I can find. Maybe I shall find them among the dead. Hear me, my chiefs, I am tired; my heart is sick and sad. From where the sun now stands, I will fight no more forever.[56]

After the surrender, the Nez Perce were sent back to the reservation at Lapwai (where they still live). Joseph, whose only crimes were seeking peace and protecting his people, was not allowed to return to his homeland. He was assigned to the Colville Reservation, where he died in 1904.

With the subjugation of the Nez Perce, the Great Plains and the Rocky Mountains were nearly clear of "hostile" Indians. Only the conquering of a few small groups remained and this vast area of land would be available for the total exploitation of the rapidly expanding United States.

In 1878, the small Bannock tribe from Ft. Hall Reservation became angry because white settlers had destroyed the camass roots, a mainstay in the diets of the Bannocks and other Plateau tribes. Enlisting the aid of a few Pauite and western Shoshoni, they began attacking settlers in the area. It only took General Howard a few months to bring this small rebellion under control and the Bannocks were thoroughly broken.

Outrages perpetrated against the Utes in Colorado sent them on the warpath the next year. In an attempt to force them to adopt farming as their method of subsistence, the Ute agent plowed up the pasture land used to sustain the horses and cattle of the tribe. The small uprising in protest to the plowing was all the Coloradoans needed to drive out the Utes. With ferocity reminiscent of Chivington, the military overwhelmed the small group of Indians and drove them to the barren wastelands of Utah.[57] Only a small group was allowed to remain in the southwestern corner of the state where the Southern Ute Reservation now exists.

With the conquest of these small bands of natives by the massive military might of the United States, the entire country was in the control of the dominant, conquering forces except for one area, the Great Southwest, which was still subject to disruption by a small scattered group of Indians referred to as Apache. These scattered bands of nomadic warriors had been harassed and vilified by the European invaders from the first contact with the Spanish in the sixteenth century. Because of their fierce independence and their magnificent ability to survive, they became the object of hate and depredation by the Americans. The story of the conquest of Apacheria is a pathetic account of a people subjugated by the use of every devious and inhumane act mankind has devised. The many tactics utilized in the triumphant vanquishing of small nations of Indians were all brought to bear in awesome proportions against the Apache. And still they survived![58]

The attitudes that seemed to prevail in the Southwest during the latter half of the nineteenth century indicate the sincere belief of most groups, civilian and military, that the solution to the "Apache problem" was extermination. Held in check to some degree by orders from Washington, the military attempted to control the Apache by killing the warriors and confining the others to strictly controlled reservations.

Most of the Apache bands were quite peaceful and had to be provoked into conflicts. Even after many provocations, including massacres of their people, the groups remained peaceful and sought protection from the military. Such was the case of the Aravaipas under their leader, Eskiminzin.

In 1863, a company of California Volunteers had attacked the peaceful Aravaipa Apaches, killing a large number and driving the rest into the mountains, where they hid out for nearly eight years. Finally, in February 1871, out of sheer desperation, they moved back to their homeland and settled at Camp Grant, where they were under the protection of the military. The citizens of Tucson, lusting for Apache blood, took advantage of the situation: on April 30, 1871, they—along with Mexican and Papago-Pima allies—struck while most of the men were away. They murdered about 125 Apaches, all but 8 of whom were women and children, and captured 27 children and turned them over to the Pimas and Papagos to be sold as slaves. The survivors of this atrocity were eventually sent to the San Carlos Reservation, where their descendants now live.

The Chiricahua Band, led by the renowned Cochise, had welcomed the Americans when they first entered their empire in southern Arizona. It was only after repeated violations of agreements and atrocities perpetrated by whites that Chochise went on the warpath. He virtually sealed off the territory and stopped travel across the desert until General Howard established peace once again with the Chiricahuas. Chochise, through respect for Howard, kept the peace until his death. Because of the efforts of Tom Jeffords (who had a contract to carry the mail through the area) and General Howard, the Chiricahua remained in their homeland until 1876, when most of the band were removed to San Carlos.[59]

Part of the peace agreement between Chochise and Howard included the cessation of raiding in Mexico by the Chiricahuas. One of Chochise's subchiefs, Geronimo, could not concur because of his vows of continued warfare against the Mexicans.[60] Typical to Apache democracy, he was allowed to take his followers and separate from the rest of the group.

Born about 1834 near Tularosa, New Mexico, Geronimo was one of the finest fighting men who ever lived. He was an uncanny tactician and an able practitioner of psychological warfare. He never had more than a handful of fighting men and was encumbered by the women and children of his group, yet he outwitted, outfought, and made fools of thousands of U.S. troops under the leadership of the ablest "Indian fighters" of the period. It is doubtful that he would ever have been captured if it were not for his own tribesmen, the Apache scouts, used by the Army.

Finally, in August 1886, Geronimo surrendered to General Nelson Miles and moved with his small contingent of Apaches to Fort Bowie, Arizona and then to Fort Apache Reservation. This respite was only for a short time, however, and in a few months Geronimo and about 750 other Apaches were shipped to prison in Florida. The irony of it all was that most of the Apaches were not members of the hostile group and many were scouts who had helped capture Geronimo. Their payment for service to Miles and the United States was to share the exile with their captive.

The Florida internment was disastrous for the Apaches, who were not accustomed to the low altitude and humidity. Many became sick and died. Geronimo managed to send one wife and two children back to New Mexico when it was learned she was a Mescalero.[61]

In October 1894, the remaining Apache prisoners were transferred from Florida to Fort Sill, Oklahoma. These exiles were never allowed to return to their homeland and Geronimo died in this alien land in 1909. The balance of the prisoners were given the option of remaining in Oklahoma or joining the Mescaleros on their reservation. About one-third of the Apaches remained and today inhabit the area around Fort Sill. Most of the remaining prisoners moved to Mescalero and , like their relatives, settled down to a peaceful life of herding, farming, and timber work.

With the subjugation of the Apaches, Indian opposition to white expansion ceased. Indian wars were over and the tribes were totally confined to their respective reservations, where they were at the mercy of the corrupt Indian agents, the cultural erosion by the various Christian denominations, and the manipulation of politicians, anthropologists, and social welfare workers.

Ten
The Aftermath

At last, after almost 400 years of resistance to the invasion of the repugnant European, the American Indian was totally defeated. Most of the leaders had been killed, degraded even in death by the exhibition of parts of their bodies, and then vilified in historical writings by scribes of the conquerors. The followers were separated into small bands and herded into concentration camps, where they were reduced to pitiful, starving creatures forced to beg their subjugators for the barest necessities for survival. The land, except for the generally barren and desolate reservations, had been over-run by the white hordes, and sacred Mother Earth had been denuded and defiled. And, worst of all, the spirits of the Indian people had been thoroughly broken. Their indomitable will had finally been crushed and living was more from habit than desire.

Now that Indianness had been subdued, the government began an earnest campaign to acculturate the remnants of the tribes. The bureaucracies seemed totally insensitive to the needs and desires of the Indians and used a unilateral approach in their fervor to make whites from Indians. The great acculturation tool used during this time, and still used today for the same purpose, was formal education.

The "civilizers" were equally insensitive in their determination to "educate" Indian children. The old adage, "As the twig is bent, so grows the tree," was never utilized more fully than it was by the United States in its Indian education policy. Children were forcibly removed from their homes and shipped—sometimes thousands of miles away—to federal boarding schools. Some of these Indian students did not see their parents for ten or twelve years because they were "farmed out" to white families during vacations. This, it was thought, would keep them from returning to their savage ways. In 1885, the Federal Superintendent of Indian Schools said that in order to make the Indian "a member of a new social order . . . we must recreate him, make him a new personality." This "recreating" reached far beyond the education of the children, though; it reached into the very nuclei of the tribes themselves.

One of the first moves to establish this "new personality" for the Indian was to abolish the recognition by the United States that the various tribes were legal and sovereign nations of people. Since the treaty is considered the "supreme law of the land" and the government had entered into over 400 treaties with the various Indian nations, thereby establishing them as sovereign nations, it took federal legislation to change the process. On March 3, 1871, Congress, in an obscure rider to the Indian appropriation bill, outlawed further treaty-making with Indian tribes. It stated:

. . . . That hereafter no Indian nation or tribe within the territory of the United States shall be acknowledged or recognized as an independent nation, tribe, or power with whom the United States may contract by treaty.[62]

Thus, with one swift stroke of the pen, Indians ceased to be citizens of their nations and became wards of the government. This legislative action legalized the acculturation and termination processes which followed.

From the mid-1800s the Indian policy of the United States was a confusion of regulations which basically consisted of two types of treatment. For the tribes which had resisted the white man, such as the Sioux, the policy was one of complete subjugation in a concentration camp condition. The buffalo were killed off and the tribes were totally subsidized by the government. The tribesmen were restricted to the boundaries of the reservation, and, if they strayed beyond their assigned limits, they were hunted down by the military and returned. The Apaches were probably the most notorious for refusing to be confined, and several leaders, Geronimo being the best known, led the army on a merry chase when reservation life became untenable.

This restriction and subsidization was intended to keep the warlike tribes in a state of impotence and thus render them harmless to the surrounding area populated by whites. For the most part, the policy was successful and, aside from Geronimo, the Indians were fairly docile. It was not the subsidies or the confinement that kept them under control, however; it was the complete loss of hope and the broken spirits that forced the compliance to the reservation rules.

The tribes that had been peaceable and friendly to the Americans were afforded a completely different treatment. They received little support from the government, and since it was recognized that these groups offered little or no threat to the white population, very little was done for their benefit. The Commissioner of Indian Affairs explained the government's attitude clearly in 1872 when he said:

. . . . It is not a whit more unreasonable that the Government should do much for the hostile Indians and little for friendly Indians than it is that a private citizen should, to save his life, surrender all the contents of his purse to a highwayman; while on another occasion, to a distressed, and deserving applicant for charity, he would measure his contribution by his means and disposition at the time. There is precisely the same justification for the course of the Government in feeding saucy and mischievous Indians to repletion, while permitting more tractable and peaceful tribes to gather a bare subsistence by hard work, or what to an Indian is hard work.[63]

This harsh, practical statement does much to indicate the feelings of Commissioner Francis A. Walker concerning the wards he was assigned.

This control by the government and rendering the tribes impotent was a preparatory strategy for the next major step in the Americanization of the Indian people. It was considered by many an impossible task to convert the tribes to the philosophy of the European invaders as long as they were allowed to live in communal societies with their own forms of traditional government. Another of the acculturation processes which helped prepare the Indians for the breaking of their traditional lives was the assignment of the reserva-

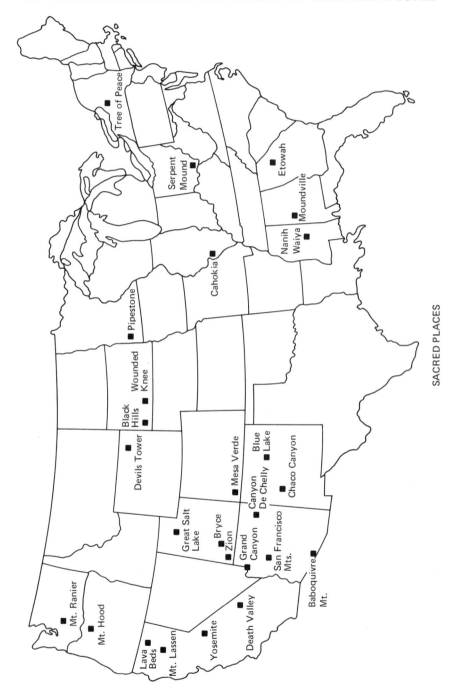

SACRED PLACES

Tree of Peace

Serpent Mound

Etowah

Moundville

Nanih Waiya

Cahokia

Pipestone

Wounded Knee

Black Hills

Devils Tower

Mesa Verde

Blue Lake

Chaco Canyon

Canyon De Chelly

Great Salt Lake

Bryce

Zion

Grand Canyon

San Francisco Mts.

Baboquivre Mt.

Mt. Ranier

Mt. Hood

Lava Beds

Mt. Lassen

Yosemite

Death Valley

tions to various religious groups for supervision. Commissioner Walker, in his Annual Report of November 1, 1872, described the apportionment as follows:

. . . . The following schedules exhibit the present apportionment of Indian agencies among the several religious associations and missionary societies. The figures refer to the number of Indians embraced in the several agencies:

Friends (Hicksite), the Northern superintendency and the agencies therein, viz: Great Nemaha, 313; Omaha, 969; Winnebago, 1440; Pawnee, 2,447; Otoe, 464; and Santee Sioux, 965; all located within the State of Nebraska.

Friends (Orthodox), the Central superintendency and the agencies therein, viz: Pottawatomie, 400; Kaw, 290; Kickapoo, 598; all located in Kansas; and Quapaw, 1070; Osage, 4,000; Sac and Fox, 463; Shawnee, 663; Wichita, 1,250; Kiowa, 5,490; and Upper Arkansas, 3,500; all located in the Indian Territory.

Baptist, the Cherokee, 18,000; Creek, 12,300, in the Indian Territory; Walker River, 6,000 and Pi-Ute, 2,500 in Nevada; and Special, 3,000, in Utah.

Presbyterian, the Choctaw 16,000; and Seminoles, 2,398 in the Indian Territory; Albiquiu or Terra Amarilla, 1,920; Navajo, 9,114; Mescalero Apache, 830; Tulerosa, or Southern Apache, 1,200, in New Mexico Territory; Moquis Pueblo, 3,000 in Arizona Territory; Nez Perce, 2,807 in Idaho Territory; and Uintah Valley, 800, in Utah Territory.

Christian, the Pueblo, 7,683, in New Mexico; Neeah Bay, 604, in Washington Territory.

Methodist, Hoopa Valley, 725; Round Valley, 1,700; and Tule River, 374, in California; Yakima, 3,000; Skokomish, 919; Quinaielt, 520, in Washington Territory; Warm Springs, 626; Siletz, 2,500; and Klamath, 4,000 in Oregon; Blackfeet, 7,500; Crow, 2,700; and Milk River, 19,755 in Montana Territory; Fort Hall, 1,037 in Idaho Territory; and Michigan 9,117, in Michigan.

Catholic, Tulalip, 3,600; and Colville, 3,349 in Washington Territory; Grand Ronde, 870; Umatilla, 837, in Oregon; Flathead, 1,780 in Montana Territory; Grand River, 6,700; and Devil's Lake, 720, in Dakota Territory.

Reformed Dutch, Colorado River, 828; Pima and Maricopa, 4,342; Camp Grant, 900; Camp Verde, 748; and White Mountain, or Camp Apache, 1,300 in Arizona Territory.

Congregational, Green Bay, 2,871; and Chippewas of Lake Superior, 5,150, in Wisconsin; and Chippewas of the Mississippi, 6,455, in Minnesota.

Protestant Episcopal, Whetstone, 5,000; Ponca, 735; Upper Missouri, 2,547; Fort Berthold, 2,700; Cheyenne River, 6,000; Yankton, 1,947; and Red Cloud, 7,000, in Dakota Territory; and Shoshone, 1,000 in Wyoming Territory.

American Board of Foreign Missions, Sisseton, 1,496, in Dakota Territory.

Unitarian, Los Pinos, 3,000; and White River, 800, in Colorado Territory.

Lutheran, Sac and Fox, 273, in Iowa. . . . [64]

Now that the Indian had been confined and "Christianized," and the children had been sent to boarding schools to be remade in the

image of the white man, the time had come to deliver the final blow against Indianness. On February 8, 1887, the federal government passed one of the most insidious legislative acts since the Removal Act of 1830. The General Allotment Act (Dawes Act) became a law for the special protection of the Indian Allottee in the enjoyment and use of his land.[65]

Undoubtedly, the leading proponents of allotment were inspired by the highest motives and regarded it as a panacea for making restitution to the Indian for all the white man had done to him in the past. The difficulty lay in the perspective used in designing this "solution." The aim of the "friends of the Indian" was to substitute white civilization for his tribal culture, with no thought to the Indian's beliefs or value systems. The concept of property ownership was the fundamental difference between white and Indian life. Whites strove for individual ownership, while Indians did everything for the good of the tribe. Members of the dominant society all agreed the white man's way was good and the Indian's way was bad. To alleviate this situation, the Allotment Act would not only give individual Indians ownership of parcels of land, but it would also break up tribal life. This would enable the Indian to acquire the "benefits of civilization."

The basic provisions of the Dawes Act was to divide the reservation land acquired by the tribes by treaty into small, individually owned tracts. These would be allotted to the several members of the tribe with a twenty-five year restriction on the owner's selling the land.[66]

Since the reservations were quite large and the Indians were so few in number, after the land was divided, there were thousands of acres left over. The Act gave the President authority to purchase the surplus land, and the proceeds accruing from such sale were to be used to further the education and civilization of the tribes. Most of the money used for education was utilized in construction and maintenance of federal boarding schools.[67]

There were other incidents connected to the allotment process that were extremely detrimental to the Indian way of life. One of the most devastating of these was the destruction of tribal government and the dissolution of tribal life. In Section 6 of the Act it was specified:

That upon the completion of said allotments and the patenting of the lands to said allotees, each and every member of the respective bands or tribes of Indians to whom allotments have been made shall have the benefits of and be subject to the laws, both civil and criminal, of the State or Territory in which they may reside. . . .

This section, in essence, made all allottees a citizen of the State or Territory and eliminated the tribal government as a governing body by excluding tribal members from its jurisdiction. This was a legal and very subtle way to destroy the tribes.

The dissolution of tribal life was obtained in a similar manner. A white agent assigned to the Yankton Sioux stated this dissolution philosophy quite succinctly when he wrote in 1877:

As long as the Indians live in their villages they will retain their old and injurious habits. Frequent feasts, community in food, heathen ceremonies and dances, constant visiting—these will continue as long as the people live together in close neighborhoods and villages—I trust that before another year is ended they will generally be located on individual lands of farms. From that date will begin their real and permanent progress.[69]

The Indian, then, was to learn to go his own independent, industrious way and he would become "civilized." As Senator George Pendleton stated in 1881: "It must be our part to seek to foster and to encourage within them (the Indians) this trinity upon which all civilization depends—family, home, and property."

Senator Dawes, the author of the Allotment Act, also made very clear the illogical white philosophy of progress and civilization, in an address in 1885 at Lake Mohunk Conference:

The head chief told us that there was not a family in the whole Nation (one of the Five Civilized Tribes) that had not a home of its own. There was not a pauper in that Nation and the Nation did not owe a dollar. It built its own capitol and it built its own schools and its hospitals. Yet the defect of the system was apparent. They have got as far as they can go, because they own their land in common. It is Henry George's system, and under that there is no enterprise to make your home any better than that of your neighbors. There is no selfishness, which is at the bottom of civilization. Till this people will consent to give up their lands, and divide them among their citizens so that each can own the land he cultivates, they will not make much more progress.[70]

The allotment of Indian land began with the Sioux and spread until nearly every tribal land base was dissolved. The Five Civilized

Tribes, the Osages, and a few others who held their land under patented title held out for a time. These patents were legal and the government hesitated to invalidate them. It was not long, however, before the federal government created the vehicle to accomplish their objective by passing the Curtis Act of 1898. This infamous legislation provided for the allotment of the patented land, the division of the tribes' other property, and the termination of their tribal government.

Between the passage of the Dawes Act in 1887 and the cessation of land allotment provided in the 1934 Indian Reorganization Act, chaos reigned in Indian country. The tribes lost nearly 100 million acres of land—about two-thirds of their holdings.[71] Tribal government was impotent and the people had no representation except that provided by a rather inept Bureau of Indian Affairs. Their children were being taken from their homes and shipped off to distant boarding schools. Their homes and lands were being confiscated by white men who had "purchased" them without the Indians understanding the transactions. There was nothing for the Indians to look forward to except a continuously unhappy situation. Even their population declined, and they seemed on the road to extinction. By 1900, only 237,000 Indians remained alive in the United States.[72] Pleasant Porter, the great Creek mixed-blood chief of the late nineteenth century, stated the situation clearly when he spoke to the Board of Indian Commissioners in 1903:

. . . There is no life in the people who have lost their institutions. Evolving a thing out of itself is natural, transplanting it is a matter of dissolution, not growth . . . the older people are dying off. There is no new disease; I don't see anything other than the lack of hope.

Thoroughly defeated by the might of the white man's armies, removed from their sacred homeland, with their leaders killed or rendered powerless, the Indians were at a point where only a spiritual revival could bring them from the depths of despair. Such was the situation of the Indians when the Ghost Dance was born. This religious exercise was developed as a psychological response of a people to intolerable stresses laid upon them by poverty and oppression.

Actually, the Ghost Dance originated in the Nevada desert on the Walker River Reservation. It was developed from a vision related by Wavoka (Jack Wilson), a Paiute spiritualist, in which he was transported in a dream to Heaven where he stood in the presence of God. He received instructions for the Paiutes "to be good and love one another and not fight, steal, or lie." God also gave Wavoka a dance for his people. By performing this five-day dance, the people would secure happiness for themselves and hasten the day when they would be reunited with dead friends and loved ones in another world. There, no evil or sadness would be experienced and only happiness would prevail.

Although the dance and the religion had been practiced by the Paiutes for a number of years, the Sioux first heard of it in the winter of 1888. Since their situation was so deplorable, the Ghost Dance was received readily by the people. And just as denominational differences occur in Christian religions over interpretation, so did they occur in the various groups embracing the Ghost Dance.

The Sioux, Cheyenne, and Arapahoe suffered extreme physical depredations at the hands of the whites and this was indicated clearly in their interpretation of the dance and the religious doctrine. They envisioned the "return of the ghosts" and the annihilation of the white man. The people were told that the Great Spirit had sent the whites to punish the Indians for their sins, and that the sins were now expiated and the time of deliverance was at hand. Their decimated ranks were to be reinforced by all the Indians who had ever died, and these spirits would bring with them huge herds of buffalo and ponies.

Shirts were made and decorated elaborately and these would turn aside the bullets of the white men. The whites would be overcome and the Indians would once again rule the land. In order to bring about this happy result, the Indians had to believe and participate in the exhaustive Ghost Dance. The tribes were ecstatic, and dance after dance was held in 1890, urged on by leaders such as Sitting Bull.

The Indians danced with such frenzy and exhibited so much excitement that the government agents became fearful of an all-out war developing. Sitting bull was killed by Indian police sent to arrest him and the situation grew more precarious every day. The whites were certain that an alliance formed around the Ghost Dance religion among the northern Plains tribes would bring about the same kind of large scale military confrontation as the one at the Little Big Horn that had killed General Custer and hundreds of men just fourteen years before. The entire Sioux Reservation became a tinder box, ready to explode.

One group of Minneconjou Sioux, under the leadership of Big Foot, fled the Cheyenne River Agency and headed for Pine Ridge and the protection of the great Oglala chief Red Cloud. They were intercepted at Wounded Knee Creek by two units of the Seventh Cavalry, Custer's old regiment, under the command of Colonel Forsyth. The troopers surrounded Big Foot's group and Forsyth demanded the surrender of the Indians' weapons. The Sioux immediately followed these orders, but somehow, in the confusion, gunfire broke out. The soldiers opened fire on the defenseless Indians with carbines, and the two Hotchkiss guns located on a hill overlooking the camp started firing explosive shells at a rate of one per second. In a few minutes, Big Foot and over half his followers were hit. Many tried to escape the massacre but were pursued by the troops and shot. Some women and children were found dead as far as three miles from the battle site. There is little doubt that the battle became a vendetta for the Custer defeat. The accepted estimate places the number of dead at nearly 300 of the 350 Sioux in the band. The Army lost 27 men, but most of them were hit by Army bullets fired in the frenzy of killing by the soldiers.

Thus ended the "Battle at Wounded Knee," more commonly known as the "Wounded Knee Massacre." This was the last semblance of resistance offered by any Indian group for many years. The Ghost Dance had not resurrected the dead Indians and the Ghost Shirts had not turned aside the white man's bullets. The buffalo were still gone and the Indians were still oppressed and confined to their reservations. Black Elk recalled the incident at Wounded Knee and recognized the horrendous ramifications of this incident. He said later:

I did not know then how much was ended. When I look back now from this high hill of my old age, I can still see the butchered women and children lying heaped and scattered all along the crooked gulch as plain as when I saw them with eyes still young. And I can see that something else died there in the bloody mud and was buried in the blizzard. A people's dream died there. It was a beautiful dream. . . . And I, to whom so great a vision was given in my youth,—you see me now a pitiful old man who has done nothing, for the nation's hoop is broken and scattered. There is no center any longer, and the sacred tree is dead.[73]

Sioux "Ghost Shirt" worn during the "Ghost Dances."

Monument at Wounded Knee—mass grave erected in 1903 by the Sioux Indians.

The mass grave at Wounded Knee. It contains the bodies of 102 adult Sioux men and women, 25 old men, 7 old women, 6 boys aged 5 to 8 years, and 7 infants.

Wounded Knee Battlefield in 1976.

Eleven
The Politicians

Prior to the twentieth century, the Indians had been primarily affected by actions of the military. When the tribes were crushed by the federal troops, the Army became a secondary force in Indian activities. From the latter part of the nineteenth century, the Indian people became the pawns of the political bureaucrat. With each new federal administration and each new Commissioner of Indian Affairs, the policies regulating the activities of the tribes changed. It was as if the Indians were puppets on the strings held by political puppeteers, each with a new tune to which the marionettes must dance.

One of the most rigid Commissioners of Indian Affairs and one who advocated withholding rations to force Indians to comply with his stringent policies, was W. A. Jones. He served in this post for about seven years, from 1897 through 1903, and strongly advocated starving his wards into complete compliance. The following letter indicates his attitudes toward those he was appointed to serve:

January 13, 1902

The Superintendent
Greenville School,
California.

Sir:

This office desires to call your attention to a few customs among the Indians which, it is believed, should be modified or discontinued.

The wearing of long hair by the male population of your agency is not in keeping with the advancement they are making, or will soon be expected to make, in civilization. The wearing of short hair by the males will be a great step in advance and will certainly hasten their progress towards civilization. The returned male student far too frequently goes back to the reservation and falls into the old custom of letting his hair grow long. He also paints profusely and adopts all the old habits and customs which his education in our industrial schools has tried to eradicate. The fault does not lie so much with the schools as with the conditions found on the reservations. These conditions are very often due to the policy of the Government toward the Indian and are often perpetuated by the superintendent's not caring to take the initiative in fastening any new policy on his administration of the affairs of the agency.

On many of the reservations the Indians of both sexes paint, claiming that it keeps the skin warm in winter and cool in summer; but instead, this paint melts when the Indian perspires and runs down into the eyes. The use of paint leads to many diseases of the eyes among those Indians who paint. Persons who have given considerable thought and investigation to the subject are satisfied that this custom causes the majority of the cases of blindness among the Indians of the United States.

You are therefore directed to induce your male Indians to cut their hair, and both sexes to stop painting. With some of the Indians this will be an easy matter; with others it will require considerable tact and perseverance on the part of yourself and your employes to successfully carry out these instructions. With your Indian employes and those Indians who draw rations and supplies it should be an easy matter as a non-compliance with this order may be made a reason for discharge or for withholding rations and supplies. Many may be induced to comply with the order voluntarily, especially the returned student. The returned students who do not comply voluntarily should be dealt with summarily. Employment, supplies, etc. should be withdrawn until they do comply and if they become obstreperous about the matter a short confinement in the guard-house at hard labor, with shorn locks, should furnish a cure. Certainly, all the younger men should wear short hair, and it is believed that by tact, perseverance, firmness, and withdrawal of supplies the superintendant cán induce *all* to comply with this order.

The wearing of citizen's clothing, instead of the Indian costume and blanket, should be encouraged.

Indian dances and so-called Indian feasts should be prohibited. In many cases these dances and feasts are simply subtrafuges to cover degrading acts and to disguise immoral purposes. You are directed to use your best efforts in the suppression of these evils.

Very respectfully,
W. A. Jones
Commissioner

Commissioner Jones was a stern taskmaster in many ways when it came to dealing with the tribes. He felt that the government should hasten their assimilation into the mainstream of society by forcing them to provide for themselves, whether a way was available or not. He strongly advocated that the agents not only encourage, but also enforce, regular labor among the Indians by withholding rations unless the Indian worked. In his report of October 1, 1900, he states:

. . . . As a method of aiding the deserving while they are learning the art of self-support the ration system is commendable. That is its aim and object. The great evil lies in the gratuitous distribution to all alike. With the necessities of life assured without effort, the incentive to labor disappears and indolence with its baleful influence reigns supreme.

It is difficult to point out a complete remedy for the evils described, but as a beginning the indiscriminate issue of rations should stop at once, a somewhat difficult thing to accomplish as long as the tribes are herded on the reservations having everything in common. The old and helpless should be provided for, but with respect to the able-bodied, the policy of reducing rations and issuing them only for labor should be strictly enforced, while those who have been educated in Indian schools should be made to depend entirely upon their own resources.

This philosophy is sound and strongly emphasizes the Puritan ethic of ''earning one's bread by the sweat of the brow.'' It does not, however, give any latitude for diversity of cultures or values; nor does it consider that there was no gainful employment available for Indians on a reservation. It does not appear that Mr. Jones knew much about conditions and circumstances of the tribesmen. If he did, he showed rather callous disregard for them.

The Commissioner also illustrated the coercive influence of his office when, in 1900, he abolished the tribal government of the Osage Nation. His reasoning was that the Osage people were divided into factions and could not agree, and that some of their elected officials were ignorant. (Sounds as if he was describing the contemporary politicians of America, doesn't it?) Mr. Jones also resented the "waste" of money in the attempt to educate the American Indian. In his report of October 15, 1901, he said:

To begin at the beginning, then, it is freely admitted that education is essential. But it must be remembered that there is a vital difference between white and Indian education. When a white youth goes away to school or college his moral character and habits are already formed and well defined. In his home, at his mother's knee, from his earliest moments he has imbibed those elements of civilization which developing as he grows up distinguish him from the savage. He goes to school not to acquire a moral character, but to prepare himself for some business or profession by which he can make his way in after life.

With the Indian youth it is quite different. Born a savage and raised in an atmosphere of superstition and ignorance, he lacks at the outset those advantages which are inherited by his white brother and enjoyed from the cradle. His moral character has yet to be formed. If he is to rise from his low estate the germs of a nobler existence must be implanted in him and cultivated. He must be taught to lay aside his savage customs like a garment and take upon himself the habits of civilized life.

. . . . He must be brought to realize that in the sweat of his face he shall eat his bread. He must be brought to recognize the dignity of labor and the importance of building and maintaining a home. He must understand that the more useful he is there the more useful he will be to society. It is there he must find the incentive to work, and from it must come the uplifting of his race.

. . . . But whatever the condition of the Indian may be, he should be removed from a state of dependence to one of independence. And the only way to do this is to take away those things which encourage him to lead an idle life, and, after giving him a fair start, leave him to take care of himself. To that it must come in the end, and the sooner steps are taken to bring it about the better. That there will be many failures and much sufferring is inevitable in the very nature of things, for it is only by sacrifice and sufferring that the heights of civilization are reached.

With this type of benevolence and understanding it is no wonder Indians sank lower and lower into the pits of despair. They had been rendered impotent in their own cultural desires, herded onto desolate reservations, totally placed at the mercy of governmental bureaucrats, and then told that if they wanted to eat, they must work according to the white man's dictates. There was no rationale to this philosophy and Indians became more and more confused and disheartened.

In 1905, however, a man with a great amount of common sense and practical thinking was appointed as Commissioner of Indian Affairs. Francis E. Leupp assumed the office in the middle of the fiscal year and set about to add some sensitivity to the handling of Indian affairs. In his first report, on September 30, 1905, he attempted to establish his new policy. He said:

> The commonest mistake made by his white well-wishers in dealing with the Indian is the assumption that he is simply a white man with a red skin. The next commonest is the assumption that because he is a non-Caucasian he is to be classed indiscriminately with other non-Caucasians, like the negro, for instance. The truth is that the Indian has as distinct an individuality as any type of man who ever lived, and he will never be judged aright till we learn to measure him by his own standards, as we whites would wish to be measured if some more powerful race were to usurp dominion over us.
>
> Suppose, a few centuries ago, an absolutely alien people like the Chinese had invaded our shores and driven the white colonists before them to districts more and more isolated, destroyed the industries on which they had always subsisted, and crowned all by disarming them and penning them on various tracts of land where they could be fed and clothed and cared for at no cost to themselves, to what condition would the white Americans of today have been reduced? In spite of their vigorous ancestry they would surely have lapsed into barbarism and become pauperized. No race on earth could overcome, with forces evolved from within themselves, the effect of such treatment. That our red brethren have not been wholly ruined by it is the best proof we could ask of the sturdy traits of character inherent in them. But though not ruined, they have suffered serious deterioration, and the chief problem now before us is to prevent it going any further.

Mr. Leupp realized that it would be a difficult task to change the older Indian people and prepare them to cope with current problems. He understood that some of the young adults could be enlisted but realized that many would not be flexible enough to adapt to a rapidly changing world. The only hope was with the young people who were still "measurably plastic." Mr. Leupp, however, did not subscribe to the tactics used in the past to bring this about:

> The task we must set ourselves is to win over the Indian children by sympathetic interest and unobtrusive guidance. It is a great mistake to try, as many good persons of bad judgement have tried, to start the little ones in the path of civilization by snapping all the ties of affection between them and their parents, and teaching them to despise the aged and non-progressive members of their families. The sensible as well as the humane plan is to nourish their love of father and mother and home—a wholesome instinct which nature planted in them for a wise end—and then to utilize this affection as a means of reaching through them, the hearts of the elders.
>
> Again, in dealing with these boys and girls it is of the utmost importance not only

that we start them aright, but that our efforts be directed to educating rather than merely instructing them. The foundation of everything must be the development of character. Learning is a secondary consideration. When we get to that, our duty is to adapt it to the Indian's immediate and practical needs. . . . Most of these [Indians]will try to draw a living out of the soil; a less—though, let us hope, an ever increasing—part will enter the general labor market as lumbermen, ditchers, miners, railroad hands, or what not. Now, if anyone can show me what advantage will come of this large body of manual workers from being able to reel off the names of the mountains in Asia, or extract the cube root of 123456789, I shall be deeply grateful. To my notion, the ordinary Indian boy is better equipped for his life struggle on a frontier ranch when he can read the simple English of the local newspaper, can write a short letter which is intelligible though maybe ill-spelled, and knows enough of figures to discover whether the storekeeper is cheating him. Beyond these scholastic acquirements his time could be put to its best use by learning how to repair a broken harness, how to straighten a sprung tire on his wagon wheel, how to fasten a loose horseshoe without breaking the hoof, and how to do the other bits of handy tinkering which are so necessary to the farmer who lives 30 miles from a town.[74] The girl who has learned only the rudiments of reading, writing, and ciphering, but knows also how to make and mend her clothing, to wash and iron, and cook her husband's dinner will be worth vastly more as mistress of a log cabin than one who has given years of study to the ornamental branches alone.

Francis Leupp also recognized the Indian as being misjudged by most Americans. He advocated getting to know the people in the rural setting who had not been contaminated by white ways. He wanted to acknowledge and preserve Indian aesthetic qualities such as music, dance, and the value systems which made the Indian unique. Mr. Leupp, long an advocate for abolition of boarding schools, started an energetic campaign for establishing on-reservation day schools. He initiated much needed improvements in Indian health care and, for a time, the situation of the Indian people was a little better.

As indicated earlier in this chapter, Indian Affairs policy was subject to change as new administrators assumed control. The vacillation of the politicians who became Commissioners of Indian Affairs was much like a pendulum, as one would be empathetic and understanding and the next would only berate the Indians for not acculturating more quickly. Such was the case when Commissioner Francis E. Leupp left office and Robert G. Valentine became the Commissioner of Indian Affairs.

In his report of 1910, Valentine reported evidence of fraud and ignorance in handling the allotment of Indian land, yet he did not question the validity of breaking up the tribal land base and conveying the land to the individual Indian. Although the Kickapoos and other Indians lost their newly allotted land through outright robbery and other groups were surely to be faced with the same experience in the future, Valentine was apparently willing to sacrifice the people he was appointed to serve in order to perpetuate the allotment psychosis.[75] By his admission of knowledge of the situation and his lack of action to alleviate it, he condoned and even encouraged the perpetuation of such activities.

Commissioner Valentine was concerned with the "immorality" of the Indian people and expended much of the resources of his office in establishing "proper moral philosophy" among the tribesmen. He attacked the Indians' use of alcohol but he only advocated treatment of the symptoms and ignored the disease. He called for stricter laws concerning the sale of alcoholic beverages to Indians and did little to alleviate the spiritual, physical, or social causes of drinking among the tribes. In his report to Congress on October 2, 1911, he stated:

> The use of intoxicating liquors is a direct and incalculable injury to Indians in undermining health and in making them undependable as workmen. . . . Moreover, it furnishes to designing white men a convenient means for carrying out questionable purposes. During the year every effort was used to enforce laws against the liquor traffic. . . .
>
> Throughout the country the necessity of keeping Indians from securing intoxicants is being appreciated. In California, Lassen County considered an ordinance prohibiting the sale of liquor alike to full and mixed bloods, and the town of Upper Lake, at which we have an agency, voted for prohibition. In connection with the situation in Minnesota . . . the Minneapolis, St. Paul, and Sault Ste. Marie Railroad issued instructions to its employees forbidding shipments of intoxicants into the territory concerned. The Legislatures of California, Montana, Washington, and Wisconsin had under consideration amendments to their present laws against the sale of liquor to Indians and the Supreme Court of Washington rendered a decision upholding the legality of the State law forbidding the traffic.

Thus, the various legislative bodies began their concerted drive to impose moral values upon the Indians by their legal processes. The continuing assumption of white moral superiority is also evident in the Bureau of Indian Affairs' investigation of the influence of the peyote bean. The peyote cult, with its all-night meetings, was seen as encroaching upon the time the Indian could be doing "useful" work. Thus, the last vestiges of traditional Indian life now came under attack. Through the boarding schools, little by little, the Indian languages, dress, social activities, and values had been seriously diminished. Now it was time to begin the erosion of the religious life in the inexorable march of the acculturation process. With their religions gone, it was thought, the Indians would have nothing more to keep them from being totally Americanized. This philosophy was clearly stated by Mr. Valentine in his 1911 report:

A relatively new intoxicant of a peculiarly insidious form has come into favor with Indians in many parts of the country. From a cactus growing wild in the arid regions of old Mexico just south of the Rio Grande the crown is cut off and dried, becoming the peyote bean of commerce. Among the tribes it is commonly known as mescal. As these beans sell for $3 or $4 a thousand and three or four beans suffice to give the full effect of the intoxicating drug in peyote, indulgence is within the reach of all.

The office has been gathering information from every available source concerning the effect of the peyote bean but still experiences some difficulty in getting complete information. Nevertheless, the information now at hand concerning the physiological and sociological results of the use of this drug is such that the office will in every way practicable prevent the Indians from indulging in it further. The physiological and toxic action of peyote places it in the same general class as opium, cocaine, Indian hemp, and chloral hydrate. The alkaloids in peyote act upon the central nervous system. This action, if repeated, unquestionably results in a fixed habit. The normal functions of the human body can not be interfered with at frequent intervals by such an agent as peyote without serious injury resulting. As used by the Indians, peyote is always taken in very considerable quantities, invariably sufficient to produce drug intoxication.

Even if the physiological effects of this drug were not serious, its use would have to be prohibited for the same sociological reasons as have led the government strongly but tactfully to modify Indian dances. As is well known, exercises which the Indians consider of a religious nature are made the occasion of taking the drug. These meetings are held as often as once a week and invariably last throughout the night. The time occupied in going to these meetings, the demoralizing effect of all night seances, and consequent nervousness and exhaustion, very considerably encroach upon the time that should normally be devoted to work. Furthermore, the effects of the drug in making the Indian contented with his present attainments seriously interfere with the progress by cutting off from him the possibility of healthful aspiration.

It is evident that Mr. Valentine was correct when he said he'd had difficulty obtaining complete information, for much of what he stated was grossly erroneous.[76] The "Puritan Work Ethic" was expressed repeatedly by Mr. Valentine in his reports. He, like so many Americans when viewing the work habits of the Indian people, was either ignorant of the cultural implications or refused to recognize them. The connotation was that the Indian must speak, think, and act like a white man, with no vestiges of his original culture. Failure to do this indicated not a flaw in the system or the methods used in dealing with Indians, but rather a flaw in the Indian himself.

One bright spot in Indian affairs did occur which can be attributed to Mr. Valentine: he resigned as Commissioner of Indian Affairs on September 12, 1912. For about nine months, the office was directed by F. H. Abbott, Acting Commissioner, and on June 4, 1913, Mr. Cato Sells was sworn in as Commissioner. Mr. Sells immediately recognized the inefficiency of the Bureau of Indian Affairs and, unlike many bureaucrats, did not seem overly optimistic about any radical change in the operation. He did proclaim, however, that "the speedy individualizing of the Indian" remained the "fixed purpose" of the Indian Bureau.

In assessing the "progress" of the Indian people, Commissioner Sells very clearly indicated his "paternalistic" concern. Although voicing a self-determination concept, he envisioned the process as one of total acculturation rather than a way of helping the Indian to function in his own realm of cultural autonomy. In other words, Mr. Sells, like so many of his peers, wanted to benevolently change Indians into whites.

On April 17, 1917, there was announced a new declaration of policy for Indian affairs. Mr. Sells set up the following rules to be observed:

1. Patents in fee.—To all able-bodied adult Indians of less than one-half Indian blood, there will be given as far as may be under the law full and complete control of all their property. Patents in fee shall be issued to all adult Indians of one-half or more Indian blood who may, after careful investigation, be found competent, provided, that where deemed advisable patents in fee shall be withheld for not to exceed 40 acres as a home.

   Indian students, when they are 21 years of age, or over, who complete the full course of instruction in the Government schools, receive diplomas and have demonstrated competency will so be declared.
2. Sale of lands.—A liberal ruling will be adopted in the matter of passing upon applications for the sale of inherited Indian lands where the applicants retain other lands and the proceeds are to be used to improve the homesteads or for

other equally good purposes. A more liberal ruling than has hitherto prevailed will hereafter be followed with regard to the applications of noncompetent Indians for the sale of their lands where they are old and feeble and need the proceeds for their support.

3. Certificates of competency.—The rules which are made to apply in the granting of patents in fee and the sale of lands will be made equally applicable in the matter of issuing certificates of competency.

4. Individual Indian moneys.—Indians will be given unrestricted control of all their individual Indian moneys upon issuance of patents in fee or certificates of competency. Strict limitations will not be placed upon the use of funds of the old, the indigent, and the invalid.

5. Pro-rata shares—trust funds.—As speedily as possible their pro-rata shares in tribal trust or other funds shall be paid to all Indians who have been declared competent, unless the legal status of such funds prevents. Where practicable the pro-rata shares of incompetent Indians will be withdrawn from the Treasury and placed in banks to their individual credit.

6. Elimination of ineligible pupils from the Government Indian schools.—In many of our boarding schools Indian children are being educated at Government expense whose parents are amply able to pay for their education and have public school facilities at or near their homes. Such children shall not hereafter be enrolled in Government Indian schools supported by gratuity appropriations, except on payment of actual per capita cost and transportation.

Mr. Sells reveals his misconception of the Indians' desires and point of view, as well as his own myopic view of the situation, when he further states:

These rules are hereby made effective, and all Indian Bureau administrative officers in Washington and in the field will be governed accordingly.

This is a new and far-reaching declaration of policy. It means the dawn of a new era in Indian administration. It means that the competent Indian will no longer be treated as half ward and half citizen. It means reduced appropriation by the Government and more self-respect and independence for the Indian. *It means the ultimate absorption of the Indian race into the body politic of the Nation. It means, in short, the beginning of the end of the Indian problem.* (Emphasis added by the author.)

And so it continued. The driving urge to acculturate the American Indian and force him into the "melting pot" whether he wanted to or not was evident in the most empathetic and seemingly understanding American. This attitude became even more prevalent as the dawn of America's entry into World War I brought about an added emphasis on patriotism and the "American way of life."

Just as the American Indian helped fight the "White Man's

Wars" in 1776, 1812, and 1861, he also was ready to do the same in 1917. Before the draft was established, over 2,000 Indians had enlisted in the armed services of Canada and the United States. After the draft was put into effect, Indians continued to distinguish themselves in their show of patriotism. Not only did they register for service, but thousands volunteered. Of the 17,313 American Indians who registered, only 228 claimed exemption from military service. Most of these were claims of age or of the claimant occupying a high religious office in his tribe. Over half of those who registered served in the military forces, a much higher percentage than that of any other group.

Indians did not restrict their patriotism to military service. Over 10,000 subscribed to Red Cross membership, and Indians purchased over $15,000,000 in Liberty Bonds, making a per capita subscription of over $50. It is incorrect to assume that Indians contributed so much in manpower and money from their meager sources primarily for the lust for adventure. Indians participated so fully in the war effort for several reasons: (1) the military did provide an outlet for the restlessness of Indian youth, allowing him an opportunity to "prove" himself; (2) World War I provided the first opportunity many Indian men had ever had to hold a steady job and to earn a living for their families; and (3) it provided a vehicle to display the fierce loyalty of the Indians, not necessarily to the United States, but to each of their own Indian nations as a part of the United States.

Indian men had a very deep reverence for bravery, and the war gave many of them an opportunity to display this facet of their culture. Many of the World War participants were sons or grandsons of veterans of the Little Big Horn or other battles of "Indian wars." They were undoubtedly thrilled by the stories told by their elders of these "days of glory," and welcomed the chance to display their courage. Although Indian warfare was not waged as Europeans fought, to seek conquest or to subjugate another people, the tribesmen were eager to run the risks in order to obtain the status of warriors with their tribes.

The economic advantage of joining the military service during the war was a pragmatic consideration for many Indians. In his report of 1913, Commissioner of Indian Affairs Cato Sells pointed out the lack of economic stability on Indian reservations. Confined for the most part on unproductive lands, Indians were unable to pursue an agricultural vocation, and the educational system had not equipped them to function in the industrial society. It was quite attractive to many of the young men, therefore, to enlist in a military organization which not only allowed them to establish their manhood in war, but at the same time, paid them on a regular basis for doing it.

Many Indians also reasoned that if it was necessary for the United States to go to war to defend itself, it was only logical that their nations, the Cherokee, Sioux, Choctaw, etc., were also endangered. Therefore, not only to prove their manhood and participate in the cultural fulfillment of warfare, or to provide economic stability to their lives by being self-sufficient, but also to defend their homeland, Indians enlisted in military service.

American Indian servicemen were exceptionally good soldiers and distinguished themselves in many ways during the war. Their bravery under fire was never doubted, but many accomplishments went far beyond the "warrior" activity. Many Indians became leaders and proved to be outstanding in initiative and battlefield strategy. Others provided communicative tactics which baffled the enemy.

The Germans were adept in "tapping" the American telephone lines and then out-maneuvering the Allies because they knew the plan of action. Indian soldiers were used to alleviate this situation, as indicated in a report by Colonel A. W. Bloor, commander of the 142nd Infantry Regiment, 36th Division:[77]

In the first action of the 142nd Infantry at St. Etienne, it was recognized that of all the various methods of liaison, the telephone presented the greatest possibilities. The field of rocket signals is restricted to a small number of agreed signals. The runner system is slow and hazardous. T.P.S. is always an uncertain quantity. It may work beautifully and again, it may be entirely worthless. The available means, therefore, for the rapid and full transmission of information are the radio, buzzer, and telephone, and of these the telephone was by far the superior—provided it could be used without let or hindrance,—provided straight to the point information could be given.

It is well understood that the German was a past master in the art of "listening in." Moreover, from St. Etienne to the Aisne we had travelled through a country netted with German wires and cables. We established P.C.'s in dugouts and houses, but recently occupied by him. There was every reason to believe every decipherable message or word going over our wires also went to the enemy. A rumor was out that our Division had given false coordinates of our supply dump, and that in thirty minutes the enemy shells were falling on that point. It was, therefore, necessary to code every message of importance and coding and decoding took valuable time.

While comparatively inactive at Baux-Champagne, it was remembered that the regiment possessed a company of Indians, who spoke twenty-six different languages or dialects, only four or five of which were ever written. It was hardly possible that Fritz would be able to translate these dialects, and the plan to have these Indians transmit telephone messages was adopted. The regiment was fortunate to have two Indian officers who spoke several of the dialects. Indians from the Choctaw tribes were chosen and one placed in each P.C.

The first use of the Indians was made in ordering a delicate withdrawal of two companies of the 2nd Battalion from Chumfilly to Chardeny on the night of October 26th. The movement was completed without mishap, although it left the 3rd Battalion greatly depleted in previous fighting, without support. The Indians were used repeatedly on the 27th in preparation for the assault on Forest Farm. The enemy's complete surprise is evidence that he could not decipher the message.[78]

It was also a common practice during the conflict to assign American Indians to duties as scouts for their units. It was assumed in some cases that the Indian had some inherent talent which would enable him to always keep his bearings and to slip across the terrain without revealing his location to the enemy. Perhaps by living close to nature and observing it, Indians did have a little edge on many of their non-Indian peers. However, it is highly unlikely that any geneticist would concur that inherited tendencies of the Indian provided him with any innate characteristics which would make him a "natural" scout.

Indian soldiers did serve with excellent military capabilities and many performed great feats of valor. Commissioner of Indian Affairs Cato Sells provided high praise for Indian bravery and courage in his report to Congress of September 30, 1919:

. . . . As a rule the Indian bears his honors very modestly and his reluctance to any display has somewhat hindered definite information in many cases. I shall, however, give a few instances as of representative significance:

It is reported that Francis Lequire, a young Chippewa, in the company with two or three others, attacked a machine gun nest, and when left as the only survivor, faced all that remained of the machine gunners and killed or captured the entire group. He was said to be recovering from 11 wounds received in action.

James M. Elson (deceased) of the Tulalip Reservation, was cited by his commanding officer for guiding sentry squads to an isolated post in no man's land, and for guiding patrols to outskirts of Brieulles, securing information of enemy occupation, and showing exceptional skill, courage, and coolness under fire.

The superior officer of Richard Bland Breeding, a young Creek of Oklahoma said of him, "He was the most capable, daring, and fearless platoon leader in the division."

Among those who won the Croix de Guerre was volunteer John Harper, a full-blood Uncompahgre Ute, of which details are lacking at this time; Chester Armstrong Fourbear, a full-blood Sioux of South Dakota, cited for bravery in swift running as a messenger at Bellicourt; Ordinance Sergt. James M. Gordon, of Wisconsin, cited for rescuing while under shell fire a second lieutenant of the French Army who was wounded while on an inspection tour; Nicholas E. Brown, a full-blood Choctaw, who when killed was a corporal in the 142nd Infantry composed largely of Oklahoma Indians, the honor being posthumously awarded; Marty Beaver, an orphan boy who enlisted in Company F, 142nd Infantry, 36th Division, details at present lacking.

Alfred G. Bailey, a Cherokee of Oklahoma, had been in regular service with Gen. Pershing in Mexico. He was a sergeant when killed in action in France and was awarded the Distinguished Service Cross for creeping into the enemy's lines alone far in advance of his regiment where, unaided, he killed two German machine gunners and captured a third with his gun.

Walter G. Sevalia, of Brule, Wisconsin, a corporal in Company F, 7th Engineers, was cited for "extraordinary heroism" in action near Breuilles, France in November, 1918. He swam the Meuse under terrific fire with a cable for a pontoon bridge, and later carried another cable over the Est Canal and across an open field covered by enemy machine guns. At this time he was wounded but returned bearing a message of great importance.

Sergt. O. W. Leader, a three-fourths Choctaw, was foreman of a cattle ranch in Oklahoma when he entered the war. Greatly to his chagrin an idle rumor gained currency that he was a Hun spy. He quit the cattle business at once and enlisted as proof of his American loyalty. He was cited for bravery in battle in the course of a brilliant record of which the following is a synopsis: Fought at Cantigny, May 23, 1918; fought at Soissons, Chateau-Thierry, July 18, 1918; fought in St. Mihiel Saleint, September 12, 1918; fought at Argonne Forest, October 1, 1918. Twice wounded and twice gassed. In addition to this military record is the interesting fact that Sergt. Leader was selected by the French Government as the model original American soldier of whom an oil painting should be made to hang on the walls of the French Federal building where will be displayed types of all the allied races.

Probably no more brilliant instance is recorded than that furnished by Pvt. Joseph Oklahombi, a full-blood Choctaw, of Company D, 141st Infantry, whose home is at Bismarck, Oklahoma, and who received the Croix de Guerre under the order of Marshall Petain, commander in chief of the French Armies of the East. A translation of the order follows:

Under a violent barrage, dashed to the attack of an enemy position, covering about 210 yards through barbed-wire entanglements. He rushed on machine gun-nests, capturing 171 prisoners. He stormed a strongly held position containing more that 50 machine guns, and a number of trench mortars. Turned the captured guns on the enemy and held the position four days, in spite of a constant barrage of large projectiles and of gas shells. Crossed no man's land many times to get information concerning the enemy, and to assist his wounded comrades.[79]

As a "reward" for their patriotism and their contributions to the war effort, American Indians who had served in the military or naval establishments of the United States, and who had received or who should receive thereafter an honorable discharge, were offered the opportunity of being granted citizenship. Many Indians rejected this offer for fear of losing their identity as Indians and seeing their tribes swallowed up by America.[80]

This act of "benevolence" by the government and its rejection by the Indians set the stage for new and less subtle methods in the great Americanization effort.

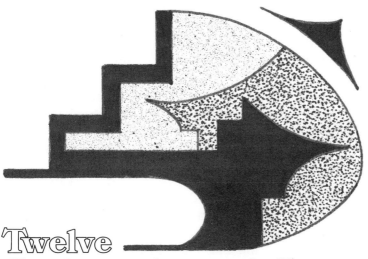

Twelve
Confrontation and Change

By the 1920s, the condition of Indians in the United States was extremely serious. Through the machinations of the Dawes Act (Allotment Act), they were rapidly losing their land. Reformers, both governmental and individual, continued their unrelenting attack on Indian cultures, insisting that they must be assimilated into white society. Indian arts and crafts were dying out or being taken over by white materialistic artisans. Indian children were being shipped to distant boarding schools where they could be deculturized more rapidly and thoroughly, despite strong parental protestations. The erosion of the last obstacle to the "Americanization" of Indians—their native religious practices—was accelerated, since the government judged them pagan ceremonies that hindered the acceptance of Christianity. The basic concepts of freedom of religion and separation of church and state were completely disregarded. As with so many activities in the area of Indian affairs, any operation used to manipulate the tribes was acceptable, regardless of legality or morality.

One of the centers of forced acculturation was in the Rio Grande Pueblos. Controversies had raged for many years over Pueblo ownership of land. Encouraged by an 1871 Supreme Court ruling

135

that Pueblo Indians were not wards of the government and that their lands were not under Federal guardianship, white squatters had invaded the Pueblo territory. In 1913, the Supreme Court reversed the decision and ruled the Pueblo title to the land was perfect and unimpaired. This decision prompted the Indians to attempt to legally recover their lands from the white dispossessors and, of course, this action caused furor which reached the highest political offices in the government.

Albert B. Fall was appointed to the office of Secretary of the Interior in 1921 by newly elected President Warren G. Harding.[81] Fall initiated action to counter the Pueblos by promoting a bill to Congress which would transfer Pueblo title from the Indian owners to white squatters. The Bursum Bill, named for the Senator who introduced it, not only transferred ownership with a very blatant disregard for morality, but also had other equally damaging ramifications. It brought the internal affairs of the Pueblos under the jurisdiction of the United States District Court, thus making the Pueblo leaders directly responsible to the court. The proposed law would have had the effect of establishing a religious inquisition, for the internal affairs of the Pueblos were completely involved with their religion. Among the Rio Grande Pueblos, the rule of secrecy is inviolable. Leaders were bound by custom not to divulge the workings of the tribal council. Under the Bursum Bill, the Indian Bureau would have been able to keep priests, governors, and other leaders of the tribes in jail for contempt of court if they refused to reveal council information. The loss of the privilege of secrecy and the subversion of leadership by the court would have brought these independent groups completely under the control of white politicians, ending their traditional way of life.

None of the Pueblo Indians even knew of this bill, for it had been carefully guarded since its inception. Through the intervention of John Collier, who later became Commissioner of Indian Affairs, the Pueblos were informed of the pending legislation. He provided them with copies of the bill and participated in meetings to assist in opposing it.

A council meeting was called and all nineteen Pueblos were represented. They reactivated the All-Pueblo Council—for the first time in 242 years—on November 22, 1922.[82] The entire New Mexico

Wine house in the Sacred Papago Wine Village in southern Arizona.

Shrine of the Children on the Papago Reservation in southern Arizona.

San Xavier del Bac Mission, Tucson, Arizona, founded by Father Kino, Jesuit Priest.

Indian community was aflame, and non-Indians joined them in their fight against the legislation.

This unification by the Pueblos and the support by non-Indians had the desired results. The United States Senate, on a motion of Senator William Borah of Idaho, recalled the Bursum Bill from the House of Representatives. The Senate implied it had passed the bill on the strength of a misrepresentation by its sponsor. In March 1923, the Bursum Bill was killed.

The defeat of the insidious Bursum Bill did not stop the Bureau from its attempt to put these "upstarts" in their place. Almost immediately, a counter-attack against the traditional Pueblos was launched. The Indians and their supporters were accused of being racketeers and of taking money from sympathetic contributors under false pretenses. They were called anti-American and subversive and even accused of being Communist agents. The religions were again attacked as cults of Indian paganism, and accusations included gross untruths that the "pagan cults" were horrible, sadistic, and obscene. The Indians were even said to be seeking to discredit and weaken the United States government.

Such vile and flagrantly untrue statements by a governmental bureau merely acted as a catalyst for Indian tribes all over America. At no time in history had they been more united than in defense of the Pueblo people against the Indian Bureau.

The destruction of the remaining native religions was viewed by the Bureau of Indian Affairs as a political necessity, for the religions made the tribes strong and made the individual Indians inpervious to intimidation or corruption. The Bureau attacked all the Pueblo native religions as well as the rapidly growing Native American Church. Using political strategies, the Bureau lobbied enactments against the Native American Church through federal and state legislatures. The religious activities of the organization were outlawed in most areas and the church was forced to go underground. More lurid and vulgar methods were used to denigrate the traditional Pueblo religions.

Bureau of Indian Affairs' inspectors were sent out to collect pornographic gossip about the tribal activities, much of which was unprintable. It was known by Indians, ethnologists, and others knowledgeable in the conduct of the tribes that the morals of these people were extremely high and no pornography existed. However, no one from these groups was allowed to examine the reports of the inspectors. A report was developed from false information and circulated, under the seal of confidence, to leading editors, churchmen, and heads of women's organizations. Bureau publicists stated that these "agents of Moscow" (the Pueblos and their supporters) were advocates of these pagan religions which were unspeakably bloody and foul. The smear campaign was as its height in 1923.

The incongruity of the attitude toward the American Indian was vividly illustrated when, in 1924, in the midst of the extreme denigration, the Congress of the United States granted citizenship to all Indians who were not yet citizens by virtue of treaty, military service, or naturalization. This act of benevolence was performed because the Indians "fought so well" in World War I.[83]

The Indians, with the Pueblos heading the effort, attempted to alleviate some of the pressure of hostile publicity by appealing to thinking people around America. In 1926, the Bureau changed its tactics from defamation to action. Commissioner Charles H. Burke, while visiting Taos Pueblo, accused the elders—the religious leaders—of being "half animals" because of their religion. The

Bureau refused to allow Pueblo boys to be excused from school to participate in their initiation ceremonies, an extremely important facet of Pueblo culture and religion. The Pueblos unanimously agreed that the ceremonies would continue no matter what penalty they suffered. The entire governing body of Taos Pueblo was thrown into prison for violating the Bureau's religious crime code. The Indians took their case to the religious press and to the United States Congress.

James Frear, Representative from Wisconsin, became an advocate for the tribes in Washington and gave the issue much publicity. Public indignation grew, and Senator William King of Utah pressed for a Senate investigation of Indian matters as a whole. In 1927, under mounting pressures and in the face of a threatened Senate investigation of Indian affairs, something was done about the situation. Secretary of the Interior Hubert Work engaged the Institute for Government Research (Brookings Institution) to make an investigation of Indian affairs. The committee, headed by Lewis Meriam and operating under a private grant of $125,000, developed a monumental report setting forth the social and economic conditions of American Indians and presenting detailed recommendations for solutions to the problems discovered.

The major conclusions of the report were that (1) Indians were excluded from managment of their own affairs, and (2) Indians were receiving a poor quality of services (especially health and education) from public officials who were supposed to be serving their needs. The wording was very concise and the condemnation was so clear that many government officials, including Secretary Work, resigned rather than attempt an explanation. In part, the report stated:

The most fundamental need in Indian education is a change in point of view. Whatever may have been the official governmental attitude, education for the Indian in the past has proceeded largely on the theory that it is necessary to remove the Indian child as far as possible from his home environment; whereas the modern point of view in education and social work lays stress on upbringing in the natural setting of home and family life. The Indian educational enterprise is peculiarly in need of the kind of approach that recognizes this principle; that is, less concerned with a conventional school system and more with the understanding of human beings. It is impossible to visit Indian schools without feeling that on the whole . . . that they are distinctly below the accepted social and educational standards of school systems in most cities and the better rural communities.

The report further states, in regard to education preparing Indians to be functional:

.... A standard course of study, routine classroom methods, traditional types of schools, even if they were adequately supplied—and they are not—would not solve the problem. The methods of the average public school in the United States cannot safely be taken over bodily and applied to Indian education. Indian tribes and individual Indians within the tribes vary so much that a standard content and method of education, no matter how carefully they might be prepared, would be worse than futile.

In the preparation of recommendations, the committee illustrated a clearer understanding of the Indian's psychological approach to modern life than had heretofore been expressed by any other organization dealing with the concept of acculturation. They dealt with the idea that Indians deserve the prerogative of deciding for themselves which route they should take:

.... The position taken, therefore, is that the work with and for the Indian must give consideration to the desires of the individual Indians. He who wishes to merge into the social and economic life of the prevailing civilization of this country should be given all practicable aid and advice in making the necessary adjustments. He who wants to remain an Indian and live according to his old culture should be aided in doing so. The question may be raised, "Why aided? Just leave him alone and he will take care of himself." The fact is, however, as has been pointed out, that the old economic basis of his culture has been to a considerable extent destroyed and new problems have been forced upon him by contacts with the whites. Adjustments have to be made, economic, social, and legal. Under social is included health. The advent of white civilization has forced on the Indian new problems of health and sanitation that they, unaided, can no more solve than can a few city individuals solve municipal problems. The presence of their villages in close proximity to white settlements make the health and sanitary conditions of those villages public questions of concern to the entire section. Both the Indians and their white neighbors are concerned in having those Indians who want to stay Indians and preserve their culture, live according to at least a minimum standard of health and decency. Less than that means not only that they themselves will go through a long drawn out and painful process of vanishing. They must be aided for the preservation of themselves.

Whichever way the individual Indian may elect to face, work in his behalf must be designed not to do for him but to help him to do for himself. The whole problem must be regarded as fundamentally educational.

The admonishment was then given which established a pattern of action used in Indian affairs for many years:

. . . . In every activity of the Indian Service the primary question should be, how is the Indian to be trained so that he will do this for himself. Unless this question can be clearly and definitely answered by an affirmative showing of distinct educational purpose and method the chances are that the activity is impeding rather than helping the advancement of the Indian. . . .[84]

The Meriam Report of 1928 came at an opportune time politically. With the retirement of Hubert Work as Secretary of the Interior and Charles Burke as Commissioner of Indian Affairs, the way was open for officials more empathetic to Indians and willing to follow the Meriam recommendations. President Hoover appointed Ray Lyman Wilbur and Charles J. Rhodes and a new day of promise dawned for the Indain people. At once, they began to reform the Bureau of Indian Affairs. Secretary Wilbur denounced the allotment of Indian land and called for reorganization of tribal governments to allow Indians some voice in their own destiny. Unfortunately, although the political climate was favorable for reformation of the Bureau, the Meriam Report came at an extremely inopportune time economically. The Hoover administration soon found itself handcuffed in its efforts to alleviate some of the Indian problems, since the Great Depression loomed on the horizon and those in power were faced with enormous tasks of attempting to combat the economic instability in the dominant society. This naturally placed Indian problems quite low on the priority list. Millionaires were losing their fortunes overnight, the stockmarket was in a shambles, and no one had the time or inclination to concern themselves too much with a few indians. Consequently, the innovations brought on by the Meriam Report were halted and, for a time, Indians were forgotten in Washington.

During the presidential campaign in 1932, Franklin D. Roosevelt promised that if he were elected America would get a "new deal." This promise entailed a comprehensive program to bring the country out of the throes of the Great Depression. Included in his "new deal" were the American Indians, and Roosevelt did his best to keep his promise. He was sincerely interested in assisting the Indians, and the years encompassing his administration were the best yet for Indians.

One of Roosevelt's first moves was to appoint the long-time friend to Indians, John Collier, as Commissioner of Indian Affairs. Collier was a well-known anthropologist and had led the fight against the Bursum Bill in the 1920s. He was mandated to develop a new Indian policy and initiate the programs necessary to put it into effect.

One of the first acts of legislation introduced affecting Indians was the Johnson-O'Malley Act of 1934. This bill was designed to provide prompt relief to the Indian people by authorizing the Secretary of the Interior to negotiate contracts with states whereby the federal government would pay for educational, medical, and other services provided Indians by the states. With these contracts, it was possible to obtain needed services for Indians without the prolonged red tape involved in building facilities, staffing and supplying an installation, and the operation of the unit. It also decreased the duplication of services and made possible the use of existing facilities.

In part, the Johnson-O'Malley Act states:

Be it enacted . . . . That the Secretary of the Interior is hereby authorized, in his discretion, to enter into a contract or contracts with any State or Territory having legal authority so to do, for the education, medical attention, agricultural assistance, and social welfare, including relief of distress, of Indians in such State or Territory, and to expend under such contract or contracts moneys appropriated by Congress for the education, medical attention, agricultural assistance, and social welfare, including relief of distress, of Indians in such State.

Sec. 2. That the Secretary of the Interior, in making any contracts herein authorized with any State or Territory, may permit such State or Territory to utilize for the purpose of this Act, existing school buildings, hospitals, and other facilities, and all equipment therein or appertaining thereto, including livestock and other personal property owned by the Government, under such terms and conditions as may be agreed upon for their use and maintenance.

Sec. 3. That the Secretary of the Interior is hereby authorized to perform any and all acts and to make such rules and regulations, including minimum standards of service, as may be necessary and proper for the purpose of carrying the provisions of this Act into effect: Provided, That such minimum standards of service are not less than the highest maintained by the States or Territories with which such contract or contracts, as herein provided, are executed.

Sec. 4. That the Secretary of the Interior shall report annually to the Congress any contract or contracts made under the provisions of this Act, and the moneys expended thereafter.

Sec. 5. That the provisions of this Act shall not apply to the State of Oklahoma.[85]

The Johnson-O'Malley Act was utilized primarily in the area of education and became one of the most used of all federal programs.

The first federal action of its kind designed exclusively to benefit Indians, the JOM program monies were channelled toward the public school systems to enable them to educate eligible Indian children. Rules were established by the government, primarily through cooperative efforts of the legislature, the Health, Education, and Welfare Department, and the Bureau of Indian Affairs. Criteria for eligibility for JOM funds for individual Indians were basically the same as for assistance from the Bureau of Indian Affairs: All children of one-quarter Indian ancestry whose parents lived on or near Indian reservations under the jurisdiction of the Bureau of Indian Affairs were eligible for assistance. Although this definition was rather limited,[86] it was a start toward bringing a "new deal" to the Indian people. The Johnson-O'Malley Act, however, was just the first step in the Collier administration's attempt to alleviate the situation in Indian affairs.

Realizing that the assimilationist viewpoint had created numerous failures whenever it was included in Indian programs, John Collier promoted the concept of cultural survival as a means of bringing the Indian tribes into the modern era. In 1934, he re-introduced the idea of Indian self-government via the Wheeler-Howard Act, officially known as the Indian Reorganization Act (IRA). This legislative action also stopped the erosion of Indian land, since it provided for the stopping of all allotment of tribal holdings and the restoration of some of the lost acreage.

This restoration was aimed at both the economic and spiritual rehabilitation of Indians. The loss of nearly 100 million acres of their land since the beginning of the allotment in 1887, about two-thirds of their total holdings, had robbed the Indian people of the necessary basis for self-support. This loss, combined with the effort to break up all tribal relations by outlawing Indian governments, had condemned large numbers of Indians to lose their spiritual dignity by forcing them to become chronic recipients of charity. Collier realized that a major portion of the Indian people, because of the ramifications of the Allotment Act, had become ruined economically and pauperized spiritually.

Under the IRA, 2,540,307 acres of land were restored to Indian ownership by purchases by the government from non-Indians. Education was enhanced by establishing funds for loans to Indian students. Appropriations of $10 million were made to establish a revolving fund for loans to Indian corporations for the purpose of promoting economic development of such tribes and of their members. Tribes were encouraged to establish constitutions and become legal entities under the law. These and other provisions were generally welcomed by the tribes, and most followed the provisions prescribed.

This does not mean, however, that Collier and his Reorganization Act were without opposition. Several tribes refused the invitation to come under the jurisdiction of the IRA and developed constitutions independently. Others had misgivings concerning various portions of the legislation.[87] Flora Seymour, an avid observer of the social conditions of her time, opposed Collier's attempts to perpetuate the Indians' customs and denounced them as "a unique program of regimentation which in several basic features is the most extreme gesture yet made by the administration toward a Communistic experiment."

Incorporated in the IRA and in Collier's directives to his employees were provisions which allowed the Indians free practice of their native religions. This action naturally brought reaction from missionary groups and Christian church leaders, who viewed this as a backward step in "civilizing" the Indians. However, Collier recognized that religious sensitivity in communities bound people together more than did any other factor. He also understood and respected the rights of Indians to freedom of choice in religious persuasion as accorded all Americans under the fourteenth amendment to the Constitution.

Early in his tenure as Commissioner of Indian Affairs, Collier began a reorganization of government Indian schools. He was a strong advocate for education which would allow Indian children to live at home. Recognizing the deleterious effect of removal of children from parental influence, he began a concerted effort to close boarding schools and establish day schools on the reservations. In 1933, ten Indian boarding schools were either closed or converted to community day schools:

The Mount Pleasant School, Mount Pleasant, Mich., was transferred by act of Congress to the State of Michigan, and the Indian children are in public schools, some under foster-home care. The school at Rapid City, S. Dak. was closed, and most of the children returned to Sioux reservation schools, with a few to other boarding schools. From the school at Hayward, Wis., now closed, the Indian children are being accommodated in local public schools, with the eventual help of additional day school facilities furnished under the Public Works program. Indian children formerly in the Genoa Indian School, Genoa, Nebr., have been absorbed in local schools, both Federal and State, in Nebraska and South Dakota. Other boarding schools were closed during the year, including Fort Belknap, Mont., where the children are to be cared for in local public schools; Mescalero, N. Mex., where a complete community program waits upon necessary home rehabilitation; Browning, Mont., where public school authorities are taking over the local educational enterprise, including partial dormitory residence for some high school pupils not able to come every day from their homes; Red Lake, Minn., where whites and Indians are combining forces in a single large school plant now under construction with Public Works funds; Standing Rock, N. Dak., where additional new construction of day schools is taking care of most of the former boarding pupils; and Tohatchi, N. Mex., where a Navajo boarding school of some two hundred children becomes a community day school of about the same number, with transportation furnished for the children living at a distance.[88]

Collier indicated that changing from boarding to day school facilities would not totally solve the Indian education problems. He did feel, however, that it was an essential first step which had to be taken before reconstruction of the Indian educational program in terms of basic Indian needs could go forward. He also mandated that, contrary to common practice in the past, the best resources in personnel, equipment, and teaching methods and materials should be placed at the disposal of the day schools.

Collier also recognized the strong tendency in the Indian schools to impress upon Indian children that Indian customs, language, and ways of life were not acceptable in modern society and must be eliminated as part of the educational process. Calling attention to this, and noting that some Indian Service officials and employees, some missionaries, and some Indians were unsympathetic to Indian religious, ceremonial, and art expressions and the use of Indian languages, Collier issued the following instructions:

There are Government schools into which no trace of Indian symbolism or art or craft expression has been permitted to enter. There are large numbers of Indians who believe that their native religious life and Indian culture are frowned upon by the Government, if not actually banned. . . .

No interference with Indian religious life or expression will hereafter be tolerated. The cultural history of Indians is in all respects to be considered equal to that of any non-Indian group. And it is desirable that Indians be bilingual—fluent and literate in the English language, and fluent in their vital, beautiful, and efficient native languages. . . .

. . . The Indian arts are to be prized, nourished, and honored.[89]

This change of attitude which the boarding schools were forced to adopt, along with the other Collier innovations, began to bring about a revitalization of the Indian spirits. Another contributing factor in the positive change in Indian affairs was initiated by the most unlikely stimulus imaginable, the Great Depression.

For many years, the kind of depression which struck America in 1929 had been the way of life to most reservation Indians. Poverty was not a new institution for the Indians, and the fact that the rest of the nation was now experiencing it had little negative effect on the tribes. In fact, it had the opposite effect for several reasons. The Collier administration had introduced an agricultural improvement program which increased the Indians' harvest from the land, especially in raising livestock. Construction of roads and dams, irrigation projects, and assistance in argricultural education improved the lot of Indians all over the country.

Federal programs, such as Public Works projects, created jobs that gave many Indians their first experience with full-time employment. Many, for the first time in years, were able to provide an adequate living for their families because of the special government-sponsored programs. Large numbers of Indian young people enrolled in college under the guidance of the Bureau of Indian Affairs; tribal governments established economic development projects; traditional religions, now permitted by the government, flourished; and, all around—strange as it may be—the best days of Indian life in the twentieth century were experienced during the depression.

Social, political, and economic progress continued under John Collier's administration until the beginning of World War II, when the impetus for internal development was changed to the "war effort." Funds usually appropriated for schools, public works, and social and economic development were needed for guns, tanks, and airplanes. Indians who were planning to attend college found themselves in the armed services. The nation's people, Indian and non-Indian alike, converted all their energies toward one common objective, the defeat of the Axis powers.

Thirteen
World War II

On December 7, 1941, the Japanese attacked Pearl Harbor, Hawaii, and the United States became officially involved in World War II. However, long before the surprise attack, the American Indians had responded to the call of the country. In numbers far exceeding the contribution of the white population, the Indians had enlisted in all branches of the armed services. They had also given of their particular skills in many fields of the civilian defense industry. In the aircraft industry, they had established themselves as perhaps the most precise and skillful workers anywhere available. The aircraft plants, after only a few months of experience with Indian employees, placed standing orders with the Bureau of Indian Affairs for all the Indians that could be recruited. "Probably no other race, including the white, has such a record of loyal and efficient service in the vital war industries," was the comment made by Floyd W. LaRouche in 1942, while he was in charge of the Information and Publications Office of the Bureau of Indian Affairs.

By October 1941, two months before the actual outbreak of hostilities, the total number of Indians in the Army alone was 4,062—one out of every ten Indians between the ages of twenty-one and thirty-five. These statistics may have startled those who thought of Indians in the stereotypical manner, but to those who knew better, the figures were not at all surprising. In World War I, as indicated in Chapter 11, Indians responded readily in defense of the country for various reasons. More than 8,000 entered military service during that conflict, most of them voluntarily, and over 17,000 registered for selective service, though they were not required to do so.

Indian participation in World War II was a natural reaction, but it was also stimulated to some degree by John Collier, Commissioner of Indian Affairs. Mr. Collier had instituted sweeping changes in Indians' lives and was generally respected by the tribes. In an effort to enlist the cooperation of the Indians in the American war effort, Collier delivered stirring addresses and wrote moving commentaries. In a radio address in 1941, he warned that Hitler had plans for slavery or extinction for the Indians in the Americas:

The Indians are a Mongoloid race. They are not Aryans. Hitler's plan dooms them to eternal slavery if they do not resist the slave-master and to total extinction if they do resist the slave-master. . . . Freedom is the passion of the Indian and there can be no doubt in the side which the Indian will take in world struggle which involves us all.

On December 8, 1941, Mr. Collier wrote a letter which was sent out with the Bureau of Indian Affairs publication, "Indians at Work." The letter said:

We are in the World War.

The stake is everything—literally everything—that we as Americans (white and Indian) hold dear. The World War is indivisible; we irrevocably have been sucked into its vortex. It is the most desperate war—not merely the hugest but the most ruthless and desperate—that our planet has ever known. No thought or imagination has been informed enough or strong enough to anticipate the ruthlessness, the desperation, the all-penetrating nature of this World War. On its outcome depends not merely the future of republics and empires, not merely the physical shape of a thousand years to come, but the actual biological survival of whole races. But something far more terrible depends on the outcome. It is whether the human spirit shall remain alive—whether the spirit and heart of mankind shall go on with much beauty and tender power, growing slowly to a more all-sufficing beauty and tenderness, or shall become a thing and a force of horror. Whether the breath of God shall blow on the waters of human life, as in ages gone and until now has blown, or through the hardness of man's own malignly organized will, shall blow on the waters of life no more.

It is going to be a long war. It can have no indecisive ending. What we love will go down for a long age, or its enemy will go down for a long age.

A long war, requiring of us more than any of us yet can foresee. Unless we give that *more* which will be required, all that we live by and care for will be sunk.

In what spirit shall we—Indian and white Americans—do what has to be endured? Let it be the spirit which wakens when we think deeply and long about what it is that makes us men; what it is that Christs and Platos lived and died to give to men; what it is that we are the keepers of, the messengers, carrying it on to boundless future time. Loveliness and greatness are our heritage, we will save them now for future men, and fighting to save them, we *will not* be changed by what we have to do into the image of their fearful antagonist. Not like the Japanese in their homeland or in horror-ridden China, not like the Nazis in their homeland or in tortured, dying Poland or Greece. Not like these shall we become through what we have to do. The increase of the good spirit within us, through the very agony of the struggle, now upon us, to save it for the world, it is possible. Let us accomplish *that* result, and not only our country, but the soul within us will have its victory.

John Collier
Commissioner of Indian Affairs

Spurred by this eloquence and the presentation of the alternatives of losing, any group of people would almost unanimously become fired with the zeal of patriotism. Such was the effect on the American Indian people.

The story of the Indians' contribution to winning the war will never by fully told, but what is known makes a very impressive record. By the spring of 1945, there were 21,767 Indians in the Army, 1,910 in the Navy, 121 in the Coast Guard, and 723 in the Marines. These figures do not include officers or women, for whom no statistics are available. However, several hundred more are known to have served.

The Bureau of Indian Affairs records seventy-one awards of the Air Medal, fifty-one of the Silver Star, forty-seven of the Bronze Star Medal, thirty-four of the Distinguished Flying Cross, and two of the Congressional Medal of Honor. There were undoubtly many more which were not reported. Many of these ribbons were decorated with oak leaf clusters in lieu of additional medals, and it was not unusual to see an Air Medal with eight or ten oak leaf clusters.

One of the Congressional Medal of Honor Medals was awarded to Lt. Jack Montgomery, a Cherokee from Sallisaw, Oklahoma. On

January 10, 1945, he received the award from President Franklin Roosevelt at the White House. The official citation read:

> For conspicuous gallantry and intrepidity at risk of life beyond and above the call of duty, on February 22, 1944, near Padiglione, Italy. Two hours before daybreak, a strong force of enemy infantry established themselves in three echelons at 50 yards, 100 yards, and 300 yards respectively in front of the rifle platoons commanded by Lieutenant Montgomery. The closest position, consisting of four machine-guns and one mortar, threatened the immediate security of the platoon position. It was now daybreak, and the enemy observation was excellent across the flat, open terrain which led to Lieutenant Montgomery's objective.
>
> When the artillery barrage had lifted, Lieutenant Montgomery ran fearlessly toward the strongly defended position. As the enemy started streaming out of the house, Lieutenant Montgomery, unafraid of treacherous snipers, exposed himself daringly to assemble the surrendering enemy and send them to the rear.
>
> His fearless, aggressive, and intrepid actions that morning accounted for a total of eleven dead, 32 prisoners, and an unknown number of wounded. The selflessness and courage exhibited by Lieutenant Montgomery in alone attacking three strong enemy positions inspired his men to a degree beyond estimation.[90]

The other Congressional Medal of Honor winner was Lt. Ernest Childers, a Creek Indian from Broken Bow, Oklahoma. His award was presented on April 12, 1944, in Italy, by Gen. Jacob L. Devers, Allied Deputy Commander of the Mediterranean Theater. The General complimented Lt. Childers for doing a "swell job."

The "swell job" was done on September 25, 1943, near Oliveto, Italy. In the dark before dawn, Lt. Childers, while advancing with his platoon, stepped in a hole and seriously injured his foot. Back at a first-aid station an hour or so later, he heard that his platoon was in a tough spot under machine-gun and mortar fire. Ignoring the doctors who wanted to remove him from duty, he hobbled back to his men. With eight of his comrades, he advanced up a hill to a wall where German machine-gunners were concealed. Ordering his men to maintain a covering fire, he advanced alone. The citation describes what followed:

> Moving along the edge of the field under mortar and artillery shelling, he was fired upon by two German riflemen from a nearby house. Returning the fire, Childers killed both. Continuing his advance he moved behind an enemy machine-gun nest and killed its two occupants with his carbine. He then made his way to a spot near the second nest and using rocks as simulated grenades caused the gunners

to stand up. He killed one with his carbine while the other German was accounted for by one of Childer's men who had moved around to the left side of the field. Childers continued his advance up the hill and arrived at a house where, single-handed, he captured a German mortar observer. Childers' indomitable courage and coolness under deadly fire from a determined enemy enabled his battalion to continue its advance.

Not all the Indian servicemen were accorded recognition for their ability, though, and many received derogatory treatment from unthinking or unfeeling companions. When a Indian found himself the only one of his race in an outfit, he could prepare himself for such names as "Chief" or "Geronimo," no matter what his tribal affiliation may have been. Many times, Indians, victimized by stereotype, were sent on missions where return probability was quite low because of their assumed genetic ability to travel over the terrain without fear of detection.[91]

The news media and service publications also exploited the Indian G.I.'s by printing ridiculous photographs of them in action. One such picture shows Sgt. Red Eagle, a Creek, leading a combat squad of the 45th Division through Italian underbrush while they were all clothed in their dress uniforms.[92] Another picture in the same publication shows Pfc. Ira Hayes, a Pima Marine,[93] posed as a paratrooper, ready to jump, complete with his chute, while dressed in khaki uniform, soft cap, and low-cut dress shoes.

Some Indians did receive recognition for what they did while in the armed sevices, and one of the best-known incidents of World War II involved the use of the "Navajo Code Talkers" in the Pacific Theater. Following the example set by the Army's 36th Division during World War I (using Choctaw Indians to confuse the enemy), the Marine Corps trained Navajo Indians to transmit battlefield messages in their native language. Navajo is one of the unique languages of the world, and embellished with improvised words and phrases for military use, it produced a code which the Japanese never broke.[94]

Through the Solomons, the Marianas, on Peletiu and Iwo Jima, and on almost every island where Marines stormed ashore, the Japanese heard this strange language gurgling in their earphones. The activities of these Navajo Indians undoubtedly saved the lives of many American fighting men and helped shorten the war.

The story of the American Indian and his efforts in the second great world struggle was not limited to the exploits of soldiers and sailors. Men and women too old or too young for service with the armed forces worked in war industries as well as in food production.

By 1943, in the Rio Grande Valley of New Mexico, Indians were leaving their homes for military service. Ten percent of the Pueblo Indians, in spite of the United States government's pressures to take their land and suppress their religions (as discussed in the previous chapter), had gone into uniform. In the neighboring cities and towns, help of all kinds was urgently needed because of the shortage of able-bodied men. Older men of the Pueblos, recognizing the emergency, advertised in the local papers, offering their sevices for part-time work in near-by areas. Soon, trucks were pouring into the villages to pick up workers, some from as far away as Colorado.

The Navy was building a huge supply depot at Clearfield, Utah, and emissaries were sent to the Pueblos to recruit labor. An agreement was reached which provided the Pueblo men be allowed to go home during the summer to plant and harvest their crops. This arrangement worked out for all concerned; the Indians were steadily employed and contributing to the war effort and the Navy had a work force of responsible people.

The great problem of production, absenteeism, was unknown among the Indian workers. They were constantly on the job. Indian participation in War Bond campaigns was 100 percent—another indication that the Indians were whole-hearted in their devotion to the cause for which their sons were fighting.

Indians sacrificed more than most who were employed in war industries. They left their land—an extremely important part of their lives—and traveled to strange places where people did not understand them and their way of living. In most cases, families—the central axis around which Indian life revolves—were divided. Indians had to forego attending dances and other religious ceremonials that are so much a part of their lives. They had to work under supervision and conditions which were totally alien to anything previously experienced, causing an adjustment far more difficult than those made by the white workers. In their quiet way, American Indians showed that they, too, had a stake in the conflict.

Indian women also did their part in the defense of America.

Thousands left home to work in factories, on ranches and farms, and even as section-hands on the railroads to replace men who were vitally needed elsewhere. They joined the nurse's corps, the military auxiliaries, the Red Cross, and the American Women's Voluntary Service.

Great numbers of Indian women gave their services in more unusual ways. More that 500 Eskimo and Indian women and girls worked day and night manufacturing skin clothing, mukluks, mittens, moccasins, snowshoes, and other articles of wearing apparel for our forces serving in cold climates. Alaskan women ran trap lines to make money to buy war bonds.

Cherokee girls wove and sold baskets, buying war stamps with the money. On the eastern Cherokee reservation, women and girls drove tractors and planted and harvested the crops. Forty Chippewa women formed a rifle brigade for home defense. An old Kiowa woman gave $1,000 to the Navy Relief Fund as her contribution. Osage women, draped in their blankets, spent long hours at sewing machines for the Red Cross.

In the West, a Pueblo woman drove a truck between Albuquerque and Santa Fe (a distance of about 62 miles), delivering milk to the Indian school. She not only serviced her own truck, but also helped at the school garage as a mechanic. Many Indian women became silversmiths and made insignias for the armed forces. At the military installation, Fort Wingate, New Mexico, the Navajo women's work ranged from that of chemists to truck drivers. Two Indian women in California served at a lonely observation post, driving the 12 miles to their position in a rickety old automobile. The war plants had many Indian women on their rolls, working a riveters, inspectors, sheet metal workers, and machinists.

Indians also supplied other resources to the federal government during World War II. One and one-half million acres of Indian land in seven states and Alaska was transferred for military purposes; a school, a hospital, and other buildings at Tomah, Wisconsin were turned over to the War Department. Over 800 leases for oil and gas operations were approved, as were 80 permits to develop deposits of coal, copper, lead, zinc, tungsten, vanadium, and helium-bearing gas on Indian land. Almost two billion board feet of lumber each year was cut from Indian-owned forests.

In 1942, Indians planted 5,100 more victory gardens than they had the year before, making a total of 36,200 gardens or, roughly, one garden for every two Indian families. In addition, 1942 field crops were increased by eighteen percent, and approximately a twenty-five percent increase in cattle sales was experienced. Indians sold enough sheep that year to clothe 12,000 soldiers and to furnish hundreds of tons of mutton.

The war also had its lighter side. Numerous incidents of Indian G.I. humor also came out of the war years. One story concerns a rather portly Indian who tried to join the Army, and, told by the recruiting officer he was too fat to qualify, tartly replied, "Don't want to run. Want to fight."

Another tale is of a Cherokee soldier who saluted his commanding officer in the morning, but refused to do so in the afternoon because, as he put it, "Back where I live, if you speak to a man in the morning, you speak to him no more that day."

There is also the story of the female radio producer who asked the Indian soldiers to record their native songs and wanted background information about the music so she could introduce them intelligently to her listening audience. The task of informing the young lady fell to the bayonet specialist, Sgt. Matlock. He had a somber face and a couple of scars on his head from college football which convinced the woman she was dealing with an honest-to-goodness Indian. Timidly, she outlined with two-syllable words and sign language that she wanted him to explain the background of his tribal songs. "Madam," said Sgt. Matlock in the mellifluous Oklahoma tone that is a combination of soft Southern and slow Western drawl, "the easiest way for me to explain our Indian songs is to tell you they are similar to a series of progressions in Chaucer's 'Canterbury Tales'," and then he proceeded to quote example from the prologue while the young lady's chin dropped.

Although the war industries and military activities were the primary consideration with most Indians, other activities took place in the early 1940s which had an effect on their lives. Although attended by little fanfare, there was an event of historic importance which occurred in the fall of 1944. Eighty delegates from thirty Indian tribes met at Denver, Colorado, from November 15 to 18, to form the National Congress of American Indians (NCAI). This convention and the resulting organization presented dramatic proof that American Indians could overcome barriers of isolation and cultural enmity and ban together in order to plan and work for their common good.

Realizing that unity was critical if Indians were to survive, NCAI was the result of years of thinking, talking, and planning by Indian leaders from all over the country. In the ground thus prepared, the members of the Denver convention laid the cornerstone of an organization which eventually grew to the largest and most influential of all Indian groups. Their philosophy was outlined clearly in the preamble to the constitution unanimously adopted, which reads as follows:

We, the members of Indian Tribes of the United States of America in convention assembled on the 16th day of November, 1944, at Denver, Colorado, in order to secure for ourselves and our descendants the rights and benefits to which we are entitled under the laws of the United States, the several states thereof, and the territory of Alaska; to enlighten the public toward a better understanding of the Indian race; to preserve Indian cultural values; to seek an equitable adjustment of tribal affairs; to secure and to preserve rights under Indian treaties with the United States; and otherwise to promote the common welfare of the American Indians—do establish this organization and adopt the following Constitution and By-Laws. . . .

The need for national Indian unity had been recognized for many years by a number of Indians and non-Indian friends. Many groups, mainly of non-Indian ancestry themselves, had formed associations to defend Indian rights. Nevertheless, the ultimate goal could not be reached until full Indian participation in the conduct of their own affairs and the affairs of the Nation was accomplished. Through an organization, national in scope, with membership limited to persons of Indian ancestry, Indians would have an opportunity to speak for themselves, work for themselves, and assume responsibilities in areas where this was not previously possible.

The program adopted by the Denver Convention was both broad and challenging. The goals were for the organization to be an all-embracing organization to represent the Indians of the United States along non-partisan political lines and to be the instrument through which Indian views could be expressed. They hoped to have an advisory and recommendatory function in all agencies and organizations related to Indian work, and to promote research and education in such fields as nutrition, native medicine, tribal customs, and other aspects of Indian culture. The initial program pointed in that direction and included legislative activities and projects devoted to purposes of education, research, and welfare. The NCAI represented one of the most positive moves by Indians ever attempted.

One of the most damaging blows to Indians occurred on January 19, 1945, when Commissioner of Indian Affairs John Collier submitted a letter of resignation to President Franklin D. Roosevelt. In the letter, Mr. Collier detailed the specific causes for his resignation:

> . . . the burdens upon the Indian Commissionership have increased almost beyond the power of description. The headquarters of the Indian Service has been moved to Chicago . . . . yet the most critical parts of the Indian Service job have to be carried out in Washington. . . . . The Indian Commissioner must try to operate one hundred per cent at each of the two headquarters. . . .
>
> Added to the above is the trend of Congressional appropriations in recent years. It has been an unfortunate trend. This trend . . . . has been in the direction of staking all of the hope of the Indians on the relatively costly institutional services, particularly schools and hospitals . . . but they are not enough. The trend has been toward denial of funds for needed work, which is imperative and which would be controlling, at the adult level and in the Indian economic need. . . .
>
> The creative development of Indian life is not being stopped, but it is being hampered and retarded by these factors.

President Roosevelt accepted the letter of resignation "with particular regret" and praised Mr. Collier for his outstanding work. The president expressed his hope "that, in the future as in the past . . . you will continue to achieve lasting benefits for the descendants of those misunderstood and misused human beings who originally possessed this great land of ours and who were displaced involuntarily, all too often with a selfish disregard of their right to live their own lives in their own way."

Although Collier's successors followed his general policy for a number of years, they were not as dedicated or as aggressive as he had been. Conditions underwent a radical change, also, as World War II came to a close. Indians were faced with another crisis situation as some 65,000 men and women who had left the reservations to enter military service or work in war industries began to make their way back home.

The Indian Reorganization Act had in part prepared them for this experience. The Commissioner's report for 1941 states:

One of the matters causing concern to the Office of Indian Affairs is the task of making provision now to take care of the several thousand Indians who will return to reservations at the end of the emergency. . . . The Indians will be among the first to be affected by the shrinkage of employment opportunities subsequent to the war, and, if the past is any guide, they will return in large numbers to their home reservations. With resources inadequate to meet the needs of those already there, the problem of providing employment opportunities and a means of livelihood for each of the returning soldiers and workers will prove a staggering task.

In Collier's report of 1942, he brings attention to this problem again:

Should economic conditions after the war continue to offer employment opportunities in industry, many Indians will undoubtedly choose to continue to work away from the reservations. Never before have they been so well prepared to take their places among the general citizenry and to become assimilated into the white population.

Most Indians in the armed forces as well as those in industry found they were accepted by their peers as a part of the total unit. When the war ended, they returned home with a differnt view of the world and the people in it. To some this brought a time of great opportunity; to others, a time of despair.

Indians returning from service had varied plans for their futures. Some had learned trades and desired to continue to work in them. For the most part, this meant moving to an urban setting. Others wanted to take advantage of the G.I. Bill and continue their education. Many were just anxious to get home and settle down in the peace and quiet of their small communities, and of these, some wanted loans to build homes, to start small businesses, to improve their property, or to buy livestock. They had seen the outside world and many wanted to incorporate part of its niceties in their lives.

The Indian Service realized the wants and needs of these Indians and was concerned. They knew that, at best, the existing reservation land base could support only a part of the returning population and it would be necessary to find a place for thousands of Indians in the general national economy.

In the Commissioner's report of 1946, he indicated that what the Bureau had anticipated had begun to occur:

Cessation of hostilities marked the beginning of a profound change in their fortunes. Wages from war vanished. Dependency allotments sent home by servicemen and women began to dwindle as the armed forces diminished. A downward trend in family incomes set in.

As the veterans returned, the Bureau attempted to work with them and keep them informed of their privileges and opportunities. They assisted in obtaining loans for homes, livestock, and improvements, as well as directing many toward the educational and vocational training benefits to which they were entitled. Even though much resource was expended in these areas, the Bureau had neither the money or the personnel to adequately handle the situation. Although reservation resources were adequate during the war years, serious economic needs became evident after 1945. This situation was brought to national attention and programatic changes began to be designed to alleviate the problems.

Fourteen
Paper Genocide

Following World War II, the federal government, realizing the economic situation on Indian reservations, attempted to strengthen the financial base for the tribes. In 1946, Congress passed the Indian Claims Commission Act, partially growing out of a desire to "solve the Indian problem" by increasing the assets of the tribes themselves. This Act provided the Indians with a court to award indemnity for past wrongful acts of the government. The Commision and its Court of Claims was established for five years to hear Indian complaints and award damages. At the end of five years, Indian claims were to be adjudicated in the same process as non-Indian claims.

Some 800 cases were filed in the first five-year period. These covered a great many subjects and were not all simple land cession revisions, as most people had anticipated. Thus, the Indian Claims Commission began to sift through the wrongs of over a century and a half and it became clear that it would be impossible to settle these in the original time alotted. Today, after over thirty years of existence, the Commission still has a tremendous backlog of cases, with more inequities being discovered all the time.

It was originally thought that the Commission's duties would be fairly easy to carry out. It was imagined that the tribes would present claims and facts supporting the claims, and decisions could be rendered quickly on the basis of those facts. It did not turn out to be such a simple operation, though, for the parties involved began to battle over legal technicalities, listings of minor discrepancies, and judicial nit-picking. Consequently, during the first twenty-five years of arbitration, less than half the claims had been settled.

It has been the practice of the Claims Commission to make monetary awards for lands illegally taken from the Indian tribes. The only exception to this practice was the decision of September 8, 1965, which recognized the Taos Indians' claim to the Blue Lake area. The Commission ruled that the tribe had aboriginal title to the lake and that the area had been wrongfully taken from them on November 6, 1907, when the lands were incorporated into the Taos National Forest.

Even with the Claims Commission's award of the land to the Taos Indians, legal and congressional procrastination held off the actual return of the sacred lake. It was not until Richard Nixon's administration took office in 1969 that the Taos people were actually given the area.

Other awards by the Claims Commission have had deleterious effects on tribes, as will be discussed in later chapters. The awards to the Klamaths, Menominee, and other tribes in the 1950s carried with them termination decrees which were disastrous. As we shall see, political manipulations changed the original intent of the Claims Commission from economic assistance and moral atonement to a tool for termination and assimilation of the Indian tribes.

In 1944, before the formation of the Indian Claims Commission, a House Select Committee on Indian Affairs offered recommendations on achieving "the final solution of the Indian problem." The committee called for a return to the pre-Meriam and pre-Collier policies, especially in education. It criticized the reservation day schools, developed under Collier's administration, for adapting education to the Indian and to his reservation lifestyle. It said "real progress" would be made only when Indian children were once again taken from their homes and placed in off-reservation boarding schools. According to the committee, "The goal of Indian education should be to make the Indian child a better American rather than to equip him to be a better Indian.''

This committee and its recommendations clearly indicate the change in attitude of the federal government toward the Indian. The vacillation is like the pendulum of a clock: one decade shows a swing to an empathetic approach to Indian affairs and the next decade demonstrates a shift to an anti-Indian philosophy. With these dichotomous concepts, there could be no continuum, and therefore, little, if any, progress in establishing a valid program of self-determination for Indian tribes.

In 1947, the Senate Civil Service Committee held hearings on ways to reduce government expenditures. Naturally, since the Bureau of Indian Affairs had always come under criticism for spending large amounts of money with comparatively little results, the office was scrutinized closely by this committee. Acting Commissioner William Zimmerman was asked to testify on ways the Bureau could reduce spending by terminating tribes.

His testimony included dividing the Indian tribes into three categories: (1) the few tribes which were, in his opinion, ready for termination (these included groups having rich natural resources and a stable reservation population); (2) most of the tribes served by the Bureau of Indian Affairs, which with proper training and development, could be terminated within a definite period of time; and (3) those tribes suffering from abject poverty and isolation, which would not be able to sever governmental ties for an indefinite period of time. When the Committee evaluated the recommendations outlined by Commissioner Zimmerman, it decided that even if the tribes who were "ready" were terminated, very little money would be saved. These Indian groups were already contributing much to their own operation and government subsidy was probably less expensive in the long run than the costs of termination.

The following year, the Hoover Commission Report on the reorganization of the federal government was issued. Although it presented good reports on the impact of the Indian Reorganization Act on Indian tribes, it still advocated that Indian responsibility be turned over to the states and that the federal government get out of the "Indian business." This report convinced many legislators that they could, in all good conscience, promote Indian termination.

They concluded that the federal government could sever the unique relationship with Indian tribes without seriously changing the status of Indian treaty rights.

Coinciding with the "termination psychosis" that was developing in the federal government was the increasing desire of well-meaning but ignorant religious and social organizations to "free the Indian" and "make him a first-class citizen." Like so many politicians who could affect changes in the lives of Indians, these "bleeding hearts" gave little or no thought to the needs or desires of the recipients of their benevolences. With no knowledge of Indian cultures or values, they went blithely on their way, "saving the savages" and attempting to remake them in the white man's mold.

By 1952, it seemed as if everyone who had the remotest connection with Indian affairs had caught the "termination fever." McCarthyism reigned supreme and anything which did not reek with "the flag, mom, and apple pie" was termed "Communistic." Both political parties in 1952 pledged to free the Indians from their shackles and make them first-class citizens with "all the rights and prerogatives pertaining to American citizenship." Whether the Indians wanted this "freedom" or the prerogatives and responsibilities it entailed was not considered. Indians were not included in the decision-making, for white America knew what was best for them. The concepts sounded fine to short-sighted Americans, but they had no basis in historic reality.

In treaty after treaty, the long range vision of most of the Indian leaders from the different tribes dictated the necessity of provisions to prevent the loss of special protection of the federal government. "Freeing" the Indians, as connoted in the dominant society's desires, simply meant that these long-standing protections would be denied to the tribes in violation of the United States' pledged honor that it would never leave them at the mercy of private citizens or state courts. The feelings of Indians toward these "permanent temporary" promises are well illustrated in the following poem:

The Promise Is Dead Grass

In eighteen hundred thirty-one
Spoke the Man in Washington:

"Relocation—
Build a new Nation,

A Nation independent and free."
(A home for you and me,)
"As long as the grass shall grow
And the waters flow. . . ."

(Been terribly dry this past century hasn't it?)[95]

On August 1, 1953, the Eighty-third Congress blatantly established an official change in the Indian policy of the United States government. Totally reversing the Collier concept and the recommendations of his successor, William Zimmerman, House Concurrent Resolution 108 was passed. This Act declared it to be the policy of the United States to abolish federal supervision over the tribes as soon as possible and to subject the Indians to the same laws, privileges, and responsibilities as other citizens. It read as follows:

Whereas it is the policy of Congress, as rapidly as possible, to make the Indians within the territorial limits of the United States subject to the same laws and entitled to the same privileges and responsibilities as are applicable to the other citizens of the United States, to end their status as wards of the United States, and to grant them all the rights and prerogatives pertaining to American citizenship; and

Whereas the Indians within the territorial limits of the United States should assume their full responsibilities as American citizens: Now, therefore, be it

Resolved by the House of Representatives (the Senate concurring),

That it is declared to be the sense of Congress that, at the earliest possible time, all of the Indian tribes and the individual members thereof located within the States of California, Florida, New York, and Texas, and all of the following named Indian tribes and the individual members thereof, should be freed from Federal supervision and control and from all disabilities and limitations specially applicable to Indians: The Flathead Tribe of Montana, the Klamath Tribe of Oregon, the Menominee Tribe of Wisconsin, the Potowatamie Tribe of Kansas and Nebraska, and those members of the Chippewa Tribe who are on the Turtle Mountain Reservation, North Dakota. It is further declared to be the sense of Congress that, upon the release of such tribes and the individual members thereof from such disabilities and limitations, all offices of the Bureau of Indian Affairs whose primary purpose was to serve any Indian tribe or individual Indian freed from Federal supervision should be abolished. It is further declared to the sense of Congress that the Secretary of Interior should examine all existing legislation dealing with such Indians, and treaties between the government of the United States and each such tribe, and report to Congress at the earliest practicable date, but not later than January 1, 1954, his recommendations for such legislation as, in his judgment, may be necessary to accomplish the purpose of this resolution.

One of the designers of H.R. 108 and one of its strongest proponents was the Commissioner of Indian Affairs, Dillon S. Myer. Myer was appointed, in part at least, as a reward for his outstanding service during World War II, when he was in charge of the Japanese internment camps in the United States. With his experience in handling the Japanese-Americans, confined because of their ethnicity—regardless of citizenship or actions—he was well qualified to deal with Indians.

By 1952, the Bureau of Indian Affairs was following a pattern diametrically opposite to the Collier policy. Commissioner Myer, in his report of June 30, outlined the actions taken to "free" the Indians, not only from the supervision of the Bureau, but from the protection of their trust status. Greatly increased emphasis on the ultimate transfer of the Indian Bureau function to the Indians themselves or to appropriate state or local agencies was reflected in almost every phase of activity. These policy changes were implemented to strengthen and support the change to policy outlined in House Resolution 108.

The Commissioner also enunciated the policy of working with tribes desirous of "freedom," even partial release of Bureau direction, in the following three-part manner:

1. If any Indian tribe is convinced the Bureau of Indian Affairs is a handicap to its advancement, I am willing to recommend to the Secretary of Interior that legislative authority be obtained from the Congress to terminate the Bureau's trusteeship responsibility with respect to that tribe.
2. If any Indian tribe desires modification of the existing trusteeship in order that some part or parts thereof be lifted (such as the control of tribal funds, the leasing of tribal land, as examples), and if the leaders of the tribe will sit down with Bureau officials to discuss the details of such a program of partial termination of trusteeship, we will be glad to assign staff members to work with the group with a view to developing appropriate legislative proposals.
3. If there are tribes desiring to assume themselves some of the responsibilities the Bureau now carries with respect to the furnishing of services, without termination of the trusteeship relationship, we are prepared to work with such tribes in the

development of an appropriate agreement providing for the necessary safeguards to the tribe and its members.

This statement constituted a standing offer by the Bureau to assist any tribe which wished to terminate partially or wholly its special relationship with the government. The rhetoric of this proposal, as with most dealing with termination, was subtly constructed to sound attractive to many interested persons without articulating any of the negative ramifications of the offer. A few tribes succumbed to these politically ambiguous propositions, only to find themselves in a much more deprived situation than before. (Examples of these incidents will be illustrated later.)

The Bureau of Indian Affairs, although supposedly an advocate for the Indian people, because of the nature of the structure of our government, must carry out the policies of Congress. If the Bureau developed a policy contrary to Congress, it would find itself attempting to function without adequate funds and under extreme pressure. This realization prompted Commissioner Myer to instruct Bureau officials to only develop programs which would promote the termination concept. In his memorandum of August 5, 1952, Myer said, "I think it may be fairly said that current congressional actions with regard to the Bureau of Indian Affairs and Indian appropriations indicate future appropriations will be limited largely to financing items which will facilitate withdrawal." He also urged his officials to explain to the Indians what was happening and to try to obtain their cooperation in designing "withdrawal programs" for the tribes. He did stipulate, however, that "We must proceed, even though Indian cooperation may be lacking in certain cases." Most of the termination activities, consequently, were carried on without the consent of—and often without the knowledge of—the various Indian tribes.

On August 15, 1953, just two weeks after House Resolution 108 was introduced, the first termination bill was enacted: Public Law 280 reared its ugly head to threaten the Indian world. It read, in part, as follows:

. . . . Sec. 2. Title 18, United States Code, is hereby amended by inserting in Chapter 53 thereof immediately after section 1161 a new section, to be designated as section 1162, as follows: "No.1162. State jurisdiction over offenses committed by or against Indians in the Indian country.

(a) Each of the States listed in the following table shall have jurisdiction over offenses committed by or against Indians in the areas of Indian country listed opposite the name of the State to the same extent that such State has jurisdiction over offenses committed elsewhere within the State, and the criminal laws of such State shall have the same force and effect within such Indian country as they have elsewhere within the State:

State of	Indian country affected
California	All Indian country within the State
Minnesota	All Indian country within the State, except the Red Lake Reservation
Nebraska	All Indian country within the State
Oregon	All Indian country within the State, except the Warm Springs Reservation
Wisconsin	All Indian country within the State, except the Menominee Reservation

(b) Nothing in this section shall authorize the alienation, encumbrance, or taxation of any real or personal property, including water rights, belonging to any Indian or any Indian tribe, band, or community that is held in trust by the United States or is subject to a restriction against alienation imposed by the United States; or shall authorize regulation of the use of such property in a manner inconsistent with any Federal treaty, agreement, or statute or with any regulation made pursuant thereto; or shall deprive any Indian or any Indian tribe, band, or community of any right, privilege, or immunity afforded under Federal treaty, agreement, or statute with respect to hunting, trapping, or fishing or the control, licensing, or regulation thereof. . . .

Public Law 280 was originally designed to alleviate difficulties in law enforcement, fire protection, and other public services generally provided by local or state governments. The concept was developed in some of the small California reservation areas which were not able to support tribal police or other agencies and for whom the Bureau would not supply the needed facilities. These rancherias and tiny reservations needed protection for their inhabitants and solicited aid through the legislature.

By the time legislators, Bureau personnel, and other politically-oriented officials finished with the bill, the Indians who had conceived the idea could scarcely recognize it. The revised edition provided jurisdiction to state governments, but that jurisdiction has since been extended to county and municipal ordinances through judicial interpretation. This allows local government to impose such legal regulations as building codes, sanitation regulations, weed abatement, and other laws which are generally irrelevant to tribal and reservation life. Inability to adhere to such rules have forced many Indians to abandon allotments and a number of reservations, and to seek shelter in the urban area.[96] Controversies and legal actions are still prevalent because of the ambiguous wording of the bill and the termination policies inferred by this ambiguity as interpreted by various agencies of government. Designed to provide needed services to small tribes, Public Law 280 became an insidious termination act reaching into nearly every facet of tribal life all over America.

The Menominee Indians were one of the tribes specifically designated by Congress to be terminated. Their situation was unique because of the several termination procedures brought to bear on the tribe and deceptive strategies used to sever their relationship with the federal government. The story is quite interesting.

Shortly after the turn of the twentieth century, a violent storm destroyed much valuable Menominee timber. The Bureau of Indian Affairs elected to let the downed timber rot rather than try any salvage operations. Millions of board feet of fine lumber was thus lost to the tribe.

After the establishment of the Indian Claims Commission in 1946, the Menominees sued the federal government for damages because of the timber loss. After due time, the case was heard and decided in favor of the Indians. This seemed a simple and non-threatening situation, and so it was—until Senator Arthur Watkins of Utah entered the picture.

Early in 1954, Senator Watkins, who was chairman of the Senate Interior Subcommittee on Indian Affairs, and E. Y. Berry, Representative from South Dakota and chairman of the counterpart committee in the House of Representatives, got together. They formed a special joint subcommittee on Indian Affairs and instituted a survey of federal Indian tribes in order to ascertain, in their minds at least, which tribes were ready to be terminated. Having identified their victims, they began to write legislation to unilaterally terminate the treaty rights of several tribes.

When Watkins learned of the Menominee court victory, he was furious. The idea that alleged wards of the government could sue their trustee for blatant violations of its role as trustee was totally unacceptable to the gentleman from Utah. His concept was that any Indian tribe astute enough to file suit against the government and win did not need federal assistance. Through the efforts of Watkins and Berry, a rider was added to the claims settlement which terminated the federal trusteeship with the Menominee Tribe. Sections of the Menominee Termination Act are as follows:

An Act To provide for a per capita distribution of Menominee tribal funds and authorize the withdrawal of the Menominee Tribe from Federal jurisdiction.
. . . . Sec.3. At midnight of the date of enactment of this Act the roll of the tribe. . . . shall be closed and no child born thereafter shall be eligible for enrollment. . . .

This portion of the Act terminates the Menominee and sentences them to extinction as a people. It blatantly states that no new Menominees shall be enrolled; thus, when the last tribal member who was alive at the time of enactment dies, the Menominees will be no more.

The government, however, displaying the materialistic mentality typical of its officials, justified the transaction by the issuance of "blood money" in the following manner:

Sec. 5. The Secretary is authorized and directed, as soon as practicable after the passage of this Act, to pay from such funds as are deposited to the credit of the tribe in the Treasury of the United States $1,500 to each member of the tribe on the rolls of the tribe on the date of the Act. . . .

Not only were the Indians sold into extinction, but the money came from their own tribal funds. This was tantamount to a person being condemned to electrocution and being billed for the cost of the electricity used.

The tribe was also expected to pay for qualified management specialists who were to show them how to survive on their $1,500 nestegg and the meager income they might receive from other sources. This provision read:

Sec. 6. The tribe is authorized to select and retain the services of qualified management specialists, including tax consultants, for the purpose of studying industrial programs on the Menominee Reservation[97] and making such reports or recommendations, including appraisal of Menominee tribal property, as may be desired by the tribe. . . . Such amounts of Menominee tribal funds as may be required for this purpose shall be made available by the Secretary.

After paying for their own termination and financing experts to explain that they were in dire economic straits, the Menominees were subjected to one more ignominy; it was publicized that they had been wiped out:

> Sec.10. When title to the property of the tribe has been transferred . . . . the Secretary will publish in the Federal Register an appropriate proclamation of that fact. Thereafter individual members of the tribe shall not be entitled to any of the services performed by the United States for Indians because of their status as Indians, all statutes of the United States which affects Indians because of their status as Indians shall no longer be applicable to the members of the tribe, and the laws of the several States shall apply to the tribe and its members in the same manner as they apply to other citizens or persons within their jurisdiction. . . .

And so the Menominee Nation of American Indians were removed from existance with complete legality and finality.

Watkins did not restrict his termination mania to the Menominees alone. He also attacked the sovereignty of the Paiutes, Klamaths, Catawbas, Alabama-Coushattas, Grande Rondes, Siletz, mixed-blood Utes, and many California tribes. When tribes would refuse to agree to termination, Watkins would threaten, harass, dupe, or coerce them into compliance. He told the small bands of Paiutes in southern Utah that the Legislation was only to validate their tribal marriages in the state. When tribes refused to agree to the legislation he sometimes threatened to pass the bills anyway and to withhold their money.

Watkins browbeat Indians and non-Indians alike in his efforts to force termination legislation through Congress. Those who would oppose him were quickly trampled, and it was as if he had a blank check to do as he pleased with the Indians. It seems incongruous that the Congress of the United States would oppose despotic and tyrannical manipulation of people all over the world, even going so far as to declare war on nations to prevent such actions, and yet allow and even encourage one of its own members to utilize the same tactics against various tribes of Indians. Not since Andrew Jackson had the

Indians had such a bitter and nefarious enemy occupying a high government office.

Termination projects were not limited to Congressional activities, for the Bureau of Indian Affairs was scrupulously following the legislative moves with their own termination programs. Under the direction of Dillon Myer and his equally objectionable successor, Glenn L. Emmons, a white banker from Gallup, New Mexico, the Bureau established the "relocation" policy.

Under this concept, Indians living on reservations were recruited for relocation to the urban areas. Although relocation was started in 1951, it gained momentum through the "termination" years of 1953 to 1958. Field offices were located in large cities and Indians from all tribes began to be moved in by the Bureau.

The general pattern was for a Bureau official to encourage the Indian to move by promising economic improvement for the family in the urban setting. The Indian was provided a one-way ticket to town and little else. Disillusioned by the lack of follow-up, ill-prepared for survival in the cities, and longing for home, most Indians had an extremely difficult time adjusting to their new environment. Many returned to the reservation, turned to alcoholism in their frustration, or committed spiritual or physical suicide. A large number were able to make the transition and establish themselves successfully.[98]

One of the policies established by the Bureau was designed to break up Indian tribal affiliations in the city and to fragment the urban Indians. By not relocating two Indians in the same block and scattering them throughout the area, these purposes were accomplished and no Indian ghettos were developed. This scattering of the relocated families also hastened the assimilation, for Indians were separated not only from their tribal members but from Indians of any tribe. In order to survive, they had to become functional within the dominant society's structure.

According to Commissioner Emmons' report of June 30, 1954, within the relocation efforts of the Bureau of Indian Affairs, goals had been established in the program and prospects were bright for attainment of the quotas. He also stated:

During the 1954 fiscal year, 2,163 Indians were directly assisted to relocate under the Bureau's relocation program. . . . In addition, over 300 Indians left reservations without assistance to join relatives and friends who had been assisted to relocate. . . .

Goals were increased and recruitment efforts were stepped up in succeeding years until there was practically a steady stream of Indians moving in and out of the reservations. Many were heading for the city with high hopes for a better life, and a lesser number were heading back home, unable to cope with urban living.

Throughout Commissioner Emmons' administration, which was from 1953 to 1961, he pressed for termination but also attempted some reform activities.

In 1953, Public Law 277 was passed by Congress. This law revised the governmental regulations concerning the sale of alcoholic beverages to Indians. The long-standing federal prohibition against the sale of liquor to Indians off the reservation was ended. Within the reservations, a system of local option was provided wherever laws of affected states would permit. Although Indians had been accorded full legal citizenship by an act of Congress in 1924, it took another Congressional action to allow them, for good or ill, the prerogative of purchasing alcohol. Such "paternalistic citizenship" had never, before or since, been bestowed on any other American.

Commissioner Emmons claimed as one of his goals the improvement of Indian health care. American Indians had suffered severe health problems for many years and the Bureau of Indian Affairs' health program was not providing adequate alleviation of the conditions. Extremely high incidents of tuberculosis, respiratory diseases, gastrointestinal ailments, trachoma, and otitis-media plagued the Indians. Infant mortality was twice the national average, and if an Indian survived childhood, his life expectancy was only forty-three years. It became more and more apparent that if Indians were to have decent health services, sweeping changes were necessary.

Consequently, on August 5, 1954, Congress passed legislation which transferred responsibility for Indian health services from the Bureau of Indian Affairs to the Public Health Service of the Department of Health, Education, and Welfare. This Act carried certain vague mandates, but did not set up specific instructions for H.E.W. The Secretary of that department was assigned the authority to make the regulations for administering the program.

The transfer of responsibility did not provide any magic formula which could suddenly transform the Bureau's mess to something of national pride, but some advantages were apparent. Administration of the program would be in the hands of personnel trained in the field of public health rather than social work. It was also provided that service in the Commissioned Officer Corps of the Public Health Service could be accepted as an alternative to military service for doctors. During time of military hostilities, this provision would become quite attractive, and many young physicians accepted commissions in the Indian Health Service.

The latter half of the 1950s was a time of continued termination activity. Even though Commissioner Emmons instituted a number of changes in the Bureau, he basically did so in the sphere of termination. He seemed to be a disciple of Senator Watkins, whose dictates he tended to follow.

Watkins spent much of his energy in promoting the termination process as the solution of the problems for the Indian people. He was quite eloquent and was reminiscent of the orators of the 1800s as he spoke and wrote of his feelings on the matter. One of his articles, published in 1957, reeked of "the flag, apple pie, and mom" and gave the reader the feeling that if he opposed termination he would be a traitor to America. After berating John Collier and the Indian Reorganization Act and praising House Concurrent Resolution 108, he concluded his article with this comment:

With the aim of "equality before the law" in mind our course should rightly be no other. Firm and constant consideration for those of Indian ancestry should lead us all to work diligently and carefully for the full realization of their national citizenship with all other Americans. Following in the footsteps of the Emancipation Proclamation of ninety-four years ago, I see the following words emblazoned in letters of fire above the heads of the Indians—THESE PEOPLE SHALL BE FREE![99]

When Fred A. Seaton became Secretary of Interior, he adopted a policy which slowed the termination activity to some degree. He stated that no tribe would be terminated unless they had a clear understanding and acceptance of the plan. In his report of September 18, 1958, he said:

. . . . In my opinion, the stated intentions of the Congress to free Indian tribes from Federal supervision, and to eliminate the need for the special services rendered by the Bureau of Indian Affairs . . . was to state an objective, not an immediate goal. . . . I want to add this; under no circumstances could I bring myself to recommend the termination of the Federal relationship with any Indian tribe in this country until the members of that tribe have been given the opportunity of a sound and effective education. To me it would be incredible, even criminal, to send any Indian tribe out into the stream of American life until and unless the educational level of that tribe was one which was equal to the responsibilities which it was shouldering. . . .

As the 1950s came to an end, the Indians found themselves still threatened with loss of federal services. Although there were advocates of Indian prerogatives, such as Fred Seaton, the old nemesis—Senator Watkins—still loomed as a continuous intimidation to their peace and security.

Indians all over America began to realize that it was an absolute necessity that a Pan-Indian approach to their problems be utilized.

Fifteen
The Seeds of
Social Revolution

During the 1950s, the Indian "voice" in the fight against the termination policy of the government was heard through the National Congress of American Indians. As the membership of NCAI grew, however, it was only natural, due to the diversity among Indians, that factionalization would develop. The organization split into two primary divisions which began to spend more time fighting each other than fighting government policy.

In an attempt to present a united Indian front to the new Kennedy administration and bring about needed reforms, a conference was called at the University of Chicago. Indians from many tribes met in June 1961 and drew up the Declaration of Indian Purpose. This document outlined proposals and recommendations on economic development, health, welfare, housing, education, law, and other topics needing the attention of the federal government. Their declaration included a statement of purpose and philosophy which said:

Creed

WE BELIEVE in the inherent right of all people to retain spiritual and cultural values, and that the free exercise of these values is necessary to the normal development of any people. Indians exercised this inherent right to live their own lives for thousands of years before the white man came and took their lands. It is a more complex world in which Indians live today, but the Indian people who first settled the New World and built the great civilizations which only now are being dug out of the past, long ago demonstrated that they could master complexity.

WE BELIEVE that the history and development of America show that the Indian has been subjected to duress, undue influence, unwarranted pressures, and policies which have produced uncertainty, frustration, and despair. Only when the public understands these conditions and is moved to take action toward the formulation and adoption of sound and consistent policies and programs will these destoying factors be removed and the Indian resume his normal growth and make his maximum contribution to modern society.

WE BELIEVE in the future of a greater America, an America which we were first to love, where life, liberty, and the pursuit of happiness will be a reality. In such a future, with Indians and all other Americans cooperating, a natural climate will be created in which the Indian people will grow and develop as members of a free society.

The Conference concluded the declaration with an eloquent statement which outlined the feelings of a proud and noble people:

To complete our Declaration, we point out that in the beginning, the people of the New World, called Indians by accident of geography, were possessed of a continent and a way of life. In the course of many lifetimes, our people had adjusted to every climate and condition from the Arctic to the torrid zones. In their livelihood and family relationships, their ceremonial observances, they reflected the diversity of the physical world they occupied.

The conditions in which Indians live today reflect a world in which every basic aspect of life has been transformed. Even the physical world is no longer the controlling factor in determining where and under what conditions men may live. In region after region, Indian groups found their means of existence either totally destroyed or materially modified. Newly introduced diseases swept away or reduced regional populations. These changes were followed by major shifts in the internal life of tribe and family.

The time came when the Indian people were no longer masters of their situation. Their lifeways survived subject to the will of a dominant sovereign power. This is said, not in a spirit of complaint; we understand that in the lives of all nations of people, there are times of plenty and times of famine. But, we do speak out in a plea for understanding.

When we go before the American people, as we do in this Declaration, and ask for material assistance in developing our resources and developing our opportunities, we pose a moral problem which cannot be left unanswered. For the problem we raise affects the standing which our nation sustains before world opinion.

Our situation cannot be relieved by appropriated funds alone, though it is equally obvious that without capital investment and funded services, solutions will be delayed. Nor will the passage of time lessen the complexities which beset a people moving toward a new meaning and purpose.

The answers we seek are not commodities to be purchased, neither are they evolved automatically through the passing of time.

The efforts to place social adjustments on a money-time interval scale which has characterized Indian administration, has resulted in unwanted pressure and frustration.

When Indians speak of the continent they yielded, they are not referring only to the loss of some millions of acres in real estate. They have in mind that the land supported a universe of things they knew, valued, and loved.

With the continent gone, except for a few poor parcels they still retain, the basis of life is precariously held, but they mean to hold the scraps and parcels as earnestly as any small nation or ethnic group was ever determined to hold to identity and survival.

What we ask of America is not charity, not paternalism, even when benevolent. We ask only that the nature of our situation be recognized and made the basis of policy and action.

In short, the Indians ask for assistance, technical and financial, for the time needed, however long that may be, to regain in the America of the space age some measure of the adjustment they enjoyed as the original possessors of their native land.

The emphasis of the proposals and recommendations of the Conference centered on the Indians' desires to play decisive roles in planning and operating their own programs. The Indians also made it clear that the Bureau of Indian Affairs needed a reorganization and that they wanted to play an important role in the action. Although Indians had been asking for a voice in their affairs for many years, the Chicago Conference was the first unified request of any consequence. It planted the seeds of self-determination which would not begin to be realized for nearly another decade.

The Kennedy administration responded to the Indian people with its own study of Indian affairs. A task force was formed, with Secretary of the Interior Stewart Udall as chairman. The report of the task force was summarized by Commissioner of Indian Affairs Philleo Nash in his 1961 Annual Report:

. . . . Probably the most important single recommendation was for a shift in program emphasis away from termination of Federal trust relationships toward a greater development of the human and natural resources on Indian reservations. . . . In addition the report recommends: (1) more vigorous efforts to attract industries to reservation areas, (2) an expanded program of vocational training and placement, (3) creation of a special Reservation Development Loan Fund, (4) establishment of a statutory Advisory Board on Indian Affairs, (5) negotiations with States and counties, and resort to the courts where necessary, to make certain that off-reservation Indians are accorded the same rights and privileges as other citizens of their areas, (6) collaboration with States and tribes to bring tribal law and order codes into conformity with those of the States and counties where reservations are located, (7) acceleration in the adjudication of cases pending before the Indian Claims Commission, and (8) more active and widespread efforts to inform the public about the status of the Indian people and the nature of their problems.

The report repudiated termination and suggested that economic development on Indian reservations be the basis of a new federal Indian policy. As a result, between 1961 and 1965, the Bureau of Indian Affairs shifted its policy direction and embarked on a program of economic and community development. Although changes in policy were implemented, nothing was done to refashion the Bureau into an effective instrument for executing the new policy and programs. It maintained its old, implacable course of inefficiency.

The 1960s brought an awakening to human rights all over America. The blacks staged sit-ins, marches, rallies, and riots in an effort to obtain an equal place in American society. This activity brought much attention to their condition and some progress was made toward their goals. The Mexican-American or Chicano communities also began some violent protestations over their lot in this country. Some semblance of success came from their efforts, too. Indians, seeing the results of other groups' social revolutions, also began to become more active in their endeavor to survive as a people. One of the earliest contemporary controversies took place in the State of Washington over the fishing rights of that state's Indians.

The first confrontation had taken place in the 1950s, when the state attempted to control Indian fishing on the Puyallup River. The right to fish at "usual and accustomed" places was upheld at that time,[100] but in the early 1960s, the state game wardens began to arrest Indians fishing off the reservations. Pressures were applied by not only the state game officials, but by sport fishermen also. Nets were cut and fishing equipment destroyed. Even buyers of fish were forced to stop buying fish caught by the Indians.

Indians, prompted and led in some cases by sympathetic whites, began to organize to protect their treaty rights. They formed the Survival of American Indians Association and participated in a number of demonstrations to dramatize their situation. Early in 1964, protest fish-ins were staged on the Nisqually River. In March, the National Indian Youth Council organized a demonstration at Olympia, and actor Marlon Brando got some of his first "civil rights" publicity when he was arrested for net fishing. He was released on a technicality and not brought to trial.

Another demonstration took place at Olympia the following year, but it did not attract the publicity the previous one had. Other fish-ins were equally quiet but began to have a cumulative effect on Indians and game officials alike.

Finally, in October 1965, the smoldering volcano erupted on the Nisqually River. An Indian boat was turned over by state officers and a fight ensued. It was only a minor fracas, but several nights later, a force of officers attempted to raid an Indian fishing camp. The Indians resisted, and this time a large brawl resulted. State patrol officers had to be called in to settle the battle.

Indians and their friends continued their fish-ins and demonstrations. On October 13, another fight broke out at a well-publicized rally and seven Indians were arrested for illegal fishing and interfering with officers. After over three years of legal maneuvering, they were tried and acquitted. Their defense was that they were peacefully demonstrating and that the extensive and unnecessary show of force by the officers had threatened their safety, thereby producing the defensive reaction on their part.

The Muckleshoot, Puyallup, and Nisqually tribes were involved in a number of court cases attempting to settle the fishing rights controversy. The courts' decisions were inconsistent and the battle raged. Many northwestern Indian tribes lent moral and monetary assistance to their brothers, and commercial and sport fishermen joined in opposition to the Indians. It was not until February 1974, when Judge George Boldt in Federal Court in Tacoma rendered a decision favoring the Indians, that the situation eased. Even then, it was an uneasy peace which still is broken from time to time. (The "Fishing War" is discussed further in a later chapter.)

After the assassination of John F. Kennedy, Lyndon Johnson became president and he declared his "War on Poverty." Included in that war were the Indian people. On March 6, 1968, President

Johnson, in his Special Message to Congress, made a forceful statement of a new direction in Indian policy. He advocated self-determination for the tribes, and, in part, said:

. . . . I propose a new goal for our Indian programs: A goal that ends the old debate about "termination" of Indian programs and stresses self-determination; a goal that erases old attitudes of paternalism and promotes partnership and self-help.

Our goal must be:

—A standard of living for the Indians equal to that of the country as a whole.

—Freedom of Choice: An opportunity to remain in their homelands, if they choose, without surrendering their dignity; an opportunity to move to the towns and cities of America, if they choose, equiped with the skills to live in equality and dignity.

—Full participation in the life of modern America, with a full share of economic opportunity and social justice.

I propose, in short, a policy of maximum choice for the American Indian: a policy expressed in programs of self-help, self-development, self-determination.

. . . . To launch an undivided, Government-wide effort in this area, I am today issuing an Executive Order to establish a National Council on Indian Opportunity.

The Chairman of the Council will be the Vice President, who will bring the problems of the Indians to the highest levels of Government. The Council will include a cross section of Indian leaders, and high government officials who have programs in this field. . . .

. . . . The Council will review Federal programs for Indians, make broad policy recommendations, and ensure that programs reflect the needs and desires of the Indian people. Most important, I have asked the Vice President, as Chairman of the Council, to make certain that the American Indian shares fully in all our federal programs.

. . . . The greatest hope for Indian progress lies in the emergence of Indian leadership and initiative in solving Indian problems. Indians must have a voice in making the plans and decisions in programs which are important to their daily life.

He goes on to explain how the new policy must be affected and promises the Indians a fair share in decisions which effect their lives:

. . . . there can be no question that the government and the people of the United States have a responsibility to the Indians.

In our effort to meet that responsibility, we must pledge to respect fully the dignity and the uniqueness of the Indian citizen.

That means partnership, not paternalism.

We must affirm the right of the first Americans to remain Indians while exercising their rights as Americans.

We must affirm their right to freedom of choice and self-determination.

We must seek ways to provide Federal assistance to Indians—with new emphasis on Indian self-help and with respect for Indian culture.

And we must assure the Indian people that it is our desire and intention that the special relationship between the Indian and his government grow and flourish.

For, the first among us must not be last.

I urge the Congress to affirm this policy and to enact this program.

Congress did hear Johnson's plea for Indian rights and self-determination and responded, at least in some areas. On April 11, 1968, the Civil Rights Act of 1968,[101] Titles II to VII of which dealt with Indian matters, was passed. Although the rights of non-reservation Indians are guaranteed under the Constitution, reservation Indians have not had the same protection. Because Indian tribes traditionally have been considered separate sovereign governing bodies, the courts have tended to hold that the Constitution does not protect tribal members against the acts of tribal officials.

The Indian Bill of Rights, as the Act mentioned above is called, was passed to correct what was felt to be a double standard of justice. It guaranteed to reservation residents many of the same civil rights and liberties in relation to tribal authorities that the Constitution guarantees to all persons in relation to federal and state authorities.

Basically, three different kinds of rights are established by the Act:

1) The freedoms of religion, speech, press, and assembly—the fundamental rights of a free people to believe what they choose, and say and write what they think;

2) The right to due process of law, which exists primarily to protect the freedoms of criminal defendants, and is essential to the fair administration of justice, setting limits on the methods officials may use in enforcing the law and bringing accused persons to trial (this receives the greatest attention under the Indian Bill of Rights);

3) The guarantee of equal protection of the laws, or freedom from improper discrimination.

The passage of the act caused widespread reaction and concern among the tribes. Some Indians saw the new law as an attempt to force national standards on tribal internal affairs in violation of tribal sovereignty. To these critics, the act posed a threat to traditional Indian ways of life. Others complained that it was improper for Congress to impose new requirements on tribal governments without also providing the funds to meet them.

Many Indians, however, welcomed these new rights as long overdue. They were tired of the double standard of justice and of "being the first Americans, with second-class citizenship." They interpreted the granting of fundamental rights to reservation Indians as an effort to strengthen tribal institutions.

In passing the Act, Congress attempted to guarantee individual rights to reservation residents without severely disrupting traditional tribal culture. In enforcing the Act, the courts were faced with the serious responsibility of drawing a balance between respect for individual rights and respect for Indian custom and tradition.

Unfortunately, the standards established by the Constitution and legislation are not always met. Widespread misunderstandings and misinterpretations by enforcement officials, sometimes innocently and sometimes intentionally, have brought about long and difficult court battles to overcome the problems which prompted the passage of this Act.[102]

The Omnibus Bill of 1967 illustrates intentional misuse of authority by government officials, pointing out the necessity for clearer articulation, closer monitoring, and constant vigilance on the part of tribal officials. It is a clear example of "forked tongue" bureaucratic maneuvering.

In 1966, Stewart Udall, Secretary of the Interior, met with Indian tribal leaders in Santa Fe, New Mexico to discuss his plans for the Bureau of Indian Affairs. The meeting was originally planned for Udall and Bureau officials, but Indian leaders "crashed" the conference to demand a voice in plans which would affect their reservation programs. Udall promised major legislative action by the Johnson administration in the form of an omnibus bill. This legislation was to have incorporated all problems of Indian administration into one gigantic legislative package. The Indians were also promised a major voice in developing the project.

Historically, it had been the policy of the Interior Department to establish policy and implement programs without Indian consultation, so Udall and his staff proceeded on the same basis to draw up the Omnibus Bill to present to the Congress. This time, however, things worked a little differently. In what must be regarded as the major coup in Indian/white relations, the National Congress of American Indians somehow obtained copies of the proposed legislation and distributed them to the various tribes.

Typical of the way the Department dealt with Indian people, newly appointed Commissioner of Indian Affairs Robert Bennett was sent on the hopeless task of consulting with the tribes in order to draw up the bill (*after* it had been written!). Since the Indians already had copies, in spite of official declarations that there *was* no bill, Bennett's task merely discredited him with the Indians. Even before Bennett's consultations were completed, the legislation was given to Congress for introduction. In the winter of 1966 and again in the following spring, the Interior Department tried to fool the tribes into believing they would have some voice in the proposal to Congress. Once more NCAI found a way to obtain copies of the legislation and distribute them to the tribes.

When the bills were finally formally introduced in Congress in May 1967, not one single Senator or Congressman would sign his name to them. The Indian leadership wanted no part of the bills, for they were totally non-Indian in concept. They immediately publicized the attempted deception and began to apply pressure on Congressional delegates to boycott the legislation. Indians had learned to play the white man's game and win.

Even more important than winning was the development of Indian thinking as a result of the Omnibus Bill. Indians were no longer cowering before government officials. They had learned that they did have some influence on what happened in their lives, and they were beginning to voice their needs and desires. This type of thinking brought about a new direction for many Indian people.

One of the first appearances of this "New Indian" was in Minneapolis, Minnesota, in July 1968, when the American Indian Movement (AIM) was organized. A group of Indian activists attempted to unify over twenty Indian organizations in the city into one unit.

A catalyst for AIM in 1968 in the city of Minneapolis was the police harassment of Indians. While Indians represented only ten percent of the city's population, seventy percent of the jail inmates were Indian. To divert Indians from jails, AIM formed a ghetto partol, equipped with two-way radios which monitored the police broadcasts. When a call came through involving Indians, AIM beat the police to the scene and spirited the Indians away, and for twenty-nine successive weekends prevented any undue arrests of Indian people. As a result of AIM's activities, Indian population in the jails decreased by sixty percent. AIM exposed definite discrimination in the policing of predominantly Indian neighborhoods of Minneapolis and forced a change of policy in the police department.

With this successful campaign as a sales tool, AIM quickly expanded its activities to other cities and became the leading Indian activist organization in the country.

A similar movement began on the West Coast in 1969, when the San Francisco Indian Center, which served the Bay Area Indians, burned down. It had provided a center for cultural and social activities for many Indians who were relocated in the San Francisco area. The people were desperately trying to find another location for their center, and Alcatraz Island—desolate, deserted, and forlorn—looked inviting to some of them.

During the night of November 19, 1969, seventy-eight young students from schools in the nearby cities swam ashore and occupied the former island prison, calling themselves the Indians of All Tribes. Supported by organizations all the over the country, Indian and non-Indian alike, the small group rejected the federal government's attempts to remove them. Bureaucratic representatives used every tactic to obtain agreement with the occupants of the island, but the Indians remained firm. No amount of coercion, bribery, or intimidation could make them leave "The Rock." Finally, on Friday, June 11, 1971, after several months of what the government called "negotiations," twenty federal marshalls, armed with rifles and shotguns, raided the island. They removed the Indians and blockaded the area so they could not return.

Throughout 1970, other groups in the West Coast area, also calling themselves the Indians of All Tribes, perpetrated similar takeovers of abandoned military installations and isolated islands. The Indian "movement" began to change from defensive to offensive postures in proclaiming dissatisfaction with the "establishment." Perhaps these activist strategies were emulations of the "Black Revolt"; perhaps they were just a result of Indians finally saying, "We've had enough." Whatever the cause, the vocal and physical actions of the Indians of All Tribes and of the

American Indian Movement in 1968 to 1970 established the pattern for other confrontations in following years.

The late 1960s were not years of militant activity only; they were years of legislative action, also. As indicated earlier in this chapter, the Bureau of Indian Affairs had not instituted any sweeping changes and continued on its inefficient way, undisturbed by outside influences. Some of the more progressive members of the Senate became tired of the status quo of the entire governmental approach to Indian affairs and set out to initiate changes.

Realizing that the only route to survival for Indians was through education, Senator Paul Fannin of Arizona wrote to Senator Wayne Morris of Oregon, chairman of the Senate Committee on Labor and Public Welfare, to suggest that a Special Subcommittee on Indian Education be established. The subcommittee was authorized on August 31, 1967 (S.Res. 165), with Senator Robert Kennedy as its chairman. The purpose of the subcommittee was summarized as an effort to "examine, investigate, and make a complete study of any and all matters pertaining to the education of Indian children." Since all aspects of life impinge in some manner on the education of children, it was necessary for the subcommittee to consider the entire scope of Indian life to obtain a comprehensive picture.

In part, the summary of the report states:

For more than two years the members of this subcommittee have been gaging how well American Indians are educated. We have traveled to all parts of the country; we have visited Indians in their homes and in their schools; we have listened to Indians, to Government officials, and to experts; and we have looked closely into every aspect of the educational opportunities this Nation offers its Indian citizens. . . .

We are shocked at what we discovered.

Others before us were shocked. They recommended and made changes. Others after us will likely be shocked, too—despite our recommendations and efforts at reform. For there is so much to do—wrongs to right, omissions to fill, untruths to correct—that our own recommendations, concerned as they are with education alone, need supplementation across the whole board of Indian life.

We have developed page after page of statistics. These cold figures mark a stain on our national conscience, a stain which has spread slowly for hundreds of years. They tell a story to be sure. But, they cannot tell the whole story. They cannot, for example, tell of the despair, the frustration, the hopelessness, the poignancy, of children who want to learn but are not taught; of adults who try to read but have no one to teach them; of families which want to stay together but are forced apart; or of 9-year-old children who want neighborhood schools but are sent thousands of miles away to remote and alien boarding schools.

We have seen what these conditions do to Indian children and Indian families. The sights are not pleasant.

The subcommittee titled their report, "Indian Education: A National Tragedy—A National Challenge." They called it that because, as they said, "Past generations of lawmakers and administrators have failed the American Indian. Our own generation thus faces a challenge—we can continue the unacceptable policies and programs of the past or we can recognize our failures, renew our commitments, and reinvest our efforts with new energy."[103]

In complying with the manadate to investigate "any and all matters pertaining to the education of Indian children," the subcommittee was compelled to examine not only the federal schools, but the state and local public schools and the mission schools as well. The findings were described thusly:

> What concerned us most deeply, as we carried out our mandate, was the low quality of virtually every aspect of the schooling available to Indian children. The school buildings themselves; the course materials and books; the attitude of teachers and administrative personnel; the accessibility of school buildings—all these are of shocking quality.[104]

The committee did not restrict its research to problems, for identifying failures without recommending solutions is easy—and doesn't change anything.

> . . . . Running all through this report are many others [statistics], which are some measure of the depth of the tragedy. There are, too, specific examples of visits we made to various facilities in the Indian education system. These are too lenghty to summarize; however, the subcommittee believes that their cumulative effect is chilling.
>
> We reacted to our findings by making a long series of specific recommendations. These recommendations embrace legislative changes; administrative changes; policy changes; structural changes—all of which are geared to making Indian education programs into models of excellence, not of bureaucratic calcification. . . .

The subcommittee concurred with the Meriam Report of 1928 in its analysis of Indian input into their own programs.

. . . . One theme running through all our recommendations is increased Indian participation and control of their own education programs. For far too long, the Nation has paid only token heed to the notion that Indians should have a strong voice in their own destiny. We have made a number of recommendations to correct this historic, anomalous paternalism. . . .

At the conclusion of the summary of their report, the subcommittee made references which indicated some things Indians had been saying for years. It also illustrated the depth of thinking and the logical attitudes of the members:

In this report, we have compared the size and scope of the effort we believe must be mounted to the Marshall Plan which revitalized postwar Europe. We believe that we have, as a Nation, as great a moral and legal obligation to our Indian citizens today as we did after World War II to our European allies and adversaries.

The scope of this subcommittee's work was limited by its authorizing resolution to education. But as we traveled, and listened, and saw, we learned that education cannot be isolated from the other aspects of Indian life. These aspects, too, have much room for improvement. . . . . Economic development, job training, legal representation in water rights and oil lease matters—these are only a few of the correlative problems sorely in need of attention.

In conclusion, it is sufficient to restate our basic finding: that our Nation's policies and programs for educating American Indians are a national tragedy. They present us with a national challenge of no small proportions. We believe that this report recommends the proper steps to meet this challenge. But we know that it will not be met without strong leadership and dedicated work. We believe that with this leadership from the Congress and the executive branch of the Government, the Nation can and will meet this challenge.

Thus, in the 1960s, there was a change in many elements in the affairs of American Indians. The Indians themselves were beginning to realize that they could demand a say in their own destiny. The Government was finally at the point of admitting to its blundering through the Bureau of Indian Affairs and ready to begin to accept Indian requests and needs in their policy-making. The nation was in the throes of a social revolution, and the Senate Subcommittee's report brought home very strongly that something had to be done to rectify the situation it uncovered.

The stage was set for the radical changes to be made in the 1970s.

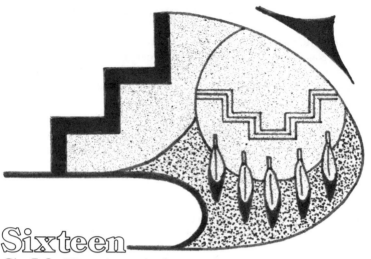

Sixteen
Self-Determination

The 1969 report of the Senate Special Subcommittee on Indian Education, called the Kennedy Report in honor of Senator Robert Kennedy, hit like a bombshell. Although much of what it said was not new (for it reiterated many of the Meriam Committee's findings of 1928), the timing was much more appropriate. The United States was in the midst of a great social change which made it expedient, both socially and politically, to respond to the recommendations set out by the subcommittee. Astute political leaders, either because of their commitments to the betterment of Indian life, or merely because it was the politically "correct" thing to do, initiated campaigns for sweeping changes in the field of Indian affairs.

On July 8, 1970, President Richard M. Nixon, in a message to Congress, recommended a policy of self-determination for Indians which included implementation of the Kennedy Report recommendations.[105] The stirring advocacy by the president prompted increased activity in the legislature, in various departments in the Cabinet, and even within the Bureau of Indian Affairs. The message said, in part:

The first Americans—the Indians—are the most deprived and most isolated minority group in our nation. On virtually every scale of measurement—employment, income, education, health—the condition of the Indian people ranks at the bottom.

This condition is the heritage of centuries of injustice. From the time of their first contact with European settlers, the American Indians have been oppressed and brutalized, deprived of their ancestral lands and denied the opportunity to control their own destiny. Even the Federal programs which are intended to meet their needs have frequently proven to be ineffective and demeaning.

But the story of the Indian in America is something more than the record of the white man's frequent aggression, broken agreements, intermittent remorse and prolonged failure. It is a record also of endurance, or survival, of adaptation and creativity in the face of overwhelming obstacles. It is a record of enormous contributions to this country—to its art and culture, to its strength and spirit, to its sense of history and its sense of purpose.

It is long past time that the Indian policies of the Federal government began to recognize and build upon the capacities and insights of the Indian people. Both as a matter of justice and as a matter of enlightened social policy, we must begin to act on the basis of what the Indians themselves have long been telling us. The time has come to break decisively with the past and create the conditions for a new era in which the Indian future is determined by Indian acts and Indian decisions. . . .

Mr. Nixon continued by saying that the policy of forced termination was wrong and that results were harmful in cases where termination had been tried. He went on to state his new policy:

. . . . I believe that both of these policy extremes are wrong. Federal termination errs in one direction, Federal paternalism errs in the other. Only by clearly rejecting both of these extremes can we achieve a policy which truly serves the best interests of the Indian people. Self-determination among the Indian people can and must be encouraged without the threat of eventual termination. In my view, in fact, that is the only way that self-determination can effectively be fostered.

This, then, must be the goal of any new national policy toward the Indian people: to strengthen the Indian's sense of autonomy without threatening his sense of community. We must assure the Indian that he can assume control of his own life without being separated involuntarily from the tribal group. And we must make it clear that Indians can become independent of Federal control without being cut off from Federal concern and Federal support. My specific recommendations to the Congress are designed to carry out this policy.

Making good his promise, Nixon did recommend many changes in the policy of the government in Indian affairs. He sponsored and signed numerous legislative acts in support of Indian self-determination and perpetuation of tribal life. Despite all the problems in his administration, Nixon did more than most of his predecessors to bring Indian life to an acceptable standard while strengthening Indian autonomy.

In summarizing his message, he said:

> . . . . In place of a long series of piece-meal reforms, we suggest a new and coherent strategy. In place of policies which simply call for more spending, we suggest policies which call for wiser spending. In place of policies which oscillate between the deadly extremes of forced termination and constant paternalism, we suggest a policy in which the Federal government and the Indian community play complimentary roles.
>
> But most importantly, we have turned from the question of *whether* the Federal government has a responsibility to Indians to the question of *how* that responsibility can best be fulfilled. We have concluded that the Indians will get better programs and that public monies will be more effectively expended if the people who are most affected by these programs are responsible for operating them.
>
> The Indians of America need Federal assistance—this much has long been clear. What has not always been clear, however, is that the Federal government needs Indian energies and Indian leadership if its assistance is to be effective in improving conditions of Indian life. It is a new and balanced relationship between the United States government and the first Americans that is the heart of our approach to Indian problems. And that is why we now approach these problems with new confidence that they will successfully be overcome.

Although Nixon's speech contained the same rhetoric as had many previous presidential proclamations, he set out immediately to fulfill his promises. One of the first indications that things might be different in the 1970s took place on December 15, 1970: the signing of the Blue Lake Restoration Act—a landmark occurrence.

In 1906, President Theodore Roosevelt had confiscated the sacred Blue Lake area from the Taos Pueblo Indians and incorporated it into the Carson National Forest. This "great humanitarian," who had no qualms about taking sacred ground from Indians, further demonstrated his freedom from racism and bigotry in a speech he made in 1886:

> I don't go so far as to think that the only good Indians are dead Indians, but I believe nine out of every ten are, and I shouldn't like to inquire too closely into the case of the tenth. The most vicious cowboy has more moral principle than the average Indian.[106]

Although the Indian Claims Commission ruled on September 8, 1965 that the land belonged to the Taos Indians and had been taken from them illegally, nothing was done to restore the area to the rightful owners. Meanwhile, the sacred lake and surrounding land was opened to tourists, sportsmen, and many others who desecrated its spirituality. Finally, after several attempts by sympathetic legislators to rectify the wrong, Congress passed a bill on December 15, 1970, with strong urging by President Nixon, to return the land to the Taos Pueblo. The significance of this action was emphasized by the president in his remarks on signing the bill:

Ladies and Gentlemen:

I want to welcome all of you here on this very special occasion during the Christmas season, and particularly our guests from the western part of the United States who have come from a long way to be with us.

We are here for a bill signing ceremony that has very special significance—the Taos-Blue Lake bill. It is a bill that has bipartisan support. Both Democrats and Republicans joined together to get it through the Congress so that the President could have the honor of signing it today.

And it is a bill which could be interpreted particularly in the Christmas season as one where a gift was being made by the United States to the Indian population of the United States.

That is not the case.

This is a bill that represents justice, because in 1906 an injustice was done in which land involved in this bill, 48,000 acres, was taken from the Indians involved, the Taos Pueblo Indians. And now, after all those years, the Congress of the United States returns that land to whom it belongs.

The bill also involves respect for religion. Those of us who know something about the background of the first Americans realize that long before any organized religion came to the United States, for 700 years the Taos Pueblo Indians worshipped in this place.

We restore this place of worship to them for all the years to come.

And finally, this bill indicates a new direction in Indian affairs in this country, a new direction in which we will have the cooperation of both Democrats and Republicans, one in which there will be more of an attitude of cooperation rather than paternalism, one of self-determination rather than termination, one of mutual respect.

I can only say that in signing the bill I trust that this will mark one of those periods in American history where, after a very, very long time, and at times a very sad history of injustice, that we started on a new road—a road which leads us to justice in the treatment of those, who were the first Americans, of our working together for the better nation that we want this great and good country of ours to become. . . .[107]

President Nixon's restoration of the Taos' sacred Blue Lake had a monumental effect on Indians all over America. This was one of the few times in the history of their dealings with the United States government when Indians received land which had been illegally taken from them. Generally, if illegality of land usurption by the government was proven, the best the tribes involved could expect was a token monetary indemnification. They were further encouraged when a bill proposed by Senators Barry Goldwater and Paul Fannin of Arizona to create a small Yavapai-Apache Indian Reservation was passed into law.

For many years, a small group of Indians had been squatting on a tiny plot of land outside Payson, Arizona. They lived in a most miserable condition in shacks which they constructed from material gathered from the refuse dump. They earned a meager survival by working in the timber industries and doing odd-jobs in the town. These Indians were remnants of the bands of Yavapai-Apache Indians that once inhabited a large part of central Arizona. On August 4, 1971, the two Arizona Senators jointly sponsored S-2422, which was passed as Public Law 92-470. This law gave federal recognition to these Indians and established a small, 85-acre federal reservation for them. Although the group only had a population of approximately 100 Indians, they were included as a federally recognized tribe. This made them eligible for federal services and benefits accorded other tribes under the jurisdiction of the Bureau of Indian Affairs. The influx of these services and benefits brought the standard of living up for these people, and in a very short time, the transformation of their community began to be evidenced. Housing development, health services, sanitation facilities, and other benefits and services were quickly established.

Nixon continued his Indian land restoration, and in 1973, he instituted one of the most unique moves in Indian affairs. He bestowed tribal identity on a small group of Pueblo Indians near El Paso, Texas, which had been a center of interest for Indian scholars for many years. Ignored by the United States government, this band of Tigua Indians had kept their identity and tribal cultures since 1680, although completely isolated from the rest of the Pueblos and surrounded by Mexican and, later, Anglo society. In a recent Department of Commerce publication, interesting commentary is made concerning this group:

．． ． ． This Tigua of Ysleta, El Paso, Texas, are a displaced Pueblo tribe originally located at the Isleta Pueblo south of Albuquerque, New Mexico. Their first contact with European civilization was in 1540 when Coronado spent the winter with them.[108] During the Spanish colonization of New Mexico, they were converted to Christianity and under the Spanish padres' direction constructed a mission in 1621 at Isleta, New Mexico dedicated to St. Anthony. During the Pueblo Revolt of 1680, the tribe was removed by the Spanish[109] during their retreat and relocated at Ysleta del Sur in what is now Texas. . . . The Tigua brought their tribal drums, their staffs of office, and Santo or Saint Anthony with them to Ysleta, where in 1682 they built the present-day Ysleta Mission. . . .

The Tigua still practice many customs no longer found among other Pueblo people. They have retained their form of tribal government, practice the same form of ceremonial dances, and continue to live in the same adobe houses. Obtaining much of their sustenance by hunting, fishing, and planting small gardens. Herbs, roots, and plants are still used for medicine.[110]

The Tiguas, approximately 500 of them, now live on the reservation. They have kept their culture intact under tremendous odds. They are living examples of the strength and tenacity some Indians have in retaining their ways of life.[111]

The years 1972 and 1973 were highlighted by land restoration and recognition by the Nixon administration of some of the legal and moral claims for survival by certain Indian groups. In addition to the Payson Yavapai-Apaches and the Tigua Indian recognition, other tribes regained land and status.

On October 9, 1972, the Stockbridge-Munsee tribe of Wisconsin regained 13,000 acres of land that had been promised them in the 1930s. These lands were dominantly submarginal,'' which meant that during the Great Depression nobody could make a living on them because they were unprofitable, thin-soiled, exhausted lands. Advised by the federal government that the land was to be theirs, the Indians worked to rehabilitate it. In the 1950s, after the Indians had improved the land for twenty years, opposition began to build against the transfer of the area to the tribe. Since the paperwork, which included the agreement to give the lands to the Indians, was "lost" in the intervening years, it took strong governmental action to make the transfer.

On October 13, 1972, an act of Congress transferred 770 acres of land for the Burns Paiutes of Burns Indian Colony, Oregon. The details of this land transfer are almost identical to that of the Stockbridge-Munsee.

President Nixon, using his power to execute special actions, on May 20, 1972, restored more than 20,000 acres of sacred timberland to the Yakima Nation in the State of Washington. This Executive Order brought to a successful conclusion the thirty-year struggle by the Pacific Northwest tribe to regain lands embracing Mt. Adams, a sacred mountain in the Yakima tribal religion.

In restoring this land, President Nixon said his action "rights a wrong going back 65 years" (to 1907, when President Theodore Roosevelt extended boundaries of a nearby forest reserve to include the Yakima acreage). Nixon's order defined explicitly the boundaries so there should be no controversy as to the control of the sacred mountain.

In March of 1973, Senator Barry Goldwater introduced a bill to the Senate which would, as one of its provisions, restore 169,000 acres of Havasupai Indian ancestral homeland to the tribe. This tiny tribe, on its 500-acre reservation deep in the confines of the Grand Canyon, had been ignored and isolated by most of America. The bill specifically involved giving tham all the waterfalls near the southern plateau lands where the tribe has traditionally enjoyed free grazing permits from the U.S. Forest Service. The 14,700 acres of Tenderfoot Plateau lands on the east would be connected with the 41,000 acres of Topocoba area lands on the west, and the sites of the tribal power station and the lone mule trial giving access into their canyon, located at Hualapai Hilltop, would also be added to the reservation. In return for the additional lands, the Havasupai would be required to give up their rights under law of grazing within the boundaries of the Grand Canyon National Park and of using park lands for agricultural purposes.

This bill, proposed by Senator Goldwater, attracted much opposition by various organizations, and it took years of arbitration and legislative bargaining before it finally became a law.

The most significant activity in terms of restoration took place on December 22, 1973, when the Menominee Indians of Wisconsin were restored to federal status. In Chapter 14, the termination of the Menominees was discussed, and the insidious manner in which it occurred was indicated. The Menominees, however, did not accept this termination and began the long struggle to make the American political process work for them. They wanted to be "Indian" and recognized the only way they could obtain that status was to overturn the Menominee Termination Bill.

In 1968, after a costly legal battle, the United States Supreme Court ruled that Menominee treaty rights to hunt and fish had "survived" termination.[112] This suit was the beginning of the Menominees' legal battle to reverse the effects of termination. The actual process of reversal, the restoration, did not begin until 1970, when a group of Menominees formed an organization known as Determination of Rights and Unity of Menominee Shareholders (DRUMS).

In late 1971, DRUMS began working with attorneys from the Native American Rights Fund (NARF), an Office of Economic Opportunity-funded legal organization. These two organizations spent more than 1,400 man-hours working on the Menominee Restoration Act over the next two years. Not wishing that the same mistakes be made as were in the termination, DRUMS and NARF carried on a series of consultations with the Menominee people concerning the provisions they wanted to see in the restoration.

On April 20, 1972, the Menominee Restoration Act was introduced into both the House and the Senate. As is the case with most complex legislation, changes were then suggested by various sources. The same kind of hearings as were held on the Termination Act were repeated. This time, however, the Menominee attended in force and made certain that there were no gaps or erasures in the record. They made sure their desires were succinctly stated and indicated they would not settle for less than complete restoration.

Full House Subcommittee hearings were held in Washington, D.C. on June 28, 1973. As had consistently been the case during the restoration effort, the Menominee people turned out in great numbers. Three busloads of tribal members arrived from Wisconsin, and many others traveled to Washington by other means.

Ironically, only a few weeks before the Menominee Restoration Act was reported out of the full Committee on Interior and Insular Affairs with unanimous bipartison support, Senator Arthur Watkins was buried in Utah. The policy of termination was to follow its architect and strongest advocate to the grave only four months later.

The Menominee Restoration Act passed the House of Representatives' roll-call vote on October 16, 1973 by an overwhelming vote of 404 to 3. It was passed to the Senate, where proceedings began to slow down. The first day of Senate Subcommittee hearings was on

September 17, 1973, with a large group of Menominee Indians there. Impressive testimony was given but the Senatorial process was still slow.

The Indians displayed their acumen in the political system by applying‑ pressure on the proper members of Congress, and on December 7, the Interior Committee gave unanimous support and the full Senate approved the bill. President Nixon signed the Menominee Restoration Act into law on Saturday, December 22, 1973.[113]

It is difficult to overestimate the significance of the Menominee Restoration Act. For the Menominee, it was the only realistic method of preserving their tribal existence, and for this reason, it became a symbol for all Indians. Restoration was not the first reversal of Indian policy, but it was probably the most important one. It provided the evidence needed to show that the American political system—imperfect as it has been and will continue to be—can be used as a tool to preserve Indian culture.

Further, after hearing evidence from the Menominee, any jury would conclude that however confining, disproportionate, and paternalistic the original treaties between Indian tribes and the United States are—those treaties have yet to be improved upon. They must be guarded and defended just as carefully as the doctrine of separation of powers, for something as important—or perhaps more important—than constitutional government is at stake: the survival of a race of people.

The passage of the Restoration Act did not solve the problems for the Menominees. Instead, in some ways, it was comparable to opening Pandora's box. Roles had to be updated, a constitution had to be written, a council had to be elected, land had to be restored, and a myriad of other mechanical operations had to be worked out. Restoration made these things possible, but much time and hard work were necessary to bring them into reality. It was, however, another step in allowing the wants and desires of the Indian people to have some meaning in shaping their destiny.

Another legislative action passed during the Nixon administration was the Indian Education Act, or Title IV of Public Law 92-318, or the 1972 Amendments to the Higher Education Act of 1965. This bill, S-659, was introduced in February 1971 by Senators Kennedy and Mondale in direct response to recommendations of the Kennedy Report. It took sixteen months of hearings, debates, revisions, and reports before, on June 13, 1972, President Nixon signed the bill into law. The following is a brief review of the act:

Part A: *Revision of Impacted Areas Program As It Relates to Indian Children.*
This section of the act amends P.L. 874 (Impact Aid Law) by providing more monies for programs designed to "meet the special needs of Indian children." Grants may be used for planning, operation and evaluation of innovative programs, as well as for equipment and minor remodeling of classrooms.
Authorized Appropriation $168 million
Approved Appropriation $ 11.5 million

Part B: *Special Programs and Projects to Improve Educational Opportunities for Indian Children.*
This portion of the act provides general education enrichment programs for Indian children including: library and instructional materials; research and planning for innovative programs; comprehensive guidance counseling; special education programs; preschool programs; and for dissemination of information relating to elementary and secondary education for Indians.
Authorized Appropriation $25 million
Approved Appropriation $ 5 million

Part C: *Special Programs Relating to Adult Education for Indians.*
This section provides additional monies for American Indians and Alaskan Natives for adult educational programs such as: planning and operating pilot projects designed to test and demonstrate the effectiveness of programs for improving employment and educational opportunities for adult Indians; assistance in the establishment and operation of programs designed to stimulate basic literacy of all Indian adults; research and curriculum design projects and for surveys and dissemination of information regarding adult education for Indians.
Authorized Appropriation $5 million
Approved Appropriation $ .5 million

Part D: *Office of Indian Education.*
In order to promote coordination and monitoring of the Indian programs in conjunction with all other Office of Education programs, a bureau of Indian Education headed by a Deputy Commissioner of Indian Education has been established in the Office of Education.

This office is assisted by a National Advisory Council for Indian Education, consisting of 15 members, all of whom are Native Americans, who are appointed by the President. They meet quarterly and are responsible for selection of the Deputy Commissioner for Indian Education; reviewing applications for assistance under any program sponsored by this act and advising the Commissioner of Education.

No specific authorizations for funding the Bureau of Indian Education and the Advisory Council were made in the original act. However, for the purpose of staffing the Bureau and providing operational funds for the Advisory Council, Congress appropriated $1 million.

Passing a bill through Congress is one action, but obtaining money to implement the legislation is another. Indian people found that this was a fact to be reckoned with, as the Indian Education Act went through the legislative procedures.

Since Nixon was involved in a re-election campaign, he was interested in cutting spending, not increasing it. Therefore, he did not request any funding for the Indian Education Act in his budget. In spite of this omission, the Senate appropriated $36 million—far short of the $200 million budget outlined in the bill. The House responded by not allocating any money for the legislation. The final decision for funding was made by a Conference Committee made up of members of both the House and the Senate Appropriations Committees. The agreement was to fund Title IV, P.L. 92–318 for $18 million. This represented less than ten percent of the original budget for the bill. However, since the appropriation was not passed until October 1972, and the year was nearly over, the $18 million was considered by the Indians involved as enough to start the program.

The amount of the funding proved immaterial, however, for in 1972, the Nixon administration came under heavy criticism for its generous spending policies and the President responded by an extreme reduction. Only critical expenditures were allocated and many projects had their appropriations "frozen." The Indian Education Act was caught in this impoundment squeeze and implementation was delayed.[114] It was not until 1974 that the programs were finally gotten underway. Since then, the Act has been amended several times and appropriations have been increased. Most of the bill's provisions have been affected, and Title IV (even though it has not totally alleviated the problems it was designed to relieve) has provided a major improvement in educational opportunities for Indians. Amendments to the Act have been made periodically by Congress to improve and update its provisions.

Even though many events which occurred during Richard Nixon's tenure as President were of a positive nature and were harmonious with the Indian people, there were also some which were strongly negative. The 1970s, besides being years of progressive social reform, were also years of social revolution which sometimes became violent. Activist organizations and militant actions were apparent in many movements, and even the normally passive Indians began to utilize the "strong-arm" strategy in dealing with the federal government. One such incident occurred in Washington, D.C., when the "Trail of Broken Treaties" caravan arrived.

The Trail of Broken Treaties was an activity designed by Indian members of several organizations as a peaceful demonstration in the nation's capitol. The purpose was to "make the general public aware of the situation of Native Americans and extract firm pledges from the Republican and Democratic parties that U.S. Indian treaties will be enforced to the letter."

On October 6, 1972, three automobile caravans departed from Seattle, San Francisco, and Los Angeles for Washington, D.C. Following different routes, the three caravans stopped at locales which had been significant in Indian history. Sites such as Sand Creek, Colorado; Wounded Knee, South Dakota; and parts of the infamous Trail of Tears were included in the itinerary. The three components were to meet in Washington on October 31 to join thousands of other American Indians. For one week, October 31 to November 7, plans had been made, permits obtained, and Washington officials briefed for a peaceful demonstration.

Activities included religious memorial services for Indian war dead, conducted at Arlington National Cemetary by Indian spiritual leaders; religious ceremonies at the Congressional Cemetery where the great Choctaw Pushmataha is buried; and religious services at the Tomb of the Unknown Soldier (since he could have been an Indian), the Iwo Jima Memorial, and other national shrines. Indian leaders, both spiritual and political, were scheduled to speak at various locations, and President Nixon was invited to address the Indian contingent. Although there were some legal problems in coordinating such a large group (over 10,000 Indians were expected), things progressed fairly smoothly and harmoniously until the caravans began to arrive.

As the Indians arrived in the capital, with expectations of a peaceful week of conferences and meetings, they were met with obstacles and problems. First, permission to hold services at Arlington was rescinded. The Indian response, indicating their intent to work within the system, was to file suit in Federal Court for permission to hold the ceremonies.[115]

Another frustrating incident occurred when the landlord of the building where the AIM offices were located and the "Trail" had set up headquarters, filed an ejectment notice. He claimed foot traffic and noise made this action necessary. (This legal action was resolved in favor of the Indians.)

The third incident, and probably the one which triggered the violence, was the failure of Washington officials to provide the housing that had been agreed to in the negotiations prior to the caravans' arrival. Indians were forced to sleep on floors, in parks, and any place they could when the expected facilities were not available.

On November 2, the Indians, angry and frustrated, occupied the Bureau of Indian Affairs' building and barricaded the entrances. All Bureau employees and others in the building were allowed to leave and the Indians prepared for a long siege.

By 6:30 AM on November 3, following an unsuccessful attempt by GSA security guards to forcibly retake the building, the Justice Department decided to turn the burden of dealing with the Indians over to the judiciary. Legal action was filed to obtain a court order to remove the Indians from the Bureau of Indian Affairs' building. Since the presidential election was only a few days off, the motive of the Justice Department officials in filing a legal action was apparently much more political than humane. Their decision was designed to minimize the impact of any possible bloodshed or violent action on President Nixon's re-election chances. The various police agencies under the Justice Department's jurisdiction needed no legal authority to retake a federal building they believed to be unlawfully occupied. Thus, the lawsuit was apparently a vehicle to shift responsibility for removal of the Indians to the courts and away from Federal officials.

By the afternoon of November 3, things had settled down to a great extent and negotiations had begun between the Indians and government officials. Commissioner of Indian Affairs Louis R.

Bruce, himself part Mohawk-Sioux, entered the building to mediate the situation. For some reason, he spent the night with the caravan members and, since he was already at odds with the Department of Interior for trying to Indianize the Bureau, he incurred the wrath of the Secretary, Rogers C.B. Morton. He was severely censured by Morton and ordered to remain totally silent on the matter and to make himself unavailable to the media. Bruce and his staff were fired from their positions a few days later.

Negotiations continued and court decisions were rendered. Finally, on November 8, the building was evacuated and the caravan members pulled out. The government had acquired $66,650 from the Office of Economic Opportunity and turned it over to the Indians to finance their return home. By 8:00 PM, they had gone and had taken with them some of the Bureau files. In their wake, they left a badly damaged and ransacked Bureau of Indian Affairs.

Webster Two Hawk, President of the National Tribal Chairman's Association, after reviewing the building, demanded the arrest and full prosecution of the leaders. He also insisted on the firing of all Interior and Indian Affairs officials who had failed to act swiftly enough to prevent the damages. Charles Trimble, Executive Director of the National Congress of American Indians, deplored the destruction of irreplaceable records but proposed that NCAI assist in the reconstruction of Indian Affairs.[116] Thus, the conservative elements of the Indian community condemned the action of the Trail of Broken Treaties. Even one of the co-chairmen of the Caravan, Robert Burnette, denounced the leadership, claiming they were totally irresponsible and guilty of irreparable harm to the Indian people.

The more activist-oriented Indians, however, praised the incident and felt it had been a blow for Indian independence. The philosophy of these Indians was expressed quite succinctly by a sign left by the Caravan over the entrance to the Bureau of Indian Affairs auditorium on November 8, 1972 when they evacuated the building.

Gentlemen: We do not apologize for the ruin nor for the so-called destruction of this mausoleum. For in building anew, one must first destroy the old. This is the beginning of a new era for the Native American people. When history recalls our efforts here, our descendants will stand with pride knowing their people were the ones responsible for the stand taken against tyranny, injustice, and gross inefficiency of

this branch of a corrupt and decadent government.
Native American Embassy.[117]

Prior to the actual Trail of Broken Treaties, October 22 to 29, in fact, a position paper stating twenty demands of the federal government was formulated. During the confrontation in Washington, the twenty-point proposal was submitted to the governmental officials. The Nixon administration responded with a promise to review and evaluate the proposal and to reply to the group. The following is a condensation of the demands of this paper:

1) Restoration of constitutional treaty-making authority.
2) Establishment of a treaty commission to make new treaties.
3) Address to the American people and joint session of Congress (by four Indian-selected spokesmen).
4) Commission to review treaty commitments and violations.
5) Resubmission of unratified treaties to the Senate.
6) All Indians to be governed by treaty relations.
7) Mandatory relief against treaty rights violations.
8) Judicial recognition of Indian right to interpret treaties.
9) Creation of a joint congressional committee on reconstructing Indian relations.
10) Land reform and restoration of a 110-million acre native land base.
11) Revision of 25 U.S.C. 163: restoration of rights to Indians terminated by enrollment and revocation of prohibition against "Dual Benefits." (If Indians are of mixed tribal lineage, blood quantum from all tribes should be used in determining eligibility for federal benefits.)
12) Repeal of state laws enacted under Public Law 280.
13) Resume Federal protective jurisdiction for offenses against Indians.
14) Abolition of the Bureau of Indian Affairs by 1976: a new structure.
15) Creation of an "Office of Federal Indian Relations and Community Reconstruction."
16) Priorities and purpose of the proposed new office.
17) Indian commerce and tax immunities.

18) Protection of Indians' religious freedom and cultural integrity.
19) National referendums, local options, and forms of Indian organization.
20) Health, housing, employment, economic development, and education.[118]

On January 8, 1973, Leonard Garment, Special Consultant to the President, and Frank Carlucci, Deputy Director of the Office of Management and Budget, responded to the twenty-point proposal. In a letter to Hank Adams, Assiniboine-Sioux, who acted as the go-between, they explained that a number of the proposed changes had already been made and that others could not be made because of conditions within the structure of the United States government. An example of this political restriction was given in answer to the first two proposals. The United States could not enter into treaty negotiations with Indian tribes since all Indians were now citizens of the country. Treaties may only be negotiated between sovereign nations and not between the United States government and particular segments of its citizenry.

Mr. Garment and Mr. Carlucci also pointed out that some of the demands would necessitate legislative action and were therefore out of the jurisdiction of the executive branch of government. There were promises made to investigate and attempt to act on some of the points. One promise which was kept was the restoration of the Menominees to federal recognition. Although they answered all twenty proposals with apparent sincerity and with an open approach, it was evident that Garment and Carlucci were representing the administration's attitude of making changes without total acquiescence to Indian demands.

An analysis of the situation one year later revealed that the government had carried out some promises; Indians had returned the confiscated records and artifacts; and some progress had been made toward settlement of some issues. Hank Adams stated conditions clearly when he said, "In the context of attitudes, Indian people are better off. But in actually securing objectives, little has happened, although there is a stronger potential than before."[119]

Although the Washington episode was settled rather peacefully and the participants in the occupation of the Bureau headquarters were allowed to go their way without prosecution, things were not tranquil in Indian country. The Pine Ridge Reservation, home of many of the leaders of the activist Indian movement, was seething with unrest. Dick Wilson, Chairman of the Oglala Sioux Tribal Council, declared "open season" on the American Indian Movement. He especially singled out Russell Means, an Oglala and one of the AIM leaders. Wilson declared the reservation "off limits" to AIM and stated, "If Russell Means sets foot on this reservation, I will personally cut his braids off."

A caravan of AIM members were stopped as they attempted to enter the Pine Ridge Reservation and turned back. Wilson deputized and armed all tribal employees and the Bureau of Indian Affairs closed their operation as Pine Ridge took on the appearance of a combat zone. Means attempted to speak at a meeting in Oglala and was stopped by an order from the "Oglala Sioux Tribal Court." Dennis Banks, another AIM leader, was arrested when he came to the reservation and escorted away. Other AIM members on the Pine Ridge Reservation were harassed by Wilson's men and the situation became extremely volatile.

The affair came to a head in late February 1973, when about 250 members of AIM took over the historic hamlet of Wounded Knee, South Dakota. There was a deep significance in choosing this site for the place of action, for it was on the banks of Wounded Knee Creek, on December 29, 1890, that the last Indian resistance to the United States government had been crushed (see Chapter 10).

After surrounding Wounded Knee, the AIM "war party" took eleven hostages and sent their demands to Washington:

1) That Senate hearings be held to look into the matter of Indian treaties which had not been observed.

2) That Congress hold hearings on the conduct of the Bureau of Indian Affairs.

3) That the Senate investigate federal treatment of Indians in its conduct.

4) That there be an inquiry into conditions on the Sioux Reservations in North and South Dakota.

Gunfire was exchanged and positions continued to harden on both sides. The government brought in armored vehicles. U.S. Marshalls, and F.B.I. agents. The Indians were supplemented by scores of sympathizers, Indian and non-Indian alike, and the area soon assumed the appearance of a Viet Nam battlefield. Newsmen, radio and television reporters, and myriads of cameramen scurried about like so many ants. Wounded Knee became the scene for a tragic comedy. As Vine Deloria, in an editorial in the *Los Angeles Times,* wrote:

The specter of the original Wounded Knee massacre of 350 Sioux Indians by U.S. soldiers has hovered over the proceedings of the past month, filling the air with a terrible dread.

Perhaps the only relief has been the bizarre parade of characters: Ralph Abernathy, the National Council of Churches, Angela Davis, and assorted hippies and well wishers who have made a valiant effort to turn the confrontation into the last rock festival and clan gathering of the New Left.[120]

Actor Marlon Brando, though of questionable Indian ancestry, refused an Oscar award and set out for Wounded Knee. Somewhere along the road he took the wrong turn and ended up in Tahiti, but he gained a lot of publicity for his efforts.[121] The basic issues of the take-over got rather obscured by the festival atmosphere promoted by some of the media.

Deloria explained the muddled mess in Indian activist incidents in the same *Los Angeles Times* editorial:

. . . . Friendly whites come in the back door, get the ears of those in power, and shut you out. . . . As you try to explain how complicated things are, a late night talk show provides an hour and a half of misinformation. . . . Wounded Knee 1973 shows one thing very clearly: American Indians are prohibited from having a modern identity.[122]

At Wounded Knee, as in many of the so-called "Indian uprisings" in modern times, many of the participants were not Indian at all. They came from various ethnic backgrounds, some seeking to assist in a "cause," and others caring only to be involved in some bizarre militant action, regardless of the cause. Many were looking for an identity and chose the "Indian" to fulfill their need.

What happened at Wounded Knee will probably never be known in its entirety. The confrontation with sporadic gunfire and negotiations lasted until May 8—about seventy days—when negotiations brought an end to the occupation. The media scourged itself for the way news was dispensed. *Harper's* published an expose of the affair in which it called the Wounded Knee plight "largely a pseudo-event to which the world press responded with all the cautiousness of sharks scenting blood." The writer continued: "We wrote good cowboy-and-Indian stories because we thought it was what the public wanted, and they were harmless, even if they were not all true."

Needless to say, Wounded Knee did not do much to improve Indian Affairs. The trials of the leaders following the cessation of hostilities were also something of a farce and, on September 16, 1974, Federal Judge Nichol dismissed the felony charges against Dennis Banks and Russell Means. He used as his reason for dismissal that he felt there had been "governmental misconduct."[123]

Was the so-called Second Battle of Wounded Knee a cynical, irresponsible piece of mischief by adventurous interlopers who pulled off a media coup for their own selfish motives? (These were, for the most part, the same militants who had been involved with the Trail of Broken Treaties and received over $66,000 for their efforts.) Had they exploited Indians and their culture to pander to television's needs: war paint, drums, braids, medicine men, buffalo skins, tepees, religious rituals? Or was this bedraggled band just what they claimed to be: a voice in the wilderness crying out for help against two hundred years of inequities, against indignities and humiliations, against land-grabs and broken treaties, against corrupt tribal governments, against poverty and disease, unemployment and illiteracy? Were the AIM occupiers spokesmen for the thousands of Indians too debilitated and too illiterate to speak for themselves? These and other questions cannot be correctly answered, for the matter is too complicated, the issues too obscure, and the information too confused. The search for truth goes on.

Totem Pole, Northwest Tribes.

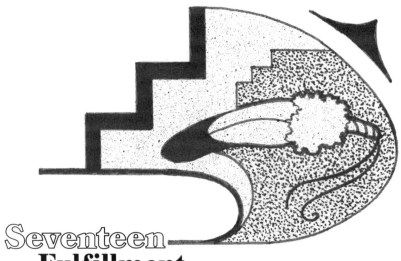

Seventeen
Fulfillment

The first few years of the 1970s saw many positive changes in the lives of American Indians with their self-determination efforts. There were some rough spots, also—the Trail of Broken Treaties and Wounded Knee, incidents which were well publicized and took the general form of Indian-white confrontations. There were, however, some covert activities taking place during this time which directly and indirectly would affect Indians in greater magnitude than either of the militant affairs.

On June 17, 1972, the break-in of the headquarters of the Democratic National Committee took place in the Watergate Hotel in Washington, D.C. The investigation of the episode uncovered misuse of power by high government officials and other acts considered by many to be serious threats to constitutional liberties. Public officials or their agents were found to be guilty of such violations of the law as burglary, perjury, conspiracy to obstruct justice, use of government agencies to harass citizens, destruction of evidence, bribery, blackmail, and many other crimes. While the incident itself did not relate to Indian people, the spin-off had a definite effect on programs dealing with them.

In an impromptu news conference on January 31, 1973, President

Nixon declared that he had the constitutional authority to impound funds appropriated by Congress if he felt it was in the nation's interest. "I will not spend money if the Congress overspends, and I will not be for programs that will raise the taxes and put a higher burden on the already overburdened American taxpayer," he said. A few days later, the White House issued a report freezing funds for many programs. One of those drastically affected was the Indian Education Act. Nixon had signed the bill, but it was impossible to implement it without money.

These impoundments by the President only widened the rift between his office and Congress and spurred the Congressional investigation of the Watergate burglary. As more and more evidence of bureaucratic discrepancies were brought to light in Washington, a "Watergate paranoia" developed. Politicians and bureaucrats became fearful of investigation and would not venture into any innovative activity and only carried on the day-to-day routine work. They hardly spoke to each other and, most certainly, would not release information to outsiders. Consequently, a news black-out descended over the many Indian programs which had been developed. The situation became so critical that the National Congress of American Indians and the Americans for Indian Opportunity, at the request of Allen Rowland, President of the Northern Cheyenne Tribe, called an emergency meeting to develop strategies to alleviate this and other problems which had developed.

On April 22 and 23, 1974, the meeting convened in the National Education Association Auditorium. Indian leaders from all over America were invited and about 200 gathered to address the problems.[124] White House representatives, as well as individuals representing many branches of the federal government, met with the Indians. These sessions were not examples of the usual bureaucratic dialogue but, instead, they were logical exchanges of ideas which resulted in a resumption of activity in Indian programs.

This meeting, however, did not resolve the Watergate problem for the administration, and the investigation continued. Eventually, a number of the Nixon administration were sentenced to prison terms and Mr. Nixon himself was forced to resign as President of the United States to avoid almost certain impeachment. Regardless of the impoundments and his political misfortunes, Richard Nixon was one of the best friends Indian people ever had in the presidency. Much of the improvement in Indian affairs initiated during his tenure in office has continued and brought about much positive change.

On August 21, 1974, just a few days after President Nixon resigned, Public Law 93–380, Education Amendments of 1974, was signed into law. This act greatly benefited Indians, for it extended through the fiscal year 1978 the Elementary and Secondary Education Act, the Impact Aid laws, and the Indian Education Act, all of which directly apply to educational opportunities for Indian children.

The Bureau of Indian Affairs also responded to the Indian conference by making significant changes in the guidelines of the Johnson-O'Malley Act funding policies. On August 16, 1974, Acting Deputy Commissioner Raymond Butler signed into effect the improved regulations to the forty-year-old law. It provided for expanded parental control at the local level, funding innovations, inclusion of early childhood education, and Indian preference in hiring.

Legislative action, which had the potential of making significant contributions to the improvement of conditions in the Indians' world, took place on January 2, 1975. Public Law 93–580, which provided for the establishment of the American Indian Policy Review Commission (AIPRC), was passed on this date. A Congressional report that led to the creation of the AIPRC said:

The Congress, after reviewing the Federal Government's historical and special legal relationship with American Indian people, finds that—

(a) The policy has shifted and changed over the years without rational design and without a consistent goal to achieve Indian self-sufficiency;

(b) There has been no general comprehensive review of the conduct of Indian Affairs since the 1928 Meriam Report; and

(c) To fulfill its Indian affairs responsibilities, Congress feels that a review should be conducted.

Congress, in its Declaration of Purpose, stated:

. . . It is essential to conduct a comprehensive review of the historical and legal developments underlying the Federal-Indian relationship in order to determine the nature and scope of necessary revisions in the formulation of policies and programs for the benefits of Indians.

The AIPRC was then created with an eleven-member composition. Congress outlined its membership as follows:

(1) *Senate Members*
Section 1(b)(1) provides that three members of the Senate shall be appointed by the President pro tempore of the Senate. There shall be two members appointed from the Democratic Party and one member appointed from the Republican Party.

(2) *House Members*
Section 1(b)(2) provides that three members of the House of Representatives shall be appointed by the Speaker of the House of Representatives. There shall be two members appointed from the Democratic Party and one member appointed from the Republican Party.

(3) *Indian Members*
Section 1(b)(3) provides that five Indian members shall be selected as provided in subsection (c) of section one.[125]

Indian members were chosen by majority vote of the Senators and Congressmen which resulted in the following selections:

From Federally-Recognized Tribes
Ada Deer, Menominee, Wisconsin
Jake Whitecrow, Quapaw-Seneca, Oklahoma
John Borbridge, Tlinget, Alaska
From Non-Federally Recognized Tribes
Adolph Dial, Lumbee, North Carolina
From Urban Indians
Louis Bruce, Mohawk-Sioux, New York

These five Indians, along with Representatives Meeds (Washington), Steiger (Arizona), and Yates (Illinois), and Senators Abourezk (South Dakota), Hatfield (Oregon), and Metcalf (Montana), made up the Commission. In order to proceed efficiently in its investigation of the designated areas, the Commission structured its work around eleven task forces created to thoroughly research and report on specific subject areas. In the development of their reports, the Task Forces utilized research, reports, studies, questionnaires, hearings, and site visits to approach the subjects in a comprehensive manner. A crucial element of the reporting process was direct consultation with all segments of the Indian community.[126]

The Task Forces and their subject areas were as follows:

Task Force # 1   Trust Responsibility and Federal Indian Relationship.

Task Force # 2   Tribal Government.

Task Force # 3   Federal Administration: Structure of Indian Affairs.

Task Force # 4   Federal, State, and Tribal Jurisdiction.

Task Force # 5   Indian Education.

Task Force # 6   Indian Health.

Task Force # 7   Reservation and Resource Development and Protection.

Task Force # 8   Urban and Rural Non-Reservation Indians.

Task Force # 9   Indian Law Revision, Consolidation, and Codification.

Task Force # 10 Terminated and Non-Federally Recognized Indians.

Task Force # 11 Alcohol and Drug Abuse.

The composition and functions of the Commission and its Task Forces were viewed rather cynically by some Indians. This mistrust was voiced by Congressman Meeds, Vice-Chairman of the Commission, when he made these remarks:

> We have had some apprehension manifested by certain people in the Indian community that a request for this Commission is just another study of Indians, and that if it functions, it will make a lengthy report, which will gather dust on the shelf, as so many in the past have. . . .[127]

It was ironic that Representative Meeds spoke of Indian apprehension, for after two years of diligent effort, hundreds of thousands of miles of travel, thousands of dollars, and untold hours of work to produce fifteen volumes of reports, Meeds cast the only dissenting voice on the Commission. He asked for and received $25,000 to prepare a minority statement concerning the Commission. One of his complaints was that the Report of the American Indian Policy Review Commission "is the product of a one-sided advocacy in favor of American Indian tribes."

Meeds went on to say:

The blunt fact of the matter is that American Indian tribes are not a third set of governments in the American federal system. They are not sovereigns. The Congress of the United States has permitted them to be self-governing entities . . . The doctrine of inherent tribal sovereignty, adopted by the Majority Report, ignores the historic reality that American Indian tribes lost their sovereignty through discovery, conquest, cession, treaties, statutes, and history.[128]

It is evident from statements in his Minority Report that Representative Meeds dismisses the moral and legal recognition of Indian tribes as a mere benevolent, paternal gesture of the federal government. He clearly indicates this in his statement:

To the extent tribal Indians exercise powers of self-government in these United States, they do so because Congress permits it. Tribes exercise powers of self-government as federal licensees, *because* and *as long* as Congress thinks it wise. More than a tribe's *external* attributes of sovereignty have been extinguished. . . . American Indian tribal governments have only those powers granted them by Congress. . . . There is no adequate theoretical basis for the assertion of inherent tribal sovereignty. . . . War, conquest, treaties, statutes, cases, and history have extinguished the tribe as a general governmental entity. All that remains is a policy. And, that policy is that American Indian tribes may govern their own internal relations by the grace of Congress.[129]

It is a good thing for Indians that Congressman Meeds does not project the sentiments of all Americans. If he did, "Indian" would be only a romantic memory or an historic reference. Mr. Meeds deserves a place in the "Indian Hall of Fame" alongside Andrew Jackson, Cotton Mather, Cortez, DeSoto, and Senator Arthur Watkins.

Besides the emphasis on tribal sovereignty, the AIPRC's report indicated that many changes were needed in the federal government's handling of the affairs of the American Indians. One of the most dramatic of these recommendations was the proposal to abolish the Bureau of Indian Affairs. The Task Force on Trust Responsibility, Federal-Indian Relations, and Treaty Review suggested replacing the Bureau with a Department of Indian Affairs, operating as an independent agency with a secretary having a cabinet-level position. The new agency would be administratively controlled by an "Indian

Board of Control" consisting of "persons appointed by the President from nomination lists submitted by Indian people in a prescribed and representative manner."

The other Task Forces also presented the government with concise views on conditions of their special areas of investigation. Their reports not only isolated the many problems in the Indian community but presented recommendations for their alleviation. As the "Kennedy Report" of 1969 brought sweeping changes in Indian education, perhaps the Policy Review Commission's report will produce an improved over-all lifestyle for America's native people.

One of the most progressive and beneficial legislative activities of recent years was enacted on January 4, 1975, when Public Law 93–638 became effective. This law was proposed when Congress, after careful review of the government's historic and special legal relationship with the American Indian, found that:

(1) the prolonged Federal domination of Indian service programs has served to retard rather than enhance the progress of Indian people and their communities. . . .;
(2) the Indian people will never surrender their desire to control their relationships both among themselves and with non-Indian governments, organizations, and persons;
(3) true self-determination in any society of people is dependant upon an educational process which will insure the development of qualified people to fulfill meaningful leadership roles;
(4) the Federal responsibility for and assistance to education of Indian children has not affected the desired level of educational achievement or created the diverse opportunities and personal satisfaction which education can and should provide; and
(5) parental and community control of the educational process is of crucial importance to the Indian people.

Recognizing the failure of the current structure of management to provide these necessary components, Congress designed and implemented Public Law 93–638, the "Indian Self-Determination and Education Assistance Act." This law was designed to:

Provide maximum Indian participation in the Government and education of the Indian people; to provide for the full participation of Indian tribes in programs and services conducted by the Federal Government for Indians and to encourage the development of human resources of the Indian people; to establish a program of assistance to upgrade Indian education; to support the right of Indian citizens to control their own educational activities; and for other purposes.[130]

This Congressional Act has brought about much needed improvements in numerous areas of Indian life.

The 1970s have brought a proliferation of legislation in American Indian affairs. Most of the activity has been of a positive nature in an attempt to fulfill unmet needs of the Indian people. Many actions were brought about because of treaty obligations and responsibilities recognized after reports such as the "Kennedy Report" and the conclusions of the AIPRC. One of the most important changes was the creation of the position of Assistant Secretary of the Interior for Indian Affairs.

Until recently, the Bureau of Indian Affairs was on a lower administrative level than the six major land and natural resources offices in the Department of Interior (which were headed by Assistant Secretaries). This structure relegated the Commissioner of Indian Affairs to report to the Secretary of Interior through one of the Assistant Secretaries, causing Indian matters to compete with land and natural resources on a day-to-day basis within the Department and for the attention of the Secretary. The result of this positioning of Indian matters within the Department of Interior had two detrimental effects.

First, it aggravated the inherent conflicts of interest which exist in the federal administration of Indian affairs. As trustee of Indian property, the United States is charged with a high fiduciary duty to protect and preserve Indian trust assets. Yet the Department of Interior is also called upon to administer the nation's resources— water, power, land, timber, oil, and minerals—for the "greatest common good." When these non-Indian national interests come into conflict with Indian trust interests, all too often the Indian interest is sacrificed or compromised in favor of the non-Indian interest.

Secondly, despite the fact that the Bureau of Indian Affairs is a unique office within the Interior Department because it deals with the direct human concerns of the Indian people, the visibility and importance of Indian matters within the Department remained at a lower level than land, water, natural resources, and power concerns.

In 1976, the Department changed the administrative structure, allowing the Commissioner of Indian Affairs to report directly to the Secretary. Congress then raised the Commissioner's status in title by creating the new Assistant Secretary position, thus demonstrating Congressional support for the departmental change.

Other bills were introduced in 1976, 1977, and 1978 which attested to the legislative agreement with the self-determination policy. Bills to improve life conditions such as health, education, child welfare, land claims, and federal recognition of tribal units have been introduced in Congress. Settlement of pending land claims was encouraged by extending the life of the Indian Claims Commission to September 30, 1978.

During the 1970s, numerous Indian-operated business organizations and professional associations have been established throughout the Indian community. Indians have formed their own Chamber of Commerce to enhance economic and business development. The Association of American Indian Physicians provides a unified and organized advocacy for improvement in health of the native peoples. Many organizations have been formed in recent years by Indians to assist in developing more validity in their children's educational programs.[131] There is now an American Indian National Bank doing business in the nation's capital. Founded in 1973, it is the keystone of a projected Indian-owned financial structure designed to assist Indian communities in establishing and developing a strong economic base.

Indians are becoming more independent in pursuing higher education. For most of the history of Indian-white relations, American Indians have been excluded from educational opportunities which would allow them to be functional in the dominant society. Higher education was a goal which was out of the reach of most Indian students. Indian college graduates were a rare commodity in America, and Indians with advanced degrees were almost nonexistent. The trend has changed in recent years and American Indian youths are going to college, remaining in school, graduating, and going into graduate studies in record numbers.

By 1974, there were seventy-two Indians attending medical school in the United States—more than the total number of Indian physicians at the time. Plans have been formulated and preparations made to establish the American Indian Medical School at Flagstaff,

Arizona. Sage Memorial Hospital on the Navajo Reservation is an Indian-operated institution. Indian medical technicians and nurses now staff many positions in the Indian Health Service and in non-government institutions, especially in Oklahoma and the Southwest.

Special Indian law programs have been established in a number of our leading universities and colleges, and Indian legal organizations handle litigation for tribes and individuals. Indian law students are graduating and entering practice all over America, and in recent years, Indian lawyers have been appointed to judicial positions.

Indian tribes with large oil reserves under their reservations are combining forces to negotiate better terms. Leasing of tribal land to coal and mineral companies has resulted in more equitable terms. Tribes have become more astute at the bargaining table and are not allowing the exploitation to continue as it has in the past. Indians are more autonomous and more in control of their destinies than at any time since the European invasion began.

Although Indian affairs seem to be at a new high and the future seems for once to be assuming a positive aspect, all is not well in America. There are still sinister forces at work and the Indian people cannot afford to be lulled into a false sense of security and become too passive in their efforts. Lloyd Meeds is still in a position of power, as are others of his kind. Judicial rulings and legislative proposals which, if allowed to be implemented, would be disastrous for Indians, are still being made.

The State of Mississippi, as recently as mid-1978, was attempting to deny the Choctaws on the reservation at Philadelphia the right to be Indian. The ruling of the State Supreme Court stated that Choctaws gave up their rights to be Indian in 1830 in the treaty of Dancing Rabbit Creek. This ruling was based on Article XIV of the treaty, which states:

> Each Choctaw head of a family being desirous to remain (in Mississippi) and become a citizen of the States, shall be permitted to do so, by signifying his intention to the Agent within six months from the ratification of this Treaty, and he or she shall thereupon be entitled to a reservation of one section of six-hundred and forty acres of land, to be bounded by sectional lines of survey. . . . If they reside upon said lands intending to become citizens of the States for five years after the ratification of this Treaty, in that case a grant in fee simple shall issue. . . . Persons who claim under this article *shall not* lose the privilege of a Choctaw citizen. . . . (Emphasis added by author.)

In spite of the clear wording that the Choctaws who remained in Mississippi would retain their Choctaw rights, and in spite of the fact that very few ever received the benefits prescribed by the treaty, the Court ruled as it did. The judge totally ignored the fact that the provisions of the treaty had not been kept by the United States government. He conveniently passed over the promises of the government that "no part of the land granted them [the Choctaws] shall ever be embraced in any Territory or State." The fact that only a handful of Choctaws ever signed the roll which signified their intentions to become citizens of Mississippi was overlooked by the judge. He apparently rendered his decision based on statements out of context, interpreted most unjudiciously, with only a one-sided approach to the question. This travesty of justice was brought about primarily to enable the State of Mississippi to collect a few dollars in state tax from Chahta Enterprises, a small tribal business operated by the Mississippi Band of Choctaw Indians. On appeal to the Supreme Court of the United States, the Choctaws won a unanimous decision, firmly establishing that the Mississippi Band of Choctaws was and had been Indian, and that the State of Mississippi had no jurisdiction to impose taxes on the tribe. This is merely an example of similar legal problems faced by other tribes around the country.

Indian struggles with the government go on, not just through the executive and judicial branches but also the legislative. Occasionally, in the midst of progressive legislation, there appears a bill which attempts to re-establish the repulsive termination process and override the self-determination policy of recent administrations. One of the most perfidious of such proposals is H.R. 9054, which at this writing has not been voted on by the House of Representatives and is still in committee. This bill, submitted by Representative Cunningham of the State of Washington, directs the President to:

. . . . abrogate all treaties entered into by the United States with Indian tribes in order to accomplish the purpose of recognizing that in the United States no individual or group possesses subordinate or special rights, providing full citizenship and equality under law to Native Americans, protecting an equal opportunity of all citizens to fish and hunt in the United States, and terminating Federal supervision over the property and members of Indian tribes, and for other purposes.

This bill not only would seriously erode the rights of Indian tribes' self-sufficient, self-governing bodies, but in reality would commit paper genocide of a complete race of people. The proposal is said to represent the growing "backlash" toward the American Indians and their treatment as special citizens of America. Actually, the bill is the fulfillment of campaign promises to about 2,000 white commercial fishermen who want complete control over the fishing industry in the State of Washington.

In 1974, Federal Judge George H. Boldt ruled that the Indians in Washington were entitled by the Treaty of 1854 to half of the annual fish harvest. This ended a monopoly in the fishing industry by white commercial fishermen and restored the fishing rights of Washington Indians, whose cultures and lifestyles revolve around fishing. As one of his campaign policies, Representative Cunningham decided to work for the repeal of the Boldt decision. He would sacrifice over one million Indians and terminate all commitments made by the federal government in over 400 treaties with the various Indian nations in order to "buy" the support of the small contingency of white fishermen. Mr. Cunningham may take his place in the "Indian Hall of Fame" with Mr. Meeds, his fellow State of Washington Congressman.

So, in spite of the apparent progress of the American Indian people, in spite of the cooperation of most of the Congressional representatives and their attempts to practice the moral philosophy provided by the founding principles of this country, some individuals in our society persist in using human lives in their games of political chess.

By the end of the nineteenth century, the American Indian people had been totally suppressed. The European invaders, the colonists, and the United States government had taken their toll, and the destruction of an entire race of people was nearly complete. Only the tenacity of these native Americans and their innate ability to survive perpetuated them. In the years since, they have recovered and are rapidly reaching their rightful place in the world. The Phoenix bird has shaken off the ashes of destruction and is rising to reach its former heights of glory.

Koi Hosh

Footnotes

1. *Handbook of Native American Studies and Chronology of Native American History* (Native American Studies, Tecumseh Center, University of California, Davis), p. 1.
2. The Book of Mormon is believed by the membership of their church to be divine translation by Joseph Smith of an historical account written by Mormon, the last of the Nephites. The translation was reported taken from the golden tablets obtained by Smith near Manchester, New York in 1827. These golden plates were delivered to Smith by Moroni, Mormon's son, who was then a "resurrected personage." The period covered by the account extends from 600 B.C. to A.D. 421.
3. Ruth Verril and Clyde Keeler, "Bulletin of Georgia Academy of Sciences," 1961-62.
4. Op cit., *Handbook,* p. 3.
5. D. G. Brinton, Library of Original American Literature, published in 1885. The Walum Olum, as translated by Brinton, shows the Lenape writing, the translation into Lenape using the Latin alphabet, and then into English.
6. A more detailed account of the Navajo creation can be found in Ruth Underhill's *Here Come The Navajo.*
7. John Lear, "Ancient Landings in America," *Saturday Review,* July 18, 1970.
8. Milton R. Hunter, *Great Civilizations and the Book of Mormon* (Salt Lake City: Bookcraft, Inc., 1970), p. 41.
9. William E. Coffer. *Spirits of the Sacred Mountains* (New York: Van Nostrand Reinhold Co., 1978).
10. Robert F. Spencer, Jesse D. Jennings, *et al, The Native Americans,* and John C. Mac Gregor, *Southwest Archeology.*
11. Grahame Clark's *World Prehistory* and Robert Silverberg's *The Mound Builders* are excellent references for study of these cultures.
12. Bernal Diaz, *The Discovery and Conquest of Mexico* (New York: Ferrar, Straus, and Cudahy, 1956).

221

13. Miguel Leon-Portilla, *The Broken Spears* (Boston: Beacon Press, 1962).
14. Op cit., Diaz.
15. Op cit., Portilla, pp. 40–41.
16. Ibid., pp. 74–76.
17. There was no need, nor is there now, for a Woman's Liberation Movement in the Indian Nations. Women have always held equal positions with the men. In many cases, women were the leaders of their groups. Today, many of the tribal units in the United States are led by women.
18. Since the author is Choctaw, he reserves the right to be slightly biased.
19. Many young Indian women had the dubious honor of being chosen by Estevanico as the recipient of his amorous activities. Although there is no evidence today, it is possible that some mixed-blood children were born in Zuni.
20. Some of the chili grown in the southwest, especially that grown in the Rio Grande River valley, is so strong it will even burn the hands as it is prepared. This proves quite painful for novice chefs on occasion. The chili from this region possesses a flavor not found in chili from anywhere else in the world.
21. Grove Day, *Coronado's Quest* (Berkeley: University of California Press, 1964), p. 64.
22. Angie Debo, *A History of the Indians of the United States* (Norman: University of Oklahoma Press, 1970), p. 30.
23. Edward Spicer, *Cycles of Conquest* (Tucson: University of Arizona Press, 1962), p. 162.
24. Today, mixed groups of Indian people get along well until some controversial subject develops. When this occurs, battle lines are formed along the ancient tribal animosities and the Pan-Indian movement reverts to inter-tribal conflict. The inability for Indians to change this type of behavior has been detrimental in establishing united efforts to alleviate problems. Non-Indians have taken advantage of this situation and utilized the "divide and conquer" tactic very successfully.
25. This is part of the statement inscribed on a brass plate currently located in Bancroft Library at the University of California at Berkeley. The plate was found in 1937 at Drake's Bay and caused a furor among historians. Extensive examination and dating tests have convinced most cynics of the authenticity of the find.
26. Virgil Vogel, *The Indian in American History* (Evanston: Northwestern University Press, 1968), p. 2.
27. Alfred Tamarin, *We Have Not Vanished* (Chicago: Follett Publishing Co., 1974). On pp. 51–54, the account of the Pequots states that Connecticut state records show thirteen Pequots still survive.
28. Peter Farb, *Man's Rise To Civilization As Shown By The Indians of North America From Primeval Times To The Coming Of The Industrial State* (New York: E. P. Dutton and Co., 1968), p. 247.
29. Cotton Mather in *Magnalia Christi Americana*.
30. Before the practice was discontinued in 1871, the United States entered into over 400 such treaties with the various Indian Nations. Innumerable treaties were written and signed by local officials and were never ratified. The treaty was the most effective tool to relieve the Indian of anything the white man wanted.
31. William E. Coffer, "Genocide of the California Indians," *The Indian Historian,* (San Francisco: The American Indian Historical Society, Spring 1977), pp. 11–12.
32. The Choctaws tell of how they defeated the British with a little help from Jackson and his poorly-trained troops.
33. The author is a descendant of some of these Choctaws who as children were informally adopted by white families.

34. Article XIV of the Treaty of Dancing Rabbit Creek states: "Each Choctaw head of a family being desirous to remain and become a citizen of the States, shall be permitted to do so, by signifying his intention to the Agent within six months from the ratification of this Treaty. . . ."

35. William Thomas, a white man who had been a friend to the Cherokees, assisted the people in the acquirement of land for farms, plant crops, and houses. They barely survived until after the Civil War, when they were recognized as a corporate body under the laws of the State of North Carolina. They became wards of the Bureau of Indian Affairs and their land became known as the Qualla Boundary, the reservation their descendants now occupy.

36. Of all the problems of dealing with the dominant society, termination is undoubtedly the foremost. This action, initiated by the federal government, removes the Indians from government recognition and from any benefits under the Bureau of Indian Affairs. The special relationship provided by law is severed and the terminated tribal members become "Americans," whatever that might mean. The land goes; the culture goes; the language dies; and genocide is complete, for there are no more Indians.

37. The Alabama-Coushatta people were the first reservation people with whom the author worked. In 1952, he began contacting local school officials, attempting to develop valid educational opportunities for the children of the tribe. From this beginning, his interest grew until he dedicated his life to these goals.

38. An account of the Tiguas is given in Chapter 2 of this book.

39. As soon as the southeastern tribes were relocated, they made compacts among themselves regulating such matters as the requisition and extradition of criminals and intertribal naturalization. These agreements were expanded to include the remnants of the tribes from the East and the old Northwest Territory.

40. William E. Coffer, *Indian Education: A Study In Self-determination,* PhD Dissertation, California Western University, 1976.

41. For more detailed descriptions of the Choctaw and Cherokee land ownership situation, read Angie Debo's *The Rise and Fall of the Choctaw Republic* and Grant Foreman's *The Five Civilized Tribes.*

42. This treatment by historians of Indians, that of highlighting their faults and ignoring their virtues, is illustrated by Virgil Vogel in *The Indian In American History* (Chicago: Integrated Education Associates, 1968), p. 5.

43. The book of Mormon, according to the members of the church, was divinely inspired and is an account of early refugees from Jerusalem who landed someplace in this hemisphere about 600 B.C. Warfare between factions developed and the rebellious group wiped out the "good guys" (one of the few admitted "Indian" victories). God cursed the winners with dark skin and, according to the book, they reverted to a primitive society. The promise of "redemption" for the "Lamanites" is one of the driving influences of the Mormon's missionary activity and their child placement program today. The Indians, or Lamanites, as they are called, are the latent saviors of mankind who must be brought into the grace of God to realize their potential, or so say the Mormons. It is preached by the church and supported by their Book of Mormon that Indians will *literally* become white through acceptance of the LDS church. Examined objectively, this philosophy and the Book of Mormon are extremely racist and denigrating to the Indian people.

44. Alexander Taylor, *The Indianology of California,* Second Series No. 89, p. 34.

45. R.I. Hayes, *Scrapbook,* Indians Vol. 42, Doc. 19.

46. Committee on Indian Affairs, Senate, on S. 1402, 76th Congress, p. 119.

47. "Forty Seven Cents." Film distributed by the University of California at Berkeley, showing interviews with descendants of California Indians of the 1848–65 era. These statements are from oral tradition passed from the early Indians to their posterity.
48. 1850 California Statutes, p. 408.
49. Senate Executive Document No. 4. (1853), p. 315.
50. H. H. Bancroft, "One of the Last Human Hunts of Civilization and the Basest and Most Brutal of Them all," *Image 3 Graphics* (San Francisco, 1971).
51. Ibid.,pp. 25–26.
52. The author's great-grandfather fought with one of these units throughout the war. He was involved in the Battle of Shepherd Mountain, in which another great-grandfather, a Cherokee, fought on the Union side.
53. For clearer understanding of the Navajo Treaty and events following the return to their homeland, read *The Book of the Navajo* by Raymond Locke and *Navajoland U.S.A.*, published by the Navajo Tribe. John Upton Terrell in *The Navajo* also deals with Bosque Redondo, as do many other authors.
54. See Chapter 7 of this book.
55. See Merrill D. Beal, *I Will Fight No More Forever* (Seattle: University of Washington, 1963), for more detailed information.
56. Ibid., p. 229.
57. While many authors have written books about the Ute Rebellion, one of the clearest descriptions is found in Marshall Sprague's *Massacre* (New York: Ballantine Books, 1957).
58. A detailed account of the relentless efforts to defeat the Apache can be found in Dan L. Thrapp's *The Conquest of Apacheria* (Norman: University of Oklahoma, 1967).
59. One of the best accounts of Cochise and his attempts to sustain peace is found in Elliott Arnold's *Blood Brother* (New York: Bantam Books, 1947). Although a novel, *Blood Brother* is based on history and is extremely accurate in historic detail.
60. Geronimo's wife and three children were brutally murdered by Mexicans and he never relaxed his hatred for all Mexican people.
61. This author was privileged to be friends with Geronimo's youngest son, Robert Geronimo. Many pleasant hours were spent talking with Robert at Apache Summit, a tourist complex operated by the Mescalero Apache Tribe. He looked amazingly like his famous father and had a great sense of humor. One of his favorite tricks was to slip up behind some unsuspecting white woman tourist. He would fold his arms and glare at her until, evidently sensing those piercing eyes, she would turn. Many times I heard the startled screams and watched the victims streaking down the highway in mortal fear, cameras and hats emblazoned with "Mexico" flying through the air. I have also seen Robert on these occasions rolling on the ground, roaring with laughter.
62. United States Statutes at Large, 16:566.
63. Extract from the *Annual Report of the Commissioner of Indian Affairs,* November 1, 1872, by Francis A. Walker, pp. 391–99.
64. Ibid., pp. 460–62.
65. "Lands in Severalty to Indians," House Report No. 1576, 46th Congress, 2nd Session, serial 1938, p. 7.
66. Pressures by non-Indian speculators soon forced removal of this twenty-five-year alienation clause and Indian allotments became saleable in a very short time. Some bright cloth, a new rifle, or a jug of cheap whiskey changed the ownership from Indian to white of a number of these parcels of land. The concept of land ownership and the ignorance of written documents made the Indian a perfect "mark" for many unscrupulous land dealers.

67. This meant more Indian children could be removed from their families and sent to boarding schools for nine to twelve months of the year. There they could be acculturated more rapidly and thus speed up the assimilation process.

68. United States Statutes at Large, 24: 388-91, or The General Allotment Act (Dawes Act), February 8, 1887, Section 6.

69. Report of the Commissioner of Indian Affairs, 1877, pp. 75-76.

70. Dawes seems to be saying that the Indian in his Utopia, with everything he needed and wanted at hand and a way of life which had existed successfully for centuries, did not know he would be better off to accept the European way of life with its jails, poor houses, poverty, indebtedness, and misery. With this egocentrism exhibited by the whites, it is no wonder the Indian people still cannot understand or accept their philosophy of life.

71. For a detailed account of the land lost from allotment, read *One Hundred Million Acres* by Kirke Kickingbird and Karen Ducheneaux.

72. United States Census of 1900 showed a total Indian population of 237,196.

73. This famous quote of Black Elk appears in many publications. For a complete version of the Ogalala holy man's ideas, read *Black Elk Speaks* by John Neihardt and *The Scared Pipe* by Joseph Epes Brown.

74. Leupp felt that Indian and white students who were going to live on the frontier needed more practical and less theoretical education in this period of time. The author feels Mr. Leupp would recognize the need for more academic and professional training if he were alive today. He truly had the welfare of Indians foremost in his heart.

75. For an excellent, concise account of the Kickapoos' land loss, read Angie Debo's *A History of the Indians of the United States,* pp. 268-283.

76. A thorough and valid presentation can be found in Weston La Barre's *The Peyote Cult.* It is quite evident to this author that Mr. Valentine assumes much more than he knows and, typical to those of his philosophical and religious inclinations, makes moral judgments based on personal bias and from a unilateral perspective.

77. The author spent some time with the 36th Division during World War II and was Operations Sergeant in the 143rd Regiment for a number of years in the 1950s. The Division was composed mainly of men from Texas and Oklahoma and many Indians were members. The unit distinguished itself in World War I and World War II.

78. Little was said of this experiment during World War I. During World War II, Navajos gained quite a bit of fame in the Pacific theater using their native language to confuse the Japanese. The subject of the "Code Talkers" is covered later in this book.

79. Had he been white, Pvt. Oklahombi might have become a national hero in America in the manner of Sgt. Alvin York. Surely, his feats were no less daring and heroic.

80. It seems utterly ludicrous that the Indian, the rightful owners of this land, should be awarded citizenship when their ancestors had inhabited the country for untold centuries. To have to legislate citizenship, when the Constitution of the United States provides it for all persons born in the territorial limits of the country, is a rather ridiculous situation. If such privileges had to be legislated, and the legislators were representatives of the people, it does not appear logical that Indians should have been the recipients of such legislation since they had no representation in Congress. Such unilateral legislation is in direct opposition to the basic tenets upon which the United States was founded—a government of, by, and for the people. The Revolutionary War was fought in part because the colonists rejected the concept of legislation without representation. Because of this concept, many tribesmen rejected the offer of citizenship and protested all efforts to include them in the action.

81. Albert Fall resigned from office in March 1923 after investigation proved he had been in-

volved in illegal oil deals with Edward Doheny and Harry Sinclair, two oil tycoons. In 1929, he was convicted of accepting a bribe of $100,000 in connection with the oil scandal and was imprisoned from 1931 to 1932.

82. The first meeting of the All-Pueblo Council was held in 1680 and initiated the Pueblo Revolt. See Chapter 4 of this book.

83. U.S. Statutes at Large, 43: 253.

84. For a complete story of the Meriam Report, read Lewis Meriam *et al, The Problem of Indian Administration* (Baltimore: Johns Hopkins Press, 1928).

85. U.S. Statutes at Large, 48:596.

86. By using the Bureau of Indian Affairs' definition of eligibility, thousands of Indian children were excluded from assistance from JOM funds. Indians from terminated tribes, Indians from the many tribes on state reservations, Indians who had migrated from their reservations, Indians who were not registered with the Bureau for whatever reason, and Indians from tribes which were not "recognized" by the Bureau were unable to utilize funds from this act. Most objective estimates conclude that more Indians were excluded than were included.

87. Beginning in August 1934 and ending in June 1935, a series of 263 elections were held by tribes all over America to decide if they would accept or reject the Indian Reorganization Act. Seventy-three tribes voted to reject the act and 172 tribes tribes voted to accept it. Sixty-two percent of the eligible voters came to the polls and cast their ballots.

88. 1933 Report of Commissioner of Indian Affairs.

89. Commissioner of Indian Affairs Circular 2970, January 1934.

90. *Indians At work,* published by the Department of Interior, Office of Indian Affairs, Vol. XII, Number 5 (Chicago, 1945), p. 30.

91. This statement is made primarily from the experience of the author and from comments of other Indian servicemen.

92. *Indians At Work,* published by the Department of Interior, Office of Indian Affairs, Vol. X, Nos. 2–6 (Chicago, 1944), p. 8.

93. Ira. H. Hayes, a Pima Indian from Bapchule, Arizona, gained fame as one of the three survivors of the historic incident on Mount Suribachi, Iwo Jima, when six marines raised the flag on the summit under heavy enemy fire. After his return home at the end of the war, he found he could not cope with the mediocrity of being just "another Indian in Arizona." He turned to alcohol and drowned in a mud puddle while in a drunken stupor, a rather ignominious end for one of our "National Heroes."

94. For details, read *The Navajo Code Talkers* by Doris A. Paul (Philadelphia: Dorrance and Co., 1973).

95. Atoni (Dr. Roy Armstrong), Choctaw, Professor of Education at California State Polytechnic University, Pomona, wrote this very appropriate poem while a graduate student at the University of Arisona. It appeared in the Fall 1977 edition of Sun Tracks, a literary publication of the Amerind Club at the University. Dr. Armstrong was managing editor at the time. The poem was awarded second place at the 1972 National Indian Arts Exhibition at Scottsdale, Arizona.

96. For a clearer explanation of the exploitation of Indians through the use of Public Law 280, read "Genocide of the California Indians," by William E. Coffer in the Spring 1977 edition of *The Indian Historian,* published by the American Indian Historical Society, San Francisco.

97. The only industry on the Menominee Reservation was one sawmill which was operated to provide jobs for the tribal members. After termination, it was operated to make a profit and about one-half the employees were dismissed.

98. In 1978, there are more Indians in the urban area than there are on reservations.
99. *Annals of the American Academy of Political and Social Science* 311 (May 1957).
100. State v. Satiacum, 50 Wn. 2d 513 (1957).
101. U.S. Statutes at Large, 82: 77–81.
102. For a detailed explanation of the provisions of this Act, read *American Indian Civil Rights Handbook,* Clearinghouse Publication No. 33, United States Commission on Civil Rights (Washington, D.C.: U.S.Government Printing Office, 1972).
103. Special Senate Subcommittee on Indian Education, "Indian Education: A National Tragedy—A National Challenge" (Washington, D.C.: U.S. Government Printing Office, 1969), p. XI.
104. Ibid., p. XII.
105. Such was the impact of the Kennedy Report that most of the recommendations were followed. A great many of the innovations of the 1970s in Indian affairs can be traced directly to this document. The death of Robert Kennedy added impetus to the report, for many felt that fulfillment of the recommendations would act as a memorial to the efforts of this popular legislator.
106. Quoted in Hermann Hagedorn, *Roosevelt in the Bad Lands* (Boston: 1921), p. 355.
107. Public papers of the President of the United States: Richard Nixon, 1970.
108. See Chapter 2 of this book.
109. Ibid.
110. U.S. Department of Commerce, *Federal and State Indian Reservations and Indian Trust Areas* (Washington, D.C.: U.S. Government Printing Office).
111. This author lived in the El Paso area for a number of years and had the privilege of spending many hours conversing with some of the Tigua elders. Many happy days were spent sitting around the plaza at the mission listening to the stories told by the revered members of the group. Some of the clearest understanding of life and its meaning was learned there.
112. Menominee Tribe v. U.S., 391 U.S. 404 (1968).
113. U.S. Statutes at Large, 87: 700ff.
114. This author spent much time in Washington lobbying for the Indian Education Act; first in 1970–71, promoting passage, and in 1972–73, encouraging legislative pressure to free the funds.
115. Permission was obtained following a ruling by the Circuit Court of Appeals, but by the time it was rendered, the situation was too tense for it to be of any value.
116. *The Native Nevadan,* "Was It Help-Or-Hindrance?" by John Tiger, American Indian Press Association release, November 1972.
117. This author was present at this incident in Washington in November 1972. He viewed the devastation and the sign and attempted to conclude the effects of the entire affair on the Indian people.
118. *Navajo Times,* November 30, 1972.
119. "BIA—One Year Later," *Akwesasne Notes,* Late Spring 1974, p. 22.
120. "Bury Our Hopes at Wounded Knee," *Los Angeles Times,* Vine Deloria, Jr., April 1, 1973.
121. A few years after this fiasco, Brando again received publicity for donating 40 acres of land to an Indian organization known as the Survival of American Indian Association. The benevolent "Godfather" neglected to mention the land had a $318,000 mortgage and the liability passed from him to the Indians upon acquisition of title.
122. Op cit., Deloria.
123. The author feels there was a more pressing reason for the dismissal of charges. If the

defendants had won the case, the precedent would have been established for more of the same type of activity. If the defendants had lost and been sentenced, they would have become martyrs to the cause. This also would have caused much more violence. In either case, AIM would have won and the government would have lost. Judge Nichol allowed the United States to save face and, since there was no victor or loser, prevented exploitation of the situation by either party.

124. This author was honored to receive an invitation to the conference and attended both days' meetings. For the first time in his experience, there was no petty inter-tribal or personal bickering. The situation was extremely serious and the Indian representatives displayed total unity of purpose to the government. This undoubtedly was at least partially responsible for the rapid response by the administration in resuming activity in Indian affairs.

125. The selection of Indian members was made by majority vote by Senators and Congressmen from three categories of Indians: Federally-Recognized Tribes, Non-Federally Recognized Tribes, and Urban Indians. Recommendations for candidates were accepted from Indian organizations, tribes, and legislators.

126. The author testified to two Task Forces and submitted written testimony to a third.

127. Hearings on H.J. Res. 881 and S.J. Res. 133 before the House Committee on Interior and Insular Affairs, 93rd Congress, 2nd Session 25 (1974).

128. The author challenges Mr. Meeds' statements and, in fact, would point out that the very items he claims disprove sovereignty, if analyzed objectively, will *prove* sovereignty for the Indian nations. With mind-sets such as expressed in his Minority Report, it is no wonder Meeds, in 1977, introduced legislation which called for the legislative genocide of Indians in America. This Congressional farce is discussed later in the chapter, but it is the opinion of this writer that Mr. Meeds would compromise the moral and legal commitments of the United States government to fulfill campaign promises to a small but influential number of constituents. He seems to be a strong advocate of "might makes right."

129. "A Racist Voice In Congress," *Wassaja* (San Francisco: Indian Historian Press, May 1977).

130. 25 USC 450.

131. One such educational organization, American Indian Educators Concerned, was co-founded in 1974 by this author. The primary objective of AIEC is to provide accurate and understandable descriptions of contemporary problems facing the American Indian. The members utilize publications, radio, television, and printed media to attain their goals.

Bibliography

Adams, Alexander B. *Geronimo*. New York: Berkeley Publishing Corp., 1971.

Aginsky, B.W. and E.G. *Deep Valley*. Briarcliff Manor: Stein and Day, 1967.

Akwesasne Notes. B.I.A. *I'm Not Your Indian Any More*. Rooseveltown: Akwesasne Notes, Mohawk Nation, 1974.

Alexander, Hartley B. *The World's Rim*. Lincoln: University of Nebraska Press, 1953.

Allen, Terry. *The Whispering Wind*. Garden City: Doubleday & Co., Inc., 1972.

Ambler, A. Richard. *The Anasazi*. Flagstaff: Museum of Northern Arizona, 1970.

American Friends Service Committee. *Uncommon Controversy*. Seattle: University of Washington Press, 1970.

Andrist, Ralph K. *The Long Death*. New York: Collier Books, 1964.

Armstrong, Virginia I. *I Have Spoken*. Chicago: Swallow Press, 1971.

Arnold, Elliot. *The Camp Grant Massacre*. New York: Simon and Schuster, 1976.

Artaud, Antouin. *The Peyote Dance*. New York: Farrar, Straus & Giroux, Inc., 1976.

Astrov, Margot. *The Winged Serpent*. Greenwich: Fawcett Publications, Inc., 1946.

Bahr, Howard M. *et al*. *Native Americans Today: Sociological Perspectives*. New York: Harper & Row, Publishers, Inc., 1972.

Baird, W. David. *Peter Pitchlynn: Chief of the Choctaws*. Norman: University of Oklahoma Press, 1972.

Baldwin, Gordon C. *Indians of the Southwest*. New York: Capricorn Books, 1970.

————. *The Warrior Apaches*. Tucson: Dale Stuart King, 1965.

Ball, Eve. *In The Days of Victorio*. Tucson: University of Arizona Press, 1970.

Barnett, Louise K. *The Ignoble Savage*. Westport: Greenwood Press, 1975.

Barrett, S. M. *Geronimo—His Own Story*. New York: Ballantine Books, 1970.

Beal, Merrill D. *I Will Fight No More Forever*. Seattle: University of Washington Press, 1963.

Bean, Lowell J. *Mukat's People*. Berkeley: University of California Press, 1972.

Bernal, Ignacio. *Mexico Before Cortez.* Garden City: Doubleday & Co., Inc., 1963.

Bierhorst, John. *The Red Swan.* New York: Farrar, Straus & Giroux, Inc., 1976.

———. *In The Trail of the Wind.* New York: Farrar, Straus & Giroux, Inc., 1971.

Blish, Helen H. *A Pictographic History of the Oglala Sioux.* Lincoln: University of Nebraska Press, 1967.

Bounds, Thelma V. *Children of Nanih Waiya.* San Antonio: The Naylor Co., 1964.

Bourke, John G. *On The Border With Crook.* Lincoln: University of Nebraska Press, 1971.

Boyd, Doug. *Rolling Thunder.* New York: Dell Publishing Co., Inc., 1974.

Brady Cyrus T. *Indian Fights and Fighters.* Lincoln: University of Nebraska Press, 1971.

Brandon, William. *The Last Americans.* New York: McGraw-Hill Book Co., 1974.

———. *The American Heritage Book of Indians.* New York: Dell Publishing Co., 1961.

———. *The Magic World.* New York: William Morrow and Co., 1971.

Braroe, Niels W. *Indian and White.* Stanford: Stanford University Press, 1975.

Brophy, William A. and Aberle, Sophie D. *The Indian: America's Unfinished Business.* Norman: University of Oklahoma Press, 1966.

Brown, Dee. *Bury My Heart at Wounded Knee.* New York: Holt, Rinehart and Winston, 1970.

———. *Fighting Indians of the West.* New York: Ballantine Books, 1975.

———. *Showdown at Little Big Horn.* New York: Berkeley Publishing Corp., 1964.

Brown, Joseph E. *The Spiritual Legacy of the American Indian.* Lebanon, PA: Sowers Printing Co., 1964.

———. *The Sacred Pipe.* Baltimore: Penguin Books, Inc., 1971.

Brown, Vinson. *Peoples of the Sea Wind.* New York: Macmillan Publishing Company, Inc., 1977.

———. *Voices of the Earth and Sky.* Harrisburg: Stackpole Books, 1974.

Burnette, Robert and Koster, John. *The Road to Wounded Knee.* New York: Bantam Books, Inc., 1974.

Burt, Jesse and Ferguson, Robert B. *Indians of the Southeast: Then and Now.* Nashville: Abingdon Press, 1973.

Cahn, Edgar S. and Hearne, David W. *Our Brothers' Keeper.* New York: New American Library, 1969.

Capps, Walter H. *Seeing With A Native Eye.* New York: Harper and Row, Publishers, Inc., 1976.

Cardenal, Ernesto. *Homage To The American Indians.* Baltimore: Johns Hopkins University Press, 1970.

Caruso, John A. *The Southern Frontier.* New York: The Bobbs-Merrill Co., Inc., 1963.

Cash, Joseph H. and Hoover, Herbert T. *To Be An Indian.* New York: Holt, Rinehart and Winston, 1971.

Casson, Lionel *et al. Mysteries of the Past.* New York: American Heritage Publishing Co., Inc., 1977.

Casteneda, Carlos. *Tales of Power.* New York: Simon and Schuster, 1974.

———. *Journey To Ixtlan.* New York: Simon and Schuster, 1974.

———. *The Teachings of Don Juan.* New York: Ballantine Books, 1968.

———. *A Separate Reality.* New York: Simon and Schuster, 1971.

Chapman, Abraham. *Literature of the American Indians.* New York: New American Library, 1975.

Chapman, Walker. *The Golden Dream.* New York: The Bobbs-Merrill Co., Inc., 1967.

Cheshire, Giff. *Thunder On The Mountain.* New York: Modern Literary Editors Publishing Co., 1960.

Claiborne, Robert. *The First Americans*. New York: Time-Life Books, 1973.

Clark, Ella E. *Indian Legends of the Pacific Northwest*. Berkeley: University of California Press, 1953.

Clum, Woodworth. *Apache Agent*. Boston: Houghton Mifflin Co., 1936.

Cochise, Ciyé. *The First Hundred Years of Niño Cochise*. New York: Pyramid Books, 1971.

Coffer, William E. *Indian Education: A Study in Self-determination,* PhD Dissertation, California Western University, September 1976.

——. "Historic Overview of Self-determination in Education by American Indians," *Vis a Vis*. Fullerton: California State University, September 1974.

——. *Spirits of the Sacred Mountains*. New York: Van Nostrand Reinhold Company, 1978.

——. "Genocide of the California Indians," *The Indian Historian*. San Francisco: Indian Historian Press, Spring 1977.

Collier, Joseph. *American History and Culture*. Los Alamitos: Hwong Publishing Co., 1977.

Collier, Peter. *When Shall They Rest?* New York: Dell Publishing Co., Inc. 1973.

Comfort, Will L. *Apache*. New York: Bantam Books, Inc., 1931.

Cook, Sherburne. *The Conflict Between the California Indian and White Civilization*. Berkeley: University of California Press, 1976.

Corle, Edwin. *Fig Tree John*. New York: Liveright Publishing Corp., 1963.

Costo, Rupert and Henry, Jeanette. *Textbooks And The American Indian*. San Francisco: The Indian Historian Press, 1970.

Cotterill, R. S. *The Southern Indians*. Norman: University of Oklahoma Press, 1954.

Council on Interracial Books for Children. *Chronicles of American Indian Protest*. Greenwich: Fawcett Publications, Inc., 1971.

Courlander, Harold. *The Fourth World of the Hopi*. Greenwich: Fawcett Publications, Inc., 1971.

Cremony, John C. *Life Among The Apaches*. Glorietta, NM: Rio Grande Press, 1868.

Cronyn George W. *American Indian Poetry*. New York: Liveright Publishing Corp., 1934.

Crosby, Alfred W. *The Columbian Exchange*. Westport: Greenwood Press, 1972.

Curtis, Edward S. *Indian Days of the Long Ago*. Yonkers: World Book Co., 1915.

——. *Visions of a Vanishing Race*. New York: Thomas Y. Crowell Co., 1976.

Cushman, Horatio B. *History of the Choctaw, Chickasaw, and Natchez Indians*. Stillwater: Redlands Press, 1962.

Custer, Elizabeth B. *Boots and Saddles*. Norman: University of Oklahoma Press, 1961.

Dale, Edward E. *The Indians of the Southwest*. Norman: University of Oklahoma Press, 1949.

Dane, Christopher. *The American Indian and the Occult*. New York: Popular Library, 1973.

Davis, Britton. *The Truth About Geronimo*. Lincoln: University of Nebraska Press, 1929.

Day, A. Grove. *The Sky Clears*. Lincoln: University of Nebraska Press, 1951.

——. *Coronado's Quest*. Berkeley: University of California Press, 1964.

de Angulo, Jaime. *The Unique Collection of Indian Tales*. New York: Ballantine Books, 1953.

Debo, Angie. *A History of the Indians of the United States*. Norman: University of Oklahoma Press, 1970.

——. *The Rise and Fall of the Choctaw Republic*. Norman: University of Oklahoma Press, 1934.

——. *And Still the Waters Run*. Princeton: Princeton University Press, 1972.

——. *Geronimo*. Norman: University of Oklahoma Press, 1976.

De Las Cases, Bartolome. *The Devastation of the Indies*. New York: The Seabury Press, 1974.

Deloria, Vine. *Of Utmost Good Faith*. San Francisco: Straight Arrow Books, 1971.

————. *Custer Died For Your Sins*. New York: Avon Books, 1969.

————. *We Talk, You Listen*. New York: Macmillan Publishing Company, Inc., 1970.

————. *God Is Red*. New York: Grosset and Dunlap, Inc., 1973.

————. *Behind the Trail of Broken Treaties*. New York: Dell Publishing Co., Inc., 1974.

————. *A Better Day For Indians*. New York: The Field Foundation, 1977.

————. *The Indian Affair*. New York: Friendship Press, 1974.

De Rosier, Arthur H. *The Removal of the Choctaw Indians*. Knoxville: University of Tennessee Press, 1970.

Dial, Adolph L. and Eliades, David K. *The Only Land I Know*. San Francisco: Indian Historian Press, 1975.

Diaz, Bernal. *The Discovery and Conquest of Mexico*. Kingsport: Kingsport Press, 1956.

Dockstader, Frederick J. *Great North American Indians*. New York: Van Nostrand Reinhold Company, 1977.

Dodge, Robert K. and McCullough, Joseph B. *Voices From Wahkontah*. New York: International Publishers, 1974.

Driver, Harold. *Indians of North America*. Chicago: University of Chicago Press, 1961.

Drucker, Philip. *Indians of the Northwest Coast*. Garden City: The Natural History Press, 1955.

Dutton, Bertha P. *The Pueblos*. Englewood Cliffs: Prentice-Hall, Inc., 1975.

Dunn, J.P. *Massacres of the Mountains*. New York: Capricorn Books, 1969.

Eastman, Charles A. *The Soul of the Indian*. Spearfish: Fenwyn Press, 1911.

————. *Indian Boyhood*. Spearfish: Fenwyn Press, 1970.

Ellis, Richard N. *The Western American Indian*. Lincoln: University of Nebraska Press, 1972.

Embree, Edwin R. *Indians of the Americas.* New York: Collier Books, 1970.

Emerson, Dorothy. *Among the Mescalero Apaches*. Tucson: University of Arizona Press, 1973.

Emerson, Ellen R. *Indian Myths*. Minneapolis: Ross and Haines, 1965.

Erdoes, Richard. *The Sun Dance People*. New York: Random House, Inc., 1972.

Farb, Peter. *Man's Rise To Civilization As Shown by the Indians of North America from Primeval Times to the Coming of the Industrial State*. New York: E.P. Dutton, 1968.

Fast, Howard. *The Last Frontier*. New York: Crown Publishers, 1968.

Fehrenbach, T.R. *Comanches*. New York: Crown Publishers, 1968.

Feldmann, Susan. *The Storytelling Stone*. New York: Dell Publishing Co., Inc., 1965.

Fergusson, Erna. *Dancing Gods*. Albuquerque: University of New Mexico Press, 1931.

Fey, Harold E. and McNickle, D'Arcy. *Indians and Other Americans*. New York: Harper & Row, Publishers, Inc., 1959.

Fiedler, Leslie A. *The Return of the Vanishing American*. New York: Drama Book Specialists, 1972.

Fleischmann, Glen. *The Cherokee Removal*. New York: Franklin Watts, Inc., 1971.

Forbes, Jack D. *The Indian In America's Past*. Englewood Cliffs: Prentice-Hall, Inc., 1964.

————. *Native Americans*. Healdsburg, CA: Naturegraph Publishers, 1968.

————. *Native Americans of California and Nevada*. Berkeley: Far West Laboratory, 1968.

————. *Aztecas Del Norte*. Greenwich: Fawcett Publications, Inc., 1973.

Foreman, Grant. *Sequoyah*. Norman: University of Oklahoma Press, 1938.

————. *Indian Removal*. Norman: University of Oklahoma Press, 1932.

————. *The Five Civilized Tribes*. Norman: University of Oklahoma Press, 1934.

Foster, J.W. *Pre-historic Races of the United States of America*. Chicago: S.C. Griggs and Co., 1874.

Fox, Hugh. *First Fire*. Garden City: Doubleday & Co., Inc., 1978.

Friar, Ralph and Natasha. *The Only Good Indian*. New York: Drama Book Specialists, 1972.

Fuchs, Estelle and Havighurst, Robert. *To Live On This Earth*. Garden City: Doubleday & Co., Inc., 1973.

Garbarino, Merwyn S. *Native American Heritage*. Boston: Little, Brown and Company, 1976.

Garfield, Viola E. and Forrest, Linn A. *The Wolf and the Raven*. Seattle: University of Washington Press, 1961.

Georgakas, Dan. *The Broken Hoop*. Garden City: Doubleday & Co., Inc., 1973.

————. *Red Shadows*. Garden City: Doubleday & Co., Inc., 1973.

Gibson, Arrell M. *The Chickasaws*. Norman: University of Oklahoma Press, 1971.

Giddings, Ruth W. *Yaqui Myths and Legends*. Tucson: University of Arizona Press, 1971.

Goodwin, Grenville. *The Social Organization of the Western Apache*. Tucson: University of Arizona Press, 1969.

Gordon, Suzanne. *Black Mesa, The Angel of Death*. New York: John Day Co., 1973.

Grinnell, George B. *The Fighting Cheyennes*. Norman: University of Oklahoma Press, 1955.

————. *By Cheyenne Campfires*. Lincoln: University of Nebraska Press, 1926.

————. *The Cheyenne Indians*. Lincoln: University of Nebraska Press, 1923.

Gunnerson, Dolores A. *The Jicarilla Apaches*. DeKalb: Northern Illinois University Press, 1974.

Guttmann, Allen. *States Rights and Indian Removal: The Cherokee Nation v. The State of Georgia*. Lexington: D.C. Heath and Co., 1965.

Hagen, William T. *American Indians*. Chicago: University of Chicago Press, 1961.

Hannum, Alberta. *Paint The Wind*. New York: Ballantine Books, 1958.

————. *Spin a Silver Dollar*. New York: Ballantine Books, 1944.

Harrington, John P. *Karuk Indian Myths*. Washington, D.C.: Smithsonian Institution, 1932.

Hassrick, Royal B. *The Colorful Story of North American Indians*. Hong Kong: Octopus Books, Ltd., 1974.

Heizer, Robert F. *They Were Only Diggers*. Ramona, CA: Ballena Press, 1974.

————. *Some Last Century Accounts of the Indians of Southern California*. Ramona, CA: Ballena Press, 1976.

————. *The Destruction of California Indians*. Santa Barbara: Peregrine Press, 1974.

———— and Whipple, M.A. *The California Indians*. Berkeley: University of California Press, 1971.

Henry, Thomas R. *Wilderness Messiah*. New York: Bonanza Books, 1955.

Highwater, Jamake. *Indian America*. New York: David McKay Co., 1975.

Hoebel, E. Adamson. *The Cheyennes*. New York: Holt, Rinehart and Winston, 1960.

Hoig, Stan. *The Sand Creek Massacre*. Norman: University of Oklahoma Press, 1961.

Hooper, Lucile. *The Cahuilla Indians*. Ramona, CA: Ballena Press, 1972.

Hoover, Dwight W. *The Red and The Black*. Chicago: Rand McNally College Publishing Co., 1976.

Horan, James D. *The McKenney-Hall Portrait Gallery of American Indians*. New York: Crown Publishers, Inc., 1972.

Howard, Helen A. and McGrath, Dan L. *War Chief Joseph*. Lincoln: University of Nebraska Press, 1941.

Hudson, Charles M. *4 Centuries of Southern Indians*. Athens: University of Georgia Press, 1975.

Hundley, Norris. *The American Indian*. Santa Barbara: Clio Press, 1974.

Hunter, John Dunn. *Memoirs of a Captivity Among the Indians of North America*. New York: Schocken Books, 1973.

Hunter, Milton R. *Great Civilizations and the Book of Mormon*. Salt Lake City: Bookcraft, Inc., 1970.

Iacopi, Robert L. *et al.*, Ed. *Look To The Mountain Top.* San Jose, CA: Gousha Publishers, 1972.

Jackson, Donald. *Black Hawk.* Urbana: University of Illinois Press, 1964.

Jackson, Helen H. *Century of Dishonor.* Minneapolis: Ross and Haines, Inc., 1964.

Jacobs, Paul and Landau, Saul. *To Serve the Devil.* New York: Random House, Inc., 1971.

Jacobs, Wilbur R. *Wilderness Politics and Indian Gifts.* Lincoln: University of Nebraska Press, 1966.

————. *Dispossessing The American Indian.* New York: Charles Scribner's Sons, 1972.

Jahoda, Gloria. *The Trail of Tears.* New York: Holt, Rinehart and Winston, 1975.

James, Wharton. *Learning From The Indian.* Philadelphia: Running Press, 1973.

Jennings, Francis. *The Invasion of America.* Chapel Hill: University of North Carolina Press, 1975.

Jones, David E. *Sanapia: Comanche Medicine Woman.* New York: Holt, Rinehart and Winston, 1968.

Josephy, Alvin M. *The Indian Heritage of America.* New York: Bantam Books, Inc., 1968.

————. *The Nez Perce Indians.* New Haven: Yale University Press, 1971.

————. *The American Heritage Book of Indians.* New York: American Heritage Publishing Co., Inc., 1961.

————. *Red Power.* New York: McGraw-Hill Book Co., 1971.

————. *The Patriot Chiefs.* New York: Penguin Books, Inc., 1969.

Kane, Robert L. and Rosalie A. *Federal Health Care (With Reservations).* New York: Springer Publishing Co., 1972.

Katz, Jane B. *I Am The Fire of Time.* New York: E.P. Dutton, 1977.

Kelley Lawrence. *Navajo Roundup.* Boulder: Pruett Publishing Co., 1970.

Kickingbird, Kirk and Ducheneaux, Karen. *One Hundred Million Acres.* New York: Macmillan Publishing Company, Inc., 1973.

Kinney, J.P. *Like Other Men.* Laurens, NY: The Village Printer, 1974.

————. *Facing Indian Facts.* Laurens, NY: The Village Printer, 1973.

Kirkpatrick, F.A. *The Spanish Conquistadores.* New York: World Publishing, 1946.

Kluckhohn, Clyde and Leighton, Dorothea. *The Navajo.* Garden City: Doubleday & Co., Inc., 1962.

Kroeber, Theodora. *The Inland Whale.* Berkeley: University of California Press, 1959.

————. *Ishi, Last of His Tribe.* Sacramento: California State Department of Education, 1967.

La Barre, Weston. *The Ghost Dance.* New York: Dell Publishing Co., Inc., 1970.

————. *The Peyote Cult.* New York: Schocken Books, 1969.

La Farge, Oliver. *A Pictorial History of the American Indian.* New York: Crown Publishers, Inc., 1956.

Lafferty, R.A. *Okla Hannali.* New York: Pocket Books, 1973.

Lame Deer, John and Erdoes, Richard. *Lame Deer Seeker of Visions.* New York: Simon and Schuster, 1972.

Landes, Ruth. *The Ojibwa Woman.* New York: W.W. Norton Co., 1971.

League of Women Voters Education Fund. *Indian Country.* Washington, D.C.: League of Women Voters, 1976.

Lee, Nelson. *Three Years Among The Comanches.* Norman: University of Oklahoma Press, 1957.

Leon-Portilla, Miguel. *The Broken Spears.* Boston: Beacon Press, 1962.

Levine, Stuart and Lurie, Nancy O. *The American Indian Today.* Baltimore: Penguin Books, Inc., 1968.

Levitan, Sar A. and Johnston, William B. *Indian Giving.* Baltimore: Johns Hopkins University Press, 1975.

Lewis, Anna. *Chief Pushmataha*. New York: Exposition Press, 1959.

Linderman, Frank B. *Plenty Coups-Chief of the Crows*. Lincoln: University of Nebraska Press, 1930.

——. *Pretty Shield*. Lincoln: University of Nebraska Press, 1932.

Locke, Raymond F. *The American Indian*. Los Angeles: Mankind Publishing Co., 1976.

——. *The Book of the Navajo*. Los Angeles: Mankind Publishing Co., 1976.

Lone Dog, Louise. *Strange Journey*. Happy Camp, California: Naturegraph Publishers, Inc., 1964.

Longstreet, Stephen. *War Cries On Horseback*. Garden City: Doubleday & Co., Inc., 1970.

Lowie, Robert H. *Indians of the Plains*. Garden City: The Natural History Press, 1954.

Lurie, Nancy O. *Mountain Wolf Woman*. Ann Arbor: University of Michigan Press, 1961.

Lyman, June and Denver, Norma. *Ute People: An Historical Study*. Salt Lake City: University of Utah Press, 1970.

Marriott, Alice and Rachlin, Carol. *American Epic*. New York: G.P. Putnam's Sons, 1969.

——. *The American Indian Speaks*. Vermillion: University of South Dakota Press, 1969.

——. *Peyote*. New York: New American Library, 1971.

Masson, Marcelle. *A Bag of Bones*. Happy Camp, California: Naturegraph Publishers, Inc., 1966.

McLuhan, T.C. *Touch The Earth*. New York: Pocket Books, 1971.

McNickle, D'Arcy. *They Came Here First*. New York: Harper & Row, Publishers, Inc., 1975.

——. *Native American Tribalism*. London: Oxford University Press, 1973.

——. *Indian Man*. Bloomington: Indiana University Press, 1971.

McReynolds, Edwin C. *The Seminoles*. Norman: University of Oklahoma Press, 1957.

Meltzer, Milton. *Hunted Like a Wolf*. New York: Farrar, Straus & Giroux, Inc., 1972.

Meyer, Roy W. *History of the Santee Sioux*. Lincoln: University of Nebraska Press, 1967.

Meyer, William. *Native Americans*. New York: International Publishers, 1971.

Meyers, J. Jay. *Red Chiefs and White Challengers*. New York: Washington Square Press, 1972.

Milton, John R. *The American Indian Speaks*. Vermillion: University of South Dakota Press, 1971.

——. *American Indian II*. Vermillion: University of South Dakota Press, 1971.

——. *Conversations With Frank Waters*. Chicago: Swallow Press, 1971.

Miner, H. Craig. *The Corporation and the Indian*. Columbia: University of Missouri Press, 1976.

Momaday, Natachee S. *American Indian Authors*. Boston: Houghton Mifflin Co., 1972.

Mooney, James. *The Ghost Dance Religion*. Chicago: University of Chicago Press, 1965.

Moquin, Wayne and Van Doren, Charles. *Great Documents in American Indian History*. New York: Praeger Publishers, 1973.

Morey, Sylvester M. *Can The Red Man Help The White Man?* New York: The Myrin Institute, 1970.

—— and Gilliam, Olivia. *Respect For Life*. Garden City: Waldorf Press, 1974.

Morgan, John S. *When The Morning Stars Sang Together*. Agincourt: The Book Society of Canada, Ltd., 1974.

Nabakov, Peter. *Two Leggins*. New York: Thomas Y. Crowell Co., 1967.

Nash, Gary B. *Red, White, and Black*. Englewood Cliffs: Prentice-Hall, Inc., 1974.

National Geographic Society. *The World of the American Indian*. Washington: National Geographic Society, 1974.

——. *Indians of the Americas*. Washington: National Geographic Society, 1955.

Neihardt, John G. *Black Elk Speaks*. New York: Pocket Books, 1972.

——. *When The Tree Flowered*. New York: Pocket books, 1973.

Newcomb, William W. *North American Indians: An Anthropological Perspective.* Pacific Palasades, CA: Goodyear Publishing Co., 1974.

Nichols, Roger L. and Adams, George R. *The American Indian.* New York: John Wiley & Sons, Inc., 1971.

Niethammer, Carolyn. *Daughters of the Earth.* Macmillan Publishing Company, Inc., 1977.

Novack, George. *Genocide Against The Indians.* New York: Pathfinder Press, 1972.

O'Donnell, James H. *Southern Indians in the American Revolution.* Knoxville: University of Tennessee Press, 1973.

Olson, James C. *Red Cloud and the Sioux Problem.* Lincoln: University of Nebraska Press, 1965.

Ortiz, Roxanne D. *The Great Sioux Nation.* New York: The American Indian Treaty Council Information Center; and San Francisco: Moon Books, 1977.

Oswalt, Wendell H. *This Land Was Theirs.* New York: John Wiley & Sons, Inc., 1973.

Otis, D.S. *The Dawes Act and the Allotment of Indian Lands.* Norman: University of Oklahoma Press, 1973.

Owen, Roger C. *et al. The North American Indians.* New York: Macmillan Publishing Company, Inc., 1967.

Pantencio, Francisco. *Stories and Legends of the Palm Springs Indians.* Palm Springs: Caroline S. Snyder, 1943.

Parkman, Francis. *The Conspiracy of Pontiac and the Indian War After the Conquest of Canada.* Boston: Little, Brown and Company, 1913.

Patterson, E. Palmer. *The Canadian Indian: A History Since 1500.* New York: Macmillan Publishing Company, Inc., 1972.

Paul, Doris A. *The Navajo Code Talkers.* Philadelphia: Dorrance and Co., 1973.

Pearce, Roy H. *Savagism and Civilization.* Baltimore: The Johns Hopkins Press, 1965.

Pearson, Keith L. *The Indian In American History.* New York: Harcourt Brace Jovanovich, 1973.

Peet, Mary R. *San Pasqual—A Crack in the Hills.* Ramona, CA: Ballena Press, 1973.

Perry, Frederick E. *Thunder On The Mountains.* Philadelphia: Dorrance and Co., 1973.

Phillips, George H. *Chiefs and Challengers.* Berkeley: University of California Press, 1975.

Poe, Charlsie. *Angel To The Papagos.* San Antonio: The Naylor Co., 1964.

Porter, C. Fayne. *Our Indian Heritage.* Philadelphia: Chilton books, 1964.

Powell, Peter J. *Sweet Medicine.* Norman: University of Oklahoma Press, 1969.

Prescott, William H. *Conquest of Mexico.* New York: The Book League of America, 1934.

———. *The World of the Aztecs.* Geneva: Editions Minerva, 1970.

Price, Monroe E. *Law and the American Indian.* New York: The Bobbs-Merrill Co., Inc., 1973.

Prucha, Francis Paul. *Documents of United States Indian Policy.* Lincoln: University of Nebraska Press, 1975.

———. *American Indian Policy in the Formative Years.* Lincoln: University of Nebraska Press, 1962.

Pryde, Duncan. *Nunaga.* New York: Walker and Co., 1971.

Quinn, Meredith M. *Dakota Proclamation.* Los Angeles: Toltecs en Aztlan, 1972.

Radin, Paul. *The Story of the American Indian.* New York: Liveright Publishing Corp., 1944.

———. *The Trickster.* New York: Schocken Books, 1972.

Rogin, Michael Paul. *Fathers and Children.* New York: Random House, Inc., 1975.

Roland, Albert. *Great Indian Chiefs.* New York: Macmillan Publishing Company, Inc., 1966.

Rosen, Kenneth. *The Man To Send Rain Clouds.* New York: Random House, Inc., 1974.

Rothenberg, Jerome. *Shaking The Pumpkin.* Garden City: Doubleday & Co., Inc., 1972.

Russell, Frank. *The Pima Indians*. Tucson: University of Arizona Press, 1975.

Sanders, Thomas E. and Peek, Walter W. *Literature of the American Indian*. Beverly Hills: Glencoe Press, 1973.

Sandoz, Mari. *These Were The Sioux*. New York: Dell Publishing Co., Inc., 1961.

———. *Crazy Horse*. Lincoln: University of Nebraska Press, 1942.

———. *Cheyenne Autumn*. New York: Avon Books, 1953.

Santee, Ross. *Apache Land*. Lincoln: University of Nebraska Press, 1947.

Satz, Ronald N. *American Indian Policy in the Jacksonian Era*. Lincoln: University of Nebraska Press, 1975.

Schellie, Don. *Vast Domain of Blood*. Los Angeles: Westernlore Press, 1968.

Schultz, J.W. *My Life As An Indian*. Greenwich: Fawcett Publications, Inc., 1935.

Schusky, Ernest L. *The Forgotten Sioux*. Chicago: Nelson-Hall, 1975.

———. *The Right To Be Indian*. San Francisco: Indian Historian Press, 1970.

Scott, Lalla. *Karnee*. Greenwich; Fawcett Publications, Inc., 1966.

Schrivner, Fielsom C. *Mohave People*. San Antonio: The Naylor Co., 1970.

Sekyaletstewa. *Indian Love Letters*. Tucson: Owen Press, 1972.

Seton, Ernest T. and Julia M. *Gospel of the Red Man*. Santa Fe: Seton Village, 1966.

Sheehan, Bernard W. *Seeds of Extinction*. New York: W.W. Norton and Co., 1973.

Shorris, Earl. *The Death of the Great Spirit*. New York: New American Library, 1971.

Silverberg, Robert. *Home of the Red Man*. New York: Washington Square Press, 1963.

Simmons, Leo W. *Sun Chief*. New Haven: Yale University Press, 1942.

Sneve, Virginia. *The Dakota's Heritage*. Sioux Falls: Brevet Press, 1973.

Sonnichsen, C.L. *The Mescalero Apaches*. Norman: University of Oklahoma Press, 1958.

Soutelle, Jacques. *Daily Life of the Aztecs*. Stanford: Stanford University Press, 1961.

Spencer, Robert F. *et al. The Native Americans*. New York: Harper & Row. Publishers, Inc., 1965.

Spicer, Edward H. *A Short History of the Indians of the United States*. New York: D. Van Nostrand Co., 1969.

———. *Cycles of Conquest*. Tucson: University of Arizona Press, 1962.

Spindler, George D. *Education and Cultural Process*. New York: Holt, Rinehart and Winston, 1974.

Sprague, Marshall. *Massacre*. New York: Ballantine Books, 1957.

Standing Bear, Luther. *My People The Sioux*. Lincoln: University of Nebraska Press, 1975.

Stands In Timber, John and Liberty, Margot. *Cheyenne Memories*. Lincoln: University of Nebraska Press, 1967.

Starkloff, Carl. *The People of the Center*. New York: The Seabury Press, 1974.

Stegner, Wallace. *Wolf Willow*. New York: Ballantine Books, 1955.

Steiner, Stan. *The Vanishing White Man*. New York: Harper & Row, Publishers, Inc., 1976.

———. *The New Indians*. New York: Dell Publishing Co., Inc., 1968.

Storm, Hyemeyohsts. *Seven Arrows*. New York: Harper & Row, Publishers, Inc., 1972.

Stout, Joseph A. *Apache Lightning*. New York: Oxford University Press, 1974.

Sutton, Imre. *Indian Land Tenure*. New York: Clearwater Publishing Co., 1975.

Svensson, Frances. *The Ethnics in American Politics*. Minneapolis: Burgess Publishing Co., 1973.

Swanton, John R. *The Indian Tribes of North America*. Washington, D.C.: Smithsonian Institution Press, 1952.

Szasz, Margaret. *Education and the American Indian*. Albuquerque: University of New Mexico Press, 1974.

Tamarin, Alfred. *We Have Not Vanished*. Chicago: Follett Publishing Co. 1974.

Tatum, Laurie. *Our Red Brothers*. Lincoln: University of Nebraska Press, 1970.

Taylor, Theodore W. *The States and Their Indian Citizens*. Washington, D.C.: U.S. Department of Interior, 1972.

Terrell, John Upton. *American Indian Almanac*. New York: Thomas Y. Crowell Co., 1961.

———. *The Navajos*. New York: Harper and Row, Publishers, Inc., 1970.

———. *Apache Chronicle*. New York: Thomas Y. Crowell Co., 1974.

———. *The Plains Apache*. New York: Thomas Y. Crowell Co., 1975.

———. *Indian Women of the Western Morning*. New York: Dial Press, 1974.

Thompson, Stith. *Tales of the North American Indian*. Bloomington: Indiana University Press, 1971.

Thrapp, Dan L. *The Conquest of Apacheria*. Norman: University of Oklahoma Press, 1967.

Tibbles, Thomas H. *The Ponca Chiefs*. Lincoln: University of Nebraska Press, 1972.

Travers, Milton A. *The Last of the Great Wampanoag Indian Sachems*. Boston: The Christopher Publishing Co., 1963.

Trennert, Robert A. *Alternative To Extinction*. Philadelphia: Temple University Press, 1975.

Turner, Frederick W., III. *The Portable North American Indian Reader*. New York: The Viking Press, 1974.

Turner, Katharine C. *Red Man Calling on The Great White Father*. Norman: University of Oklahoma Press, 1951.

Tyler, Daniel. *Red Men and Hat Wearers*. Boulder: Pruett Publishing Co., 1974.

Tyler, S. Lyman. *A History of Indian Policy*. Washington, D.C.: U.S. Department of Interior, 1973.

Underhill, Ruth M. *Red Man's America*. Chicago: University of Chicago Press, 1953.

———. *People of the Crimson Evening*. Washington, D.C.: U.S. Department of Interior, 1951.

———. *Here Come the Navajo*. Washington, D.C.: U.S. Department of Interior, 1953.

———. *Singing For Power*. Berkeley: University of California Press, 1938.

———. *Red Man's Religion*. Chicago: University of Chicago Press, 1965.

Underwood, Thomas B. *Cherokee Legends and the Trail of Tears*. Knoxville: S.B. Newman Printing Co., 1956.

———. *The Story of the Cherokee People*. Knoxville: S.B. Newman Printing Co., 1961.

Unger, Steven. *The Destruction of American Indian Families*. New York: Association on American Indian Affairs, 1977.

Utley, Robert M. *The Last Days of the Sioux Nation* New Haven: Yale University Press, 1963.

Vanderwerth, W.C. *Indian Oratory*. Norman: University of Oklahoma Press, 1971.

Van Every, Dale. *Disinherited*. New York: Avon Books, 1966.

Van Roekel, Gertrude B. *Jicarilla Apaches*. San Antonio: The Naylor Co., 1971.

Vogel, Virgil J. *This Country Was Ours*. New York: Harper & Row, Publishers, Inc., 1972.

——— . *The Indian in American History*. Chicago: Integrated Educational Associates, 1969.

Von Hagen, Vistor W. *The Aztec Man and Tribe*. New York: New American Library, 1958.

Waddell, Jack O. and Watson, O. Michael. *The American Indian in Urban Society*. Boston: Little, Brown and Company, 1971.

Walker, Deward E. *The Emergent Native Americans*. Boston: Little, Brown and Company, 1972.

Wallace, Anthony F.C. *The Death and Rebirth of the Seneca*. New York: Random House, Inc., 1972.

Washburn, Wilcomb E. *The Indian and the White Man*. New York: Doubleday & Co., Inc., 1964.

———. *Red Man's Land—White Man's Law*. New York: Charles Scribner's Sons, 1971.

——. *The Indian In America.* New York: Harper & Row, Publishers, Inc., 1975.

——. *The American Indian and the United States.* New York: Random House, Inc., 1973 (4 vols.).

——. *The Assault On Indian Tribalism.* New York: J.B. Lippincott Co., 1975.

Waters, Frank. *Book of the Hopi.* New York: Ballantine Books, 1963.

——. *Pumpkin Seed Point.* Chicago: Sage Books, 1969.

——. *Masked Gods.* New York: Ballantine Books, 1950.

Wax, Murray L. *Indian Americans.* Englewood Cliffs: Prentice-Hall, Inc., 1971.

—— and Buchanan, Robert W. *Solving "The Indian Problem."* New York: Time Books, 1976.

Weaver, Thomas. *Indians of Arizona.* Tucson: University of Arizona Press, 1974.

Weltfish, Gene. *The Lost Universe.* New York: Ballantine Books, 1965.

Wherry, Joseph H. *The Totem Pole Indians.* New York: Thomas Y. Crowell Co., 1964.

——. *Indian Masks and Myths of the West.* New York: Thomas Y. Crowell, 1974.

White, Anne T. *The False Treaty.* New York: Scholastic Books, 1970.

White, Jay V. *Taxing Those They Found Here.* Albuquerque: University of New Mexico Press, 1972.

White, Lonnie J. *Hostiles and Horse Soldiers.* Boulder: Pruett Publishing Co., 1972.

Wilkins, Thurman. *Cherokee Tragedy.* New York: Macmillan Publishing Company, Inc., 1970.

Williams, Samuel C. *Adair's History of the American Indians.* New York: Promontory Press, 1975.

Willoya, William and Brown, Vinson. *Warriors of the Rainbow.* Happy Camp, California: Naturegraph Publishing Co., 1962.

Wilson, Charles B. *Indians of Eastern Oklahoma.* Afton, Oklahoma: Buffalo Publishing Co., 1947.

Wilson, Edmund. *Apologies To The Iroquois.* New York: Random House, Inc., 1959.

Wiltse, Charles M. *Expansion and Reform.* New York: The Free Press, 1967.

Wise, Jennings C. *The Red Man in the New World Drama.* New York: Macmillan Publishing Company, Inc., 1971.

Wissler, Clark. *Red Man Reservations.* New York: Collier Books, 1971.

——. *Indians of the United States.* Garden City: Doubleday & Co., Inc., 1940.

Witt, Shirley H. and Steiner, Stan. *The Way.* New York: Random House, Inc., 1972.

Wolf, Eric. *Sons of the Shaking Earth.* Chicago: University of Chicago Press, 1959.

Woodward, Grace S. *The Cherokees.* Norman: University of Oklahoma Press, 1963.

Wright, Kathleen. *The Other Americans.* Los Angeles: Lawrence Publishing Co., 1969.

Wrone, David and Nelson, Russell. *Who's The Savage?* Greenwich: Fawcett Publications, Inc., 1973.

Young, Mary E. *Redskins, Ruffleshirts and Rednecks.* Norman: University of Oklahoma Press, 1961.

Zuni People. *The Zunis.* Albuquerque: University of New Mexico Press, 1972.

Appendix

To enable the lay reader to understand the structure and general scope of the over 400 treaties entered into by the United States government and the various Indian nations, the following are presented as typical examples. These six treaties were also selected because of their impact on the Indian world. Each of these has great historic emphasis and drastically affected the Indian–white relationship.

DELAWARE TREATY

The first treaty between the new government of the United States and an Indian nation was with the powerful Delaware (or, as they called themselves, the Lenape) Nation of Indians. Although the colonies were still at war with England and had not been recognized as a nation by most of the world, they needed the friendship of the Delaware people and needed permission from the Indians to move troops across the Delaware land.

This treaty established the pattern of diplomatic dealings between the United States and the various Indian nations. It also provided the general structural pattern which was followed throughout the succeeding ninety-three years of treaty-making—that of making promises to the tribes which were never intended to be consumated.

Delaware Indian Treaty
Fort Pitt, September 17, 1778

MADE AND ENTERED INTO BY COMMISSIONERS FOR, AND IN BEHALF OF THE UNITED STATES OF NORTH-AMERICA OF THE ONE PART, AND DEPUTIES AND CHIEF MEN OF THE DELAWARE NATION OF THE OTHER PART.

ARTICLE I

THAT ALL OFFENCES of hostilities by one, or either of the contracting parties against the other, be mutually forgiven, and buried in the depth of oblivion, never more to be had in remembrance.

ARTICLE II

That a perpetual peace and friendship shall from henceforth take place, and subsist between the contracting parties aforesaid, through all succeeding generations: and if either of the parties are engaged in a just and necessary war with any other nation or nations, that then each shall assist the other in due proportion to their abilities, till their enemies are brought to reasonable terms of accomodation: and that if either of them shall discover any hostile designs forming against the other, they shall give the earliest notice thereof, that timeous measures may be taken to prevent their ill effect.

ARTICLE III

And whereas the United States are engaged in a just and necessary war, in defence and support of life and liberty and independence, against the King of England and his adherents, and as said King is yet possessed of several posts and forts on the lakes and other places, the reduction of which is of great importance to the peace and security of the contracting parties, and as the most practicable way for the troops of the United States to some of the posts and forts is by passing through the country of the Delaware Nation, the aforesaid deputies, on behalf of themselves and their nation, do hereby stipulate and agree to give free passage through their country to the troops aforesaid, and the same to conduct by the nearest and best ways to the posts, forts or towns of the enemies of the United States, affording to said troops such supplies of corn, meat, horses, or whatever may be in their power for the accomodation of such troops, on the commanding officer's &c. paying, or engaging to pay, the full value of whatever they can supply them with. And the said deputies, on the behalf of their nation, engage to join the troops of the United States aforesaid, with such a number of their best and most expert warriors as they can spare, consistent with their own safety, and act in concern with them; and for the better security of the old men, women and children of the aforesaid nation, whilst their warriers are engaged against the common enemy, it is agreed on the part of the United States, that a fort of sufficient strength and capacity be built at the expense of the said States, with such assistance as it may be in the power of the said Delaware Nation to give, in the most convenient place, and advantageous situations, as shall be agreed on by the commanding officer of the troops aforesaid, with the advice and concurrence of the deputies of the aforesaid Delaware Nation, which fort shall be garrisoned by such a number of the troops of the United States, as the commanding officer can spare for the present, and hereafter by such numbers, as the wise men of the United States in council, shall think most conducive to the common good.

ARTICLE IV

For the better security of the peace and friendship now entered into by the contracting parties, against all infractions of the same by the citizens of either party, to the prejudice of the other, neither party shall proceed to the infliction of punishments on the citizens of the other, otherwise than by securing the offender or offenders by imprisonment, or any other competent means, till a fair and impartial trial can be had by judges or juries of both parties, as near as can be to the laws, customs and usages of the contracting parties and natural justice: The mode of such trials to be hereafter fixed by the wise men of the United States in Congress assembled, with the assistance of such deputies of the Delaware Nation, as may be appointed to act in concert with them in adjusting this matter to their mutual liking. And it is further agreed between the parties aforesaid, that neither shall entertain or give countenance to the enemies of the other, or protect in their respective states, criminal fugitives or slaves, but the same to apprehend, and secure and deliver to the State or States, to which such enemies, criminals, servants or slaves respectively belong.

ARTICLE V

Whereas the confederation entered into by the Delaware Nation and the United States, renders the first dependent on the latter for all the articles of clothing, utinsils and implements of war, and it is judged not only reasonable, but indispensibly necessary, that the aforesaid Nation be supplied with such articles from time to time, as far as the United States may have it in their power, by a well-regulated trade, under the conduct of an intelligent, candid agent, with an adequate salary, one more influenced by the love of his country, and a constant attention to the duties of his department by promoting the common interest, than the sinister purposes of converting and binding all the duties of his office to his private emolument: Convinced of the necessity of such measures, the Commissioners of the United States, at the earnest solicitation of the deputies aforesaid, have engaged in behalf of the United States, that such a trade shall be afforded said nation, conducted of such principals of mutual interest as the wisdom of the United States in Congress assembled shall think most conducive to adopt for their mutual convenience.

ARTICLE VI

Whereas the enemies of the United States have endeavoured, by every article in their power, to possess the Indians in general with an opinion, that it is the design of the States aforesaid, to extirpate the Indians and take possession of their country: to obviate such false suggestion, the United States do engage to guarantee to the aforesaid nation of Delawares, and their heirs, all their territorial rights in the fullest and most ample manner, as it hath been bounded by former treaties, as long as they the said Delaware nation shall abide by, and hold fast the chain of friendship now entered into. And it is further agreed on between the contracting parties should it for the future be found conducive for the mutual interest of both parties, to invite any other tribes who have been friends to the interest of the United States, to join the present confederation, and to form a state whereof the Delaware nation shall be the head, and have a representation in Congress: Provided, nothing contained in this article to be considered as conclusive until it meets with the approbation of Congress. And it is also the intent and meaning of this article, that no protection or countenance shall be afforded to any who are at present our enemies, by which they might escape the punishment they deserve.

In witness whereof, the Parties have hereunto interchangeably set their Hands and Seals at Fort-Pitt, September seventeenth, Anno Domini one thousand seven hundred and seventy-eight.

ANDREW LEWIS,
THOMAS LEWIS,
WHITE EYES,
THE PIPE,
JOHN KILL BUCK.

IN PRESENCE OF

LACHN. M'INTOSH, Brig. General, Commander the Western Department, DANIEL BRODHEAD, Col. 8th Pennsylvania regiment, W. CRAWFORD, Col. JOHN CAMPBELL, JOHN STEPHENSON, JNO. GIBSON, Col. 13th Virginia regiment, A. GRAHAM, Brigade Major, Pennsylvania regiment, JOHN FINLEY, Capt. 8th Pennsylvania regiment.

TREATY OF DANCING RABBIT CREEK

For a number of years following the formation of the United States, the great Choctaw Nation had withstood the pressures to move west of the Mississippi River. They had ceded land through treaty negotiations in 1786, 1801, 1802, 1803, 1805, 1816, 1820, and 1825. These treaties were unilateral examples of coercion, threats, falsehoods, and bribery and were typical of most of the treaties negotiated by the United States and her Indian neighbors.

The white government would seek to obtain Indian land by promising payment of money, exchange of land, educational facilities, and/or everlasting peace and friendship. Any concession was given to the natives, for the United States had little or no intention of fulfilling its obligations. These concessions and promises were considered only temporary, until the Indians were no longer a threat or obstacle to white settlers. The Indians, however, considered these treaties as sacred promises and lived up to the very letter of their obligations. They were constantly surprised and astounded that the whites took their word of honor so lightly.

The Choctaws were as naive in 1830 as they were in 1801, and they entered into the Treaty of Dancing Rabbit Creek in good faith. They gave up all the ancestral land they had left in Mississippi for the southern portion of Oklahoma. Their removing to the West carried promises of sovereignty and non-interference "forever." This "forever" lasted less than forty years.

Treaty with the Choctaws
Dancing Rabbit Creek
September 27, 1830

ENTERED INTO BY JOHN H. EATON AND JOHN COFFEE, FOR AND IN BEHALF OF THE UNITED STATES, AND THE MINGOES, CHIEFS, CAPTAINS AND WARRIORS OF THE CHOCTAW NATION.

WHEREAS THE GENERAL Assembly of the State of Mississippi has extended the laws of said State to persons and property within the chartered limits of the same, and the President of the United States has said that he cannot protect the Choctaw people from the operation of these laws; Now therefore that the Choctaw may live under their own laws in peace with the United States and the State of Mississippi they have determined to sell their lands east of the Mississippi and have accordingly agreed to the following articles of treaty.*

ARTICLE I

Perpetual peace and friendship is pledged and agreed upon by and between the United States and the Mingoes, Chiefs, and Warriors of the Choctaw Nation of Red People; and that this may be considered the Treaty existing between the parties all other Treaties heretofore existing and inconsistent with the provisions of this are hereby declared null and void.

*This paragraph was not ratified by the United States Senate.

ARTICLE II

The United States under a grant specially to be made by the President of the U.S. shall cause to be conveyed to the Choctaw Nation a tract of country west of the Mississippi River, in fee simple to them and their descendants, to inure them while they shall exist as a nation and live on it, beginning near Fort Smith where the Arkansas boundary crosses the Arkansas River, running thence to the source of the Canadian fork; if in the limits of the United States, or to those limits; thence due south to Red River, and down Red River to the west boundary of the Territory of Arkansas; thence north along that line to the beginning. The boundary of the same to be agreeably to the Treaty made and concluded at Washington City in the year 1825. The grant to be executed so soon as the present Treaty shall be ratified.

ARTICLE III

In consideration of the provisions contained in the several articles of this Treaty, the Choctaw nation of Indians consent and hereby cede to the United States, the entire country they own and posess, east of the Mississippi River, early as practicable, and will so arrange their removal, that as many as possible of their people not exceeding one half of the whole number, shall depart during the falls of 1831 and 1832; the residue to follow during the succeeding fall of 1833; a better opportunity in this manner will be afforded the Government, to extend to them the facilities and comforts which it is desirable should be extended in conveying them to their new homes.

ARTICLE IV

The Government and people of the United States are hereby obliged to secure to the said Choctaw Nation of Red People the jurisdiction and government of all the persons and property that may be within their limits west, so that no Territory or State shall ever have a right to pass laws for the government of the Choctaw Nation of Red People and their descendants; and that no part of the land granted them shall ever be embraced in any Territory or State; but the U.S. shall forever secure said Choctaw Nation from, and against, all laws except such as from time to time may be enacted in their own National Councils, not inconsistent with the Constitution, Treaties, and Laws of the United States; and except such as may, and which have been enacted by Congress, to the extent that Congress under the Constitution are required to exercise a legislation over Indian Affairs. But the Choctaws, should this Treaty be ratified, express a wish that Congress may grant to the Choctaws the right of punishing by their own laws, any white man who shall come into their nation, and infringe any of their national regulations.

ARTICLE V

The United States are obliged to protect the Choctaws from domestic strife and from foreign enemies on the same principles that the citizens of the United States are protected, so that whatever would be a legal demand upon the U.S. for the defence or for wrongs committed by an enemy, on a citizen of the U.S. shall be equally binding in favour of the Choctaws, and in all cases where the Choctaws shall be called upon by a legally authorized officer of the U.S. to fight an enemy, such Choctaw shall receive the pay and other emoluments, which citizens of the U.S. receive in such cases, provided, no war shall be undertaken or prosecuted by said Choctaw Nation but by declaration made in full Council, and to be approved by the U.S. unless it be in self defence against an open rebellion or against an enemy marching into their country, in which cases they shall defend, until the U.S. are advised thereof.

ARTICLE VI

Should a Choctaw or any party of Choctaws commit acts of violence upon the person or property of a citizen of the U.S. or join any war party against any neighboring tribe of Indians, without the authority in the preceding article; and except to oppose an actual or threatened invasion or rebellion, such person so offending shall be delivered up to an officer of the U.S. if in the power of the Choctaw Nation, then said Choctaw Nation shall not be held responsible for the injury done by said offender.

ARTICLE VII

All acts of violence committed upon persons and property of the people of the Choctaw Nation either by citizens of the U.S. or neighboring Tribes of Red People, shall be referred to some authorized Agent by him to be referred to the President of the U.S. who shall examine into such cases and see that every possible degree of justice is done by said Indian party of the Choctaw Nation.

ARTICLE VIII

Offenders against the laws of the U.S. or any individual State shall be apprehended and delivered to any duly authorized person where such offender may be found in the Choctaw country, having fled from any part of U.S. but in all such cases application must be made to the Agent or Chiefs and the expense of his apprehension and delivery provided for and paid by the U. States.

ARTICLE IX

Any citizen of the U.S. who may be ordered from the Nation by the Agent and constituted authorities of the Nation refusing to obey or return into the Nation without the consent of the aforesaid persons, shall be subject to such pains and penalties as may be provided by the laws of the U.S. in such cases. Citizens of the U.S. traveling peaceable under the authority of the laws of the U.S. shall be under the care and protection of the nation.

ARTICLE X

No person shall expose goods or other article for sale as a trader, without a written permit from the constituted authorities of the Nation, or authority of the laws of the Congress of the U.S. under penalty of forfeiting the Articles, and the constituted authorities of the Nation shall grant no license except to such persons as reside in the Nation and are answerable to the laws of the Nation. The U.S. shall be particularly obliged to assist to prevent ardent spirits from being introduced into the Nation.

ARTICLE XI

Navigable streams shall be free to the Choctaws who shall pay no higher toll or duty than citizens of the U.S. It is agreed further that the U.S. shall establish one or more Post Offices in said Nation, and may establish such military post roads, and posts, as they may consider necessary.

ARTICLE XII

All intruders shall be removed from the Choctaw Nation and kept without it. Private property to be always respected and on no occasion taken for public purposes without just compensation being made therefor to the rightful owner. If an Indian unlawfully take or steal any property from a white man a citizen of the U.S. the offender shall be punished. And if a white man unlawfully take or steal any thing from an Indian, the property shall be restored and the offender shall be punished. It is further agreed that when a Choctaw shall be given up to be tried for any offense against the laws of the U.S. if unable to employ counsel to defend him, the U.S. will do it, that his trial may be fair and impartial.

ARTICLE XIII

It is consented that a qualified Agent shall be appointed for the Choctaws every four years, unless sooner removed by the President; and he shall be removed on petition of the constituted authorities of the Nation, the President being satisfied there is sufficient cause shown. The Agent shall fix his residence convenient to the great body of the people; and in the selection of an Agent immediately after the ratification of this Treaty, the wishes of the Choctaw Nation on the subject shall be entitled to great respect.

ARTICLE XIV

Each Choctaw head of a family being desirous to remain and become a citizen of the States, shall be permitted to do so, by signifying his intention to the Agent within six months from the ratification of this Treaty, and he or she shall thereupon be entitled to a reservation of one section of six hundred and forty acres of land, to be bounded by sectional lines of survey; in like manner shall be entitled to one half that quantity for each unmarried child which is living with him over ten years of age; and a quarter section to such child as may be under 10 years of age, to adjoin the location of the parent. If they reside upon said lands intending to become citizens of the States for five years after the ratification of this Treaty, in that case a grant in fee simple shall issue; said reservation shall include the present improvement of the head of the family, or a portion of it. Persons who claim under this article shall not lose the privilege of a Choctaw citizen, but if they ever remove are not to be entitled to any portion of the Choctaw annuity.

ARTICLE XV

To each of the Chiefs in the Choctaw Nation (to wit) Greenwood Laflore, Nutackachie, and Mushulatubbe there is granted a reservation of four sections of land, two of which shall include and adjoin their present improvement, and the other two located where they please but on unoccupied unimproved lands, such sections shall be bounded by sectional lines, and with the consent of the President they may sell the same. Also to the three principal Chiefs and to their successors in office there shall be paid two hundred and fifty dollars annually while they shall continue in their respective offices, except to Mushulatubbe, who as he has an annuity of one hundred and fifty dollars for life under a former treaty, shall receive only the additional sum of one hundred dollars, while he shall continue in office as Chief; and if in addition to this the Nation shall think proper to elect an additional principal Chief of the whole to superintend and govern upon republican principles he shall receive annually for his services five hundred dollars, which allowance to the Chiefs and their successors in office, shall continue for twenty years. At any time when in military service, and while in service by authority of the U.S. the district Chiefs under and by selection of the President shall be entitled to the pay of Majors; the other Chief under the same circumstances shall have the pay of the Lieutenant Colonel. The Speakers of the three districts, shall receive twenty-five dollars a year for four years each; and the three secretaries, one to each of the Chiefs, fifty dollars each for four years. Each Captain of the Nation, the number not to exceed ninety-nine, thirty-three from each district, shall be furnished upon removing to the West, with each a good suit of clothes and a broad sword as an outfit, and for four years commencing with the first of their removal, shall each receive fifty dollars a year, for the trouble of keeping their people at order in settling; and whenever they shall be in military service by authority of the U.S. shall receive the pay of a Captain.

ARTICLE XVI

In wagons; and with steam boats as may be found necessary—the U.S. agree to remove the Indians to their new homes at their expense and under the care of discreet and careful persons, who will be kind and brotherly to them. They agree to furnish them with ample corn and beef, or pork for themselves and families for twelve months after reaching their new homes.

It is agreed further that the U.S. will take all their cattle, at the valuation of some discreet person to be appointed by the President, and the same shall be paid for in money after their arrival at their new homes; or other cattle such as may be desired shall be furnished them, notice being given through their Agent of their wishes upon this subject before their removal that time to supply the demand may be afforded.

ARTICLE XVII

The several annuities and sums secured under former Treaties to the Choctaw nation and people shall continue as though this Treaty had never been made.

And it is further agreed that the U.S. in addition will pay the sum of twenty thousand dollars for twenty years, commencing after their removal to the West, of which in the first year after their removal, ten thousand dollars shall be divided and arranged to such as may not receive reservations under this Treaty.

ARTICLE XVIII

The U.S. shall cause the lands hereby ceded to be surveyed; and surveyors may enter the Choctaw Country for that purpose, conducting themselves properly and disturbing or interrupting none of the Choctaw people. But no person is to be permitted to settle within the nation, or the lands to be sold before the Choctaws shall remove. And for the payment of the several amounts securred in this Treaty, the lands hereby ceded are to remain a fund pledged to that purpose, until the debt shall be provided for and arranged. And further it is agreed, that in the construction of this Treaty wherever well founded doubt shall arise, it shall be construed most favourably towards the Choctaws.

ARTICLE XIX

The following reservations of land are hereby admitted. To Colonel David Fulsom four sections of which two shall include his present improvement, and two may be located elsewhere, on unoccupied, unimproved land.

To I. Garland, Colonel Robert Cole, Tuppanahomer, John Pitchlynn, Charles Juzan, Johokebetubbe, Eaychahobia, Ofehoma, two sections, each to include their improvements, and to be bounded by sectional lines, and the same may be disposed of and sold with the consent of the President. And that others not provided for, may be provided for, there shall be reserved as follows:

First. One section to each head of a family not exceeding forty in number, who during the present year, may have had in actual cultivation, with a dwelling house thereon fifty acres or more. Secondly, three quarter sections after the manner aforesaid to each head of a family not exceeding four hundred and sixty, as shall have cultivated thirty acres and less than fifty, to be bounded by quarter section lines of survey, and to be contiguous and adjoining.

Third: One half section as aforesaid to those who shall have cultivated from twenty to thirty acres the number not to exceed four hundred. Fourth: a quarter section as aforesaid to such as shall have cultivated from twelve to twenty acres, the number not to exceed three hundred and fifty, and one half that quantity to such as shall have cultivated from two to twelve acres, the number also not to exceed three hundred and fifty persons. Each of said class of cases shall be subject to the limitations contained in the first class, and shall be so located as to include that part of the improvement which contains the dwelling house. If a greater number shall be found to be entitled to reservations under the several classes of this article, than is stipulated for under the limitation prescribed, then and in that case the Chiefs separately or together shall determine the persons who shall be excluded in the respective districts.

Fifth; Any Captain the number not exceeding ninety persons, who under the provisions of this article shall receive less than a section, he shall be entitled, to an additional quantity of half a section adjoining to his other reservation. The several reservations secured under this article, may be sold with the consent of the President of the U.S. but should any prefer it, or omit to take a reservation for the quantity he may be entitled to, the U.S. will on his removing pay fifty cents an acre, after reaching their new homes, provided that before the first of January next they shall adduce to the Agent, or some other authorized person to be appointed, proof of his claim and the quantity of it. Sixth: Likewise children of the Choctaw Nation residing in the Nation, who have neither father nor mother a list of which, with satisfactory proof of Parentage and orphanage being filed with Agent in six months to be forwarded to the War Department, shall be entitled to a quarter section of Land, to be located under the direction of the President, and with his consent the same may be sold and the proceeds applied to some beneficial purpose for the benefit of said orphans.

ARTICLE XX

The U.S. agree and stipulate as follows, that for the benefit and advantage of the Choctaw people, and to improve their condition, there shall be educated under the direction of the President and at the expense of the U.S. forty Choctaw youths for twenty years. This number shall be kept at school, and as they finish their education others, to supply their places, shall be received for the period stated. The U.S. agree also to erect a Council House for the Nation at some convenient central point, after their people shall be settled; and a House for each Chief, also a Church for each of the three Districts, to be used also as school houses, until the Nation may conclude to build others; and for these purposes ten thousand dollars shall be appropriated; also fifty thousand dollars (viz.) twenty-five hundred dollars annually shall be given for the support of three teachers of schools for twenty years. Likewise there shall be furnished to the Nation, three Blacksmiths one for each district for sixteen years, and a qualified Mill Wright for five years; Also there shall be furnished the following articles, twenty-one hundred blankets, to each warrior who emigrates a rifle, moulds, wipers and ammunition. One thousand axes, ploughs, hoes, wheels and carts each; and four hundred looms. There shall also be furnished, one ton of iron and two hundred weight of steel annually to each District for sixteen years.

ARTICLE XXI

A few Choctaw Warriors yet survive who marched and fought in the army with General Wayne, the whole number stated not to exceed twenty.

These it is agreed shall hereafter, while they live, receive twenty-five dollars a year; a list of them to be early as practicable, and within six months, made out, and presented to the Agent, to be forwarded to the War Department.

ARTICLE XXII

The Chiefs of the Choctaws who have suggested that their people are in a state of rapid advancement in education and refinement, and have expressed a solicitude that they might have the privilege of a Delegate on the floor of the House of Representatives extended to them. The Commissioners do not feel that they can under a treaty stipulation accede to request, but at their desire, present it in the Treaty, that Congress may consider of, and decide the application.

Done, and signed, and executed by the Commissioners of the United States, and the Chiefs, Captains and Head Men of the Choctaw Nation at Dancing Rabbit Creek, this 27th day of September, eighteen hundred and thirty.

JNO. H. EATON,
JNO. COFFEE.

GREENWOOD LEFLORE,
MUSHOLATUBBEE,
NITTUCACHEE,
EYARHOCUTTUBBEE,
IYACHERHOPIA,
OFFAHOOMAH,
ARCHALATER,
ONNAHUBBEE,
HOLARTERHOOMAH,
HOPIAUNCHAHUBBEE,
ZISHOMINGO,
CAPTAINHALKE,
JAMES SHEILD,
PISTIYUBBEE,
PISTIYUBBEE,
YOBALARUNEHAHUBBEE,
HOLUBBEE,
ROBERT COLE,
MOKELAREHARHOPIN,
LEWIS PERRY,
ARTONAMARSTUBBEE,
HOPEATUBBEE,
HOSHAHOOMAH,
CHUALLAHOOMAH,
JOSEPH KINCADE,
ARTOOKLUBBETUSHPAR,
METUBBEE,
ARSARKATUBBEE,
ISSATERHOOMAH,
CHOHTAHMATAHAH,
TUNNUPPASHUBBEE,

HOSHHOPIA,
WARSHARSHAHOPIA,
MAARSHUNCHAHUBBEE,
MISHARYUBBEE,
DANIEL MCCURTAIN,
TUSHKERHARCHO,
HOKTOONTUBBEE,
NUKNACRAHOOKMARHEE,
MINGO HOOMAH,
PININHOCUTTUBBEE,
TULLARHACHEE,
LITTLE LEADER,
MAANHUTTER,
COWEHOOMAH,
TILLAMOER,
IMNULLACHA,
ARTOPILACHUBBEE,
SHUPHERUNCHAHUBBEE,
NITTERHOOMAH,
OAKLARYUBBEE,
PUKUMNA,
APPALAR,
HOLBER,
HOPARMINGO,
ISPARHOOMAH,
TIEBERHOOMAO,
TISHOHOLARTER,
MAHAYCHUBBEE,
ARLARTER,
NITTAHUBBEE,
TISHONOUAN,

OKECCHARYER,
WARSHARCHAHOOMAH,
ISAAC JAMES,
HOPIAINTUSHKER,
ARYOSHKERMER,
SHEMOTAR,
HOPIAISKETINA,
THOMAS LEFLORE,
ARNOKECHATUBBEE
JOHN MCKELBERY,
SHOKEPEBUKNA,
POSHERHOOMAH,
ROBERT FOLSOM,
ARHARYOTUBBEE,
TISHOWAKAYO,
JAMES VAUGHAN,
JAMES KARNES,
TISHOHAKUBBEE,
NARLANALAR,
PAEEAHA,
INHARYYARKER,
MOTUBBEE,
NARHARYUBBEE,
ISHMARYTUBBEE,
JAMES MCKING,
LEWIS WILSON,
ISHTONARKERHARCHO,
HOINSHAMARHER,
KINSULACHUBBEE,
EMARHINSTUBBEE,
GYSALNDALRA, B.M.,
THOMAS WALL,
SAM. S. WORCHESTER,
JACOB FOLSOM,
ONTIOERHARCHO,
HUGH A. FOSTER,
PIERRE JUZAR,
JNO. PITSHLYNN,
DAVID FOLSOM,
SHOLOHOMMASTUBE,
TESHO,
LAUWECHUBBEE,
HOSHEHAMMO,
OFENOWO,
AHEKOCHE,
KALOSHOUBE,
ATOKO,
EMTHTOHABE,
SILAS D. FISHER,

PHIPLIP,
MESHAMEYE,
ISHETEHEKA,
HESHOHOMME,
BENJAMIN JAMES,
TIKBACHAHAMBE,
AHOLIKTUBE,
WALKING WOLF,
JOHN WAIDE,
BIG AXE,
BOB,
TUSHKACHABBEE,
ITTABE,
ITTABE,
CUSHONOLARTER,
FOLEHOMMO,
JOHN GARLAND,
KOSHONA,
ISHELOHAMUBE,
OKLANOWA,
NETO,
JAMES FLETCHER,
SILUS D. PITCHLYNN,
WILLIAM TRAHORN,
TOSHKAHEMMITTO,
TETHETAYO,
EMOKLOSHAHOPIE,
TISHOIMITO,
THOMAS W. FOSTER,
ZADOC BRASHEARS,
LEVI PERKINS,
ISAAC PERRY,
HIRAM KING,
OGLA ENLAH,
NULTAHTUBBEE,
TUSKA HOLLATTUH,
PANSHASTUBBEE,
P.P. PITSHLYM,
JOEL H. NAIL,
HOPIA STONAKEY,
KOCHOOMMA,
WILLIAM WADE,
PANSHSTICHUBBEE,
HOLITTANKCHAHUBBEE,
KOTHOANTCHAHUBBEE,
EYARPULUBBEE,
OKENTAHUBBEE,
JOHN JONES,
CHARLES JONES,

ISAAC FOLSOM,
HERATUBE,
HAKSECHE,
JERRY CARNEY,
JOHN WASHINGTON.

HOCKLUCHA,
HOCHLUCHA,
MUSCOGEE,
EDEN NELSON,

IN PRESENCE OF

E. BREATHITT, Secretary to the Commissioners, WILLIAM E. WARD, Agent for Choctaws, JOHN PITCHLYNN, United States Interpreter, M. MACHEY, United States Interpreter, GEO. S. GAINED, of Alabama, R.P. CURRIN, LUKE HOWARD, SAM. S. WORCESTER, JNO. N. BYRN, JOHN BELL, JNO. BOND.

SUPPLEMENTARY ARTICLES

I

Various Choctaw persons have been presented by the Chiefs of the nation, with a desire that they might be provided for. Being particularly deserving, an earnestness has been manifested that provision might be made for them. It is therefore by the undersigned commissioners here assented to, with the understanding that they are to have no interest in the reservations which are directed and provided for under the general Treaty to which this is a supplement.

As evidence of the liberal and kind feelings of the President and Government of the United States the Commissioners agree to the request as follows, (to wit) Pierre Juzan, Peter Pitchlynn, G.W. Harkins, Jack Pitchlynn, Isreal Fulsom, Louis Laflore, Benjamin James, Joel H. Nail, Hopoynjahubbee, Onorkubbee, Benjamin Laflore, Michael Laflore, and Allen Yates and wife shall be entitled to a reservation of two sections of land each to include their improvement where they at present reside, with the exception of the three first named persons and Benjamin Laflore, who are authorized to locate one of their sections on any other unimproved and unoccupied land, within their respective districts.

II

And to each of the following persons there is allowed a reservation of a section and a half of land, (to wit) James L. McDonald, Robert Jones, Noah Wall, James Campbell, G. Nelson, Vaughn Brashears, R. Harris, Little Leader, S. Foster, J. Vaughn, L. Durans, Samuel Long, T. Magagha, Thos. Everge, Giles Thompson, Tomas Garland, John Bond, William Laflore, and Turner Brashears, the two first named persons, may locate one section each, and one section jointly on any unimproved and unoccupied land, these not residing in the Nation; The others are to include their present residence and improvement.

Also one section is allowed to the following persons (to wit) Middleton Mackey, Wesley Train, Choclehomo, Moses Foster, D.W. Wall, Charles Scott, Molly Nail, Susan Colbert, who was formerly Susan James, Samuel Garland, Silas Fisher, D. McCurtain, Oaklahoma, and Polly Fillecuthey, to be located in the entire sections to include their present residence and improvement, with the exception of Molly Nail and Susan Colbert, who are authorized to locate theirs on any unimproved unoccupied land.

John Pitchlynn has long and faithfully served the Nation in character of U. States Interpreter, he has acted as such for forty years, in consideration it is agreed, in addition to what has been done for him there shall be granted to two of his children, (to wit) Silas Pitchlynn and Thomas Pitchlynn one section of land each, to adjoin the location of their father; likewise to James Madison and Peter sons of Mushulatubbee, one section of land each to include the old house and improvement where their father formerly lived on the old military road adjoining a large Prerarie.

And to Henry Groves son of the Chief Natticavhe there is one section of land given to adjoin his father's land.

And to each of the following persons half a section of land is granted on any unoccupied and unimproved lands in the Districts where they respectively live (to wit) Willis Harkins, James D. Hamilton, William Juzan, Tobias Laflore, JoDoke, Jacob Fulsom, P. Hays, Samuel Worcester, George Hunter, William Train, Robert Nail and Alexander McKee.

And there is given a quarter section of land each to Delila and her five fatherless children, she being a Choctaw woman residing out of the nation; also the same quantity to Peggy Trihan, another Indian woman residing out of the nation and her two fatherless children; and to the Widows of Pushmilaha, and Pucktshenubbee, who were formerly distinguished Chiefs of the nation and for their children four quarter sections of land, each in trust for themselves and their children.

All of said last mentioned reservations are to be located under and by direction of the President of the U. States.

III

The Choctaw people now that they have ceded their lands are solicitous to get their new homes early as possible and accordingly they wish that a party may be permitted to proceed this fall to ascertain whereabouts will be most advantageous for their people to be located.

It is therefore agreed that three or four persons (from each of the three districts) under the guidance of some discreet and well qualified persons may proceed during this fall to the West upon an examination of the country.

For their time and expenses the U. States agree to allow the said twelve persons two dollars a day each, not to exceed one hundred days which is deemed to be ample time to make an examination.

IV

John Donly of Alabama, who has several Choctaw grandchildren, and who for twenty years has carried the mail through the Choctaw Nation, a desire by the Chiefs is expressed that he may have a section of land, it is accordingly granted, to be located in one entire section, on any unimproved and unoccupied land.

Allen Glover and George S. Gaines licensed Traders in the Choctaw Nation, have accounts amounting to upwards of nine thousand dollars against the Indians who are unable to pay their said debts without distress against the families; a desire is expressed by the Chiefs that two sections of land be set apart to be sold and the proceeds thereof to be applied toward the payment of the aforesaid debts. It is agreed that two sections of any unimproved and unoccupied land be granted to George S. Gaines who will sell the same for the best price he can obtain and apply the proceeds thereof to the credit of the Indians on their account due to the before mentioned Glover and Gaines; and shall make application to the poorest Indian first.

At the earnest and particular request of the Chief Greenwood Laflore there is granted to David Haley one half section of land to be located in a half section on any unoccupied and unimproved land as a compensation, for a journey to Washington City with dispatches to the Government and returning others to the Choctaw Nation.

The foregoing is entered into, as supplemental to the treaty concluded yesterday.

Done at Dancing Rabbit Creek the 28th day of September 1830.
JNO. H. EATON,
JNO. COFFEE.

GREENWOOD LEFLORE,   HOPIAUNCHAHUBBE,
NITTUCACHEE,   DAVID FOLSOM,
MUSHOLATUBBEE,   JOHN GARLAND,
IFAHOOMAH,   HOPIAHOOMAH,
EYARHOEUTTUBBEE,   CAPTAINHALKO,
IYAEHERHOPIA,   PIERRE JUZAN,
HOLUBBEE,   IMMARSTARHER,
ONARHUBBEE,   HOSHIMAMARTAR,
ROBERT COLE.

IN PRESENCE OF

E. BREATHITT, Secty. to Coms. W. WARD, Agt. for Choctaws, M. MACKEY, U.S. Intr,
JOHN PITCHLYNN, U.S. Intr., R.P. CURRIN, JNO. W. BYRN, GEO. S. GAMES.

TREATY WITH THE CHEROKEES

The perfidy displayed by the government of the United States and its Chief Executive, Andrew
Jackson, is a matter of historic fact. The story of the defense through the courts by the
Cherokee people for their right to remain on their lands, the illegal treaty signed by a few
unauthorized Cherokee sell-outs, the cruel forced removal of the people from their homes,
and the infamous "Trail of Tears" is one of the darkest stains in the pages of American
history. Over 4,000 lives were lost during this ordeal.

Treaty with the Cherokees
New Echota, Georgia
December 29, 1835

BETWEEN GENERAL WILLIAM CARROL AND JOHN F. SCHERMERHORN COM-
MISSIONERS ON THE PART OF THE UNITED STATES AND THE CHIEFS HEAD
MEN AND PEOPLE OF THE CHEROKEE TRIBE OF INDIANS.

WHEREAS THE CHEROKEE are anxious to make some arrangements with the Government
of the United States whereby the difficulties they have experienced by a residence within the
settled parts of the United States under the jurisdiction and laws of the State Governments
may be terminated and adjusted; and with a view to reuniting their people in one body and
securing a permanent home for themselves and their posterity in the country selected by their
forefathers without the territorial limits of the State sovereignties, and where they can
establish and enjoy a government of their choice and perpetuate such a state of society as may
be most consonant with their views, habits and condition; and as may tend to their individual
comfort and their advancement in civilization.

And whereas a delegation of the Cherokee nation composed of Messrs. John Ross Richard
Taylor Danl. McCoy Samuel Gunter and William Rogers with full power and authority to
conclude a treaty with the United States did on the 28th day of February 1835 stipulate and

agree with the Government of the United States to submit to the Senate to fix the amount which should be allowed the Cherokees for their claims and for a cession of their lands east of the Mississippi river, and did agree to abide by the award of the Senate of the United States themselves and to recommend the same to their people for their final determination.

And whereas on such submission the Senate advised "that a sum not exceeding five millions of dollars be paid to the Cherokee Indians for all their lands and possessions east of the Mississippi river."

And whereas this delegation after said award of the Senate had been made, were called upon to submit propositions as to its disposition to be arranged in a treaty which they refuse to do, but insisted that the same "should be referred to their nation and there in general council to deliberate and determine on the subject in order to ensure harmony and good feeling among themselves."

And whereas a certain other delegation composed of John Ridge Elias Boudinot Archilla Smith S.W. Bell John West Wm. A. Davis and Ezekiel West, who represented that portion of the nation in favor of emigration to the Cherokee country west of the Mississippi entered into propositions for a treaty with John F. Schermerhorn commissioner on the part of the United States which were to be submitted to their nation for their final action and determination:

And whereas the Cherokee people, at their last October council at Red Clay, fully authorized and empowered a delegation or committee of twenty persons of their nation to enter into and conclude a treaty with the United States commissioner then present, at that place or elsewhere and as the people had good reason to believe that a treaty would then and there be made or at a subsequent council at New Echota which the commissioners it was well known and understood, were authorized and instructed to convene for said purpose; and since the said delegation have gone to Washington city, with a view to close negotiations there, as stated by them notwithstanding they were officially informed by the United States commissioner that they would not be received by the President of the United States and that they would transact no business of this nature with them, and that if a treaty was made it must be done in the nation, where the delegation at Washington last winter urged it would be done for the purpose of promoting peace and harmony among the people; and since these facts have also been corroborated to us by a communication recently received by the commissioner from the Government of the United States and read and explained to the people in open council and therefore believing said delegation can effect nothing and since our difficulties are daily increasing and our situation is rendered more and more precarious uncertain and insecure in consequence of the legislation of the States; and seeing no effectual way of relief, but in accepting the liberal overtures of the United States.

And whereas Genl. William Carrol and John F. Schermerhorn were appointed commissioners on the part of the United States, with full power and authority to conclude a treaty with the Cherokees east and were directed by the President to convene the people of the nation in general council at New Echota and to submit said propositions to them with power and authority to vary the same so as to meet the views of the Cherokees in reference to its details.

And whereas the said commissioners did appoint and notify a general council of the nation convene at New Echota on the 21st day of December 1835; and informed them that the commissioners would be prepared to make a treaty with the Cherokee people who should assemble there and those who did not come they should be transacted at this council and the people having met in council according to said notice.

Therefore the following articles of a treaty are agreed upon and concluded between William Carrol and John F. Schermerhorn commissioners on the part of the United States and the Chiefs and head men and people of the Cherokee nation in general council assembled this 29th day of Dec. 1835.

ARTICLE I

The Cherokee nation hereby cede relinquish and convey to the United States all the lands owned claimed or possessed by them east of the Mississippi river, and hereby release all their claims upon the United States for spoliations of every kind for and in consideration of the sum of five millions of dollars to be expended, paid and invested in the manner stipulated and agreed upon in the following articles. But as a question has arisen between the commissioners and the Cherokees whether the Senate in their resolution by which they advised "that a sum not exceeding five millions of dollars be paid to the Cherokee Indians for all their lands and possessions east of the Mississippi river" have included and made any allowance or consideration for claims for spoliations it is therefore agreed on the part of the United States that this question shall be again submitted to the Senate for their consideration and decision and if no allowance was made for spoliations that then an additional sum of three hundred thousand dollars be allowed for the same.

ARTICLE II

Whereas by the treaty of May 6th 1828 and the supplementary treaty thereto of February 14th 1833 with the Cherokees west of the Mississippi the United States guaranteed and secured to be conveyed by patent, to the Cherokee nation of Indians the following tract of country "Beginning at a point on the old western territorial line of Arkansas Territory being twenty-five miles north from the point where the territorial line crosses Arkansas river, thence running from said north point south on the said territorial line crosses the Verdigris river, thence down said Verdigris river to the Arkansas river; thence down said Arkansas to a point where a stone is placed opposite the east or lower bank of Grand river at its junction with the Arkansas; thence running south forty-four degrees west one mile; thence in a straight line to a point four miles northerly, from the mouth of the north fork of the Canadian; thence along the said four mile line to the Canadian; thence down the Canadian to the Arkansas; thence down the Arkansas to that point on the Arkansas where the eastern Choctaw boundary strikes said river and running thence with the western line of Arkansas Territory as now defined, to the southwest corner of Missouri; thence along the western Missouri line to the land assigned the Senecas thence on the south line of the Senecas to Grand river; thence up said Grand river as far as the south line of the Osage reservation, extended if necessary; thence up and between said south Osage line extended west if necessary, and a line drawn due west from the point of beginning to a certain distance west, at which a line running north and south from said due west line will make seven millions of acres within the whole described boundaries. In addition to the seven millions acres of land thus provided for and bounded, the United States further guarantee to the Cherokee nation a perpetual outlet west, and a free and unmolested use of all the country west of the western boundary of said seven millions of acres, as far west as the sovereignty of the United States and their right of soil extended:

Provided however: That if the saline or salt plain on the western prairie shall fall within said limits prescribed for said outlet, the right is reserved to the United States to permit other tribes of red men to get salt on said plain in common with the Cherokees; And letters patent shall be issued by the United States as soon as practicable for the land hereby guaranteed."

And whereas it is apprehended by the Cherokees that in the above cession there is not contained a sufficient quantity of land for the accommodation of the whole nation on their removal west of the Mississippi the United States in consideration of the sum of five hundred thousand dollars therefore hereby covenant and agree to convey to the said Indians, and their decendants by patent, in fee simple the following additional tract of land situated between the west line of the State of Missouri and the Osage reservation beginning at the southeast corner of the same and runs north along the east line of the Osage lines fifty miles to the northeast corner thereof; and thence east to the west line of the State of Missouri; thence with said line south fifty miles; whence west to the place of beginning; estimated to contain eight hundred thousand acres of land; but it is expressly understood that if any of the lands assigned the Quapaws shall fall within the aforesaid bounds the same shall be reserved and excepted out of the lands above granted and a pro rata reduction shall be made in the price to be allowed to the United States for the same by the Cherokees.

ARTICLE III

The United States also agree that the lands above ceded by the treaty of February 14, 1833, including the outlet, and those ceded by this treaty shall all be included in one patent executed to the Cherokee nation of Indians by the President of the United States according to the provisions of the act of May 28, 1830. It is however, agreed that the military reservation at Fort Gibson shall be held by the United States. But should the United States abandon said post and have no further use for the same it shall revert to the Cherokee nation. The United States shall always have the right to make and establish such post and military roads and forts in any part of the Cherokee country, as they may deem proper for the interest and protection of the same and the free use of as much land, timber, fuel and materials of all kinds for construction and support of the same as may be necessary; provided that if the private rights of individuals are interfered with, a just compensation therefor shall be made.

ARTICLE IV

The United States also stipulate and agree to extinguish for the benefit of the Cherokees the titles to the reservations within their country made in the Osage treaty of 1825 to certain half-breeds and for this purpose they hereby agree to pay to the persons to whom the same belong or have been assigned or to their agents or guardians whenever they shall execute after the ratification of this treaty a satisfactory conveyance for the same, to the United States, the sum of fifteen thousand dollars according to a schedule accompanying this treaty of the relative value of the several reservations.

And whereas by the several treaties between the United States and the Osage Indians the Union and Harmony Missionary reservations which were established for their benefit are now situated within the country ceded by them to the United States; the former being situated in the Cherokee country and the latter in the State of Missouri. It is therefore agreed that the United States shall pay the American Board of Commissioners for Foreign Missions for the improvements on the same what they shall be appraised at by Capt. Geo. Vashon Cherokee sub-agent Abraham Redfield and A.P. Chouteau or such persons as the President of the United States shall appoint and the money allowed for the same shall be expended in schools among the Osages and improving their condition. It is understood that the United States are to pay the amount allowed for the reservations in this article and not the Cherokees.

ARTICLE V

The United States hereby covenant and agree that the lands ceded to the Cherokee nation in the foregoing article shall, in no future time without their consent, be included within the territorial limits or jurisdiction of any State or Territory. But they shall secure to the Cherokee nation the right by their national councils to make and carry into effect all such laws as they may deem necessary for the government and protection of the persons and property within their own country belonging to their people or such persons as have connected themselves with them: provided always that they shall not be inconsistent with the constitution of the United States and such acts of Congress as have been or may be passed regulating trade and intercourse with the Indians; and also, that they shall not be considered as extending to such citizens and army of the United States as may travel or reside in the Indian country by permission according to the laws and regulations established by the Government of the same.

ARTICLE VI

Perpetual peace and friendship shall exist between the citizens of the United States and the Cherokee Indians. The United States agree to protect the Cherokee nation from domestic strife and foreign enemies and against intestine wars between the several tribes. The Cherokees shall endeavor to preserve and maintain the peace of the country and not make war upon their neighbors they shall also be protected against interruption and intrusion from citizens of the United States, who may attempt to settle in the country without their consent; and all such persons shall be removed from the same by order of the President of the United States. But this is not intended to prevent the residence among them of useful farmers mechanics and teachers for the instruction of Indians according to treaty stipulations.

ARTICLE VII

The Cherokee nation having already made great progress in civilization and deeming it important that every proper and laudable inducement should be offered to their people to improve their conditions as well as to guard and secure in the most effectual manner the rights guaranteed to them in this treaty, and with a view to illustrate the liberal and enlarged policy of the Government of the United States towards the Indians in their removal beyond the territorial limits of the States, it is stipulated that they shall be entitled to a delegate in the House of Representatives of the United States whenever Congress shall make provision for the same.

ARTICLE VIII

The United States also agree and stipulate to remove the Cherokees to their new homes and to subsist them one year after their arrival there and that a sufficient number of steamboats and baggage-wagons shall be furnished to remove them comfortably, and so as not to endanger their health, and that a physician well supplied with medicines shall accompany each detachment of emigrants removed by the Government. Such persons and families as in the opinion of the emigrating agent are capable of subsisting and removing themselves shall be permitted to do so; and they shall be allowed in full for all claims for the same twenty dollars for each member of their family; and in lieu of their one year's rations they shall be paid the sum of thirty-three dollars and thirty-three cents if they prefer it.

Such Cherokees also as reside at present out of the nation and shall remove with them in two years west of the Mississippi shall be entitled to allowance for removal and subsistence as above provided.

ARTICLE IX

The United States agree to appoint suitable agents who shall make a just and fair valuation of all such improvements now in the possession of the Cherokees as add any value to the lands; and also of the ferries from which they have been dispossessed in a lawless manner or under any existing laws of the State where the same may be situated.

The just debts of the Indians shall be paid out of any monies due them for their improvements and claims; and they shall also be furnished at the discretion of the President of the United States with a sufficient sum to enable them to obtain the necessary means to remove themselves to their new homes, and the balance of their dues shall be paid them at the Cherokee agency west of the Mississippi. The missionary establishments shall also be valued and appraised in a like manner and the amount of them paid over by the United States to the treasurers of the respective missionary societies by whom they have been established and improved in order to enable them to erect such buildings and make such improvements among the Cherokees west of the Mississippi as they may deem necessary for their benefit. Such teachers at present among the Cherokees as this council shall select and designate shall be removed west of the Mississippi with the Cherokee nation and on the same terms allowed to them.

ARTICLE X

The President of the United States shall invest in some safe and most productive public stocks of the country for the benefit of the whole Cherokee nation who have removed or shall remove to the lands assigned by this treaty to the Cherokee nation west of the Mississippi the following sums as a permanent fund for the purposes hereinafter specified and pay over the net income of the same annually to such person or persons as shall be authorized or appointed by the Cherokee nation to receive the same and their receipt shall be a full discharge for the amount paid to them viz: the sum of two hundred thousand dollars in addition to the present annuities of the nation to constitute a general fund the interest of which shall be applied annually by the council of the nation to such purposes as they may deem best for the general interest of their people. The sum of fifty thousand dollars to constitute an orphans' fund the annual income of which shall be expended towards the support and education of such orphan children as are destitute of the means of subsistence. The sum of one hundred and fifty thousand dollars in addition to the present school fund of the nation shall constitute a permanent school fund, the interest shall be applied annually by the council of the nation for the support of common schools and such literary institution of a higher order as may be established in the Indian country. And in order to secure as far as possible the true and beneficial application of the orphans' and school fund the council of the Cherokee nation when required by the President of the United States shall make a report of the application of those funds and he shall at all times have the right if the funds have been misapplied to correct any abuses of them and direct the manner of their application for the purposes for which they were intended. The council of the nation may by giving two years' notice of their intention withdraw their funds by and with the consent of the president and the Senate of the United States, and invest them in such manner as they may deem most proper for their interest. The United States also agree and stipulate to pay the just debts and claims against the Cherokee nation held by the citizens of the same and also the just claims of citizens of the United States for services rendered to the nation and the sum against individual persons of the nation shall be allowed and paid by the nation. The sum of three hundred thousand dollars is hereby set apart to pay spoliations of every kind, that have not been already satisfied under former treaties.

ARTICLE XI

The Cherokee nation of Indians believing it will be for the interest of their people to have all their funds and annuities under their own direction and future disposition hereby agree to commute their permanent annuity of ten thousand dollars for the sum of two hundred and fourteen thousand dollars, the same to be invested by the President of the United States as a part of the general fund of the nation; and their present school fund amounting to about fifty thousand dollars shall constitute a part of the permanent school fund of the nation.

ARTICLE XII

Those individuals and families of the Cherokee nation that are averse to a removal to the Cherokee country west of the Mississippi and are desirous to become citizens of the States where they reside and such as are qualified to take care of themselves and their property shall be entitled to receive their due portion of all the personal benefits accuring under this treaty for their claims, improvements and per capita; as soon as appropriation is made for this treaty.

Such heads of Cherokee families as are desirous to reside within the States of No. Carolina Tennessee and Alabama subject to the laws of the same; and who are qualified or calculated to become useful citizens shall be entitled, on the certificate of the commissioners to a pre-emption right to one hundred and sixty acres of land or one quarter section at the minimum Congress price; so as to include the present buildings or improvements of those who now reside there and such as do not live there at present shall be permitted to locate within two years any lands not already occupied by persons entitled to pre-emption privilege under this treaty and if two or more families live on the same quarter section and they desire to continue their residence in these States and are qualified as above specified they shall on receiving their pre-emption certificate be entitled to the right of pre-emption to such lands as they may select not already taken by any person entitled to them under this treaty.

It is stipulated and agreed between the United States and the Cherokee people that John Ross James Starr George Hicks John Gunter George Chambers John Ridge Elias Boudinot George Sanders John Martin William Rogers Roman Nose Situake and John Thimpson shall be a committee on the part of the Cherokees to recommend such persons for the privilege of pre-emption rights as may be deemed entitled to the same under the above articles and to select the missionaries who shall be removed with the nation; and that they be hereby fully empoorer and authorized to transact all business on the part of the Indians which may arise in carrying into effect the provisions of this treaty and settling the same with the United States. If any of the persons above mentioned should decline acting or be removed by death; the vacancies shall be filled by the committee themselves.

It is also understood and agreed that the sum of one hundred thousand dollars shall be expended by the commissioners in such manner as the committee deem best for the benefit of the poorer class of Cherokees as shall remove west and are entitled to the same benefits of this treaty. The same to be delivered at the Cherokee agency west as soon after the removal of the nation as possible.

ARTICLE XIII

In order to make a final settlement of all the claims of the Cherokees for reservations granted under former treaties to any individuals belonging to the nation by the United States it is therefore hereby stipulated and agreed and expressly understood by the parties to this treaty—that all the Cherokees and their heirs and descendants to whom any reservations have been made under any former treaties with the United States, and who have not sold or conveyed the same by deed or otherwise and who in the opinion of the commissioners have complied with the terms on which the reservations were granted as far as practicable in the several cases; and which reservations have been sold by the United States shall constitute a just claim against the United States and the original reservee or their heirs or descendants shall be entitled to receive the present value thereof from the United States as unimproved lands. And all such reservations as have not been sold by the United States and where the terms on which reservations were made in the opinion of the commissioners have been complied with as far as practicable, they or their heirs or descendants shall be entitled to the same. They are hereby granted and confirmed to them—and also all persons who were entitled to reservations under the treaty of 1817 and who as far as practicable in the opinion of the commissioners, have complied with the stipulations of said treaty, although by the treaty of 1819 such reservations were included in the unceded lands belonging to the Cherokee nation are hereby confirmed to them and they shall be entitled to receive a grant for the same. All such reservees as were obliged by the laws of the States in which their reservations were situated, to abandon the same or purchase them from the States shall be deemed to have a just claim against the United States for the amount by them paid to the States with interest thereon for such reservations and if obliged to abandon the same, to the present value of such reservations as unimproved lands but in all cases where the reservees have sold their reservations or any part thereof and conveyed the same by deed or otherwise and have been paid for the same, they their heirs or descendants or their assigns shall not be considered as having any claims upon the United States under this article of the treaty nor be entitled to receive any compensation for the lands thus disposed of. It is expressly understood by the parties to this treaty that the amount be allowed for reservations under this article shall not be deducted out of the consideration money allowed to the Cherokees for their claims for spoliations and the cession of their lands; but the same is to be paid for independently by the United States as it is only a just fulfillment of the former treaty stipulations.

ARTICLE XIV

It is also agreed on the part of the United States that such warriors of the Cherokee nation as were engaged on the side of the United States in the late war with Great Britain and the southern tribes of Indians, and who were wounded in such service shall be entitled to such pensions as shall be allowed them by the Congress of the United States to commence from the period of their disability.

ARTICLE XV

It is expressly understood and agreed between the parties to this treaty that after deducting the amount which shall be actually expended for the payment for improvements, ferries, claims, for spoliations, removal subsistence and debts and claims upon the Cherokee nation and for the additional quantity of lands and goods for the poorer class of Cherokees and the several sums to be invested for the general national funds; provided for in the several articles of this treaty the balance whatever the same may be shall be equally divided between all the people belonging to the Cherokee nation east according to the census just completed; and such Cherokees as have removed west since June 1833 who are entitled by the terms of their enrollment and removal to all the benefits resulting from the final treaty between the United States and the Cherokee east as shall be paid for their improvements according to their improvements and value before their removal where fraud has not already been shown in their valuation.

ARTICLE XVI

It is hereby stipulated and agreed by the Cherokees that they shall remove to their new homes within two years from the ratification of this treaty and that during such time the United States shall protect and defend them in their possessions and property and free use and occupation of the same and such persons as have been dispossessed of their improvements and houses; and for which no grant has actually issued previously to the enactment of the law of the State of Georgia, of December 1835 to regulate Indian occupancy shall be again put in possession and placed in the same situation and condition, in reference to the laws of the State of Georgia, as the people are left unprotected, then the United States shall pay the several Cherokees for their losses and damages sustained at New Echota for which no grant has been actually made previous to the passage of the above recited act if not occupied by the Cherokee people shall be reserved for the purpose of settling and closing all the Indian business arising under this treaty between the commissioners of claims and the Indians.

The United States, and the several States interested in the Cherokee lands, shall immediately proceed to survey the lands ceded by this treaty; but it is expressly agreed and understood between the parties that the agency buildings and that tract of land surveyed and laid off for the use of Colonel R. J. Meigs Indian agent or heretofore enjoyed and occupied by his successors in office shall continue subject to the use and occupancy of the United States, or such agent as may be engaged specially superintending the removal of the tribe.

ARTICLE XVII

All the claims arising under or provided for in the several articles of this treaty, shall be examined and adjucated by Gen. Wm. Carrol and John F. Schermerhorn or by such commissioners as shall be appointed by the President of the United States for that purpose and their decision shall be final and on their certificate of the ammount due the several claimants they shall be paid by the United States. All stipulations in former treaties which have not been superseded or annulled by this shall continue in full force and virtue.

ARTICLE XVIII

Whereas in consequence of the unsettled affairs of the Cherokee people and the early frosts, their crops are insufficient to support their families and great distress is likely to ensue and whereas the nation will not, until after their removal be able to advantageously to expend the income of the permanent funds of the nation it is therefore agreed that the annuities of the nation which may incrue under this treaty for two years, the time fixed for their removal shall be expended in provision and clothing for the benefit of the poorer class of the nation; and the United States hereby agree to advance the same for that purpose as soon after the ratification of this treaty as an appropriation for the same shall be made. It is however not intended in this article to interfere with that part of the annuities due the Cherokees west by the treaty of 1819.

ARTICLE XIX

This treaty after the same shall be ratified by the President and Senate of the United States shall be obligatory on the contracting parties.

In testimony whereof the commissioners and the chiefs head men and people whose names are hereunto annexed being duly authorized by the people in general council assembled have affixed their hands and seals for themselves and in behalf of the Cherokee nation.

I have examined the foregoing treaty and although not present when it was made, I approve this generally, and therefore sign it.

WM. CARROL,
J. F. SCHERMERHORN.

MAJOR RIDGE,	TE-GAH-E-SHE,
JAMES FOSTER,	ROBERT ROGERS,
TESA-TA-ESKY,	JOHN GUNTER,
CHARLES MOORE,	JOHN A. BELL,
GEORGE CHAMBERS,	CHARLES F. FOREMAN,
TAH-YESKE,	WILLIAM ROGERS,

ARCHILLA SMITH,
ANDREW ROSS,
WILLIAM LASSLEY,
CAE-TE-HEE,

GEORGE W. ADAIR,
ELIAS BOUDINOUT,
JAMES STARR,
JESSE HALF-BREED.

SIGNED AND SEALED IN PRESENCE OF

WESTERN B. THOMAS, Secry., BEN F. CURRY, Special Agent, M. WOLFE BATEMAN, 1st lt. 6th U.S.A. inf., DISBG. AGENT JNO. L. HOOPER, lt. 4th inf. C.M. HITCHCOCK, M.D. Assist, Surg., U.S.A., G.W. CURREY, WM. H. UNDERWOOD, CORNELIUS D. TERHUNE, JOHN W.H. UNDERWOOD.

ADDITIONAL ARTICLE
XX

The United States do also hereby guarantee the payment of all unpaid just claims upon the Indians without expense to them, out of the proper funds of the United States, for the settlement of which a cession or cessions of land has or have been heretofore made by the Indians, in Georgia. Provided the United States or the State of Georgia has derived benefit from the said cession or cessions of land without having made payment to the Indians therefor. It is hereby however further agreed and understood that if the Senate of the United States disapprove of this article it may be rejected without impairing any other provision of this treaty, or affecting the Indians in any manner whatever.

A. MCCOY,
W.B. THOMAS.

In compliance with the unanimous request of the Committee of the Cherokee nation in general council assembled, it is consented and agreed by the commissioner on the part of the United States that the foregoing shall be added as a supplemental article to the treaty under the express condition and stipulation that if the President or Senate of the United States disapprove of this article it may be rejected without impairing any other provision of this treaty, or affecting the Indians in any manner whatever.

J. F. SCHERMERHORN.

Whereas the western Cherokees have appointed a delegation to visit the eastern Cherokees to assure them of the friendly disposition of their people and their desire that the nation should again be united as one people and to urge upon them the expediency of accepting the overtures of the Government; and that, on their removal they may be assured of a hearty welcome and an equal participation with them in all the benefits and privileges of the Cherokee country west and the undersigned two of said delegation being the only delegates in the eastern nation from the west at the signing and sealing of the treaty lately concluded at new Echota between their eastern brethren and the United States; and having fully understood the provisions of the same they agree to it in behalf of the western Cherokees. But it is expressly understood that nothing in this treaty shall affect any claims of the western Cherokees on the United States.

   In testimony whereof, we have, this 31st day of December, 1835, hereunto set our hands and seals.

JAMES ROGERS,
JOHN SMITH.
Delegates from the western Cherokees.

SUPPLEMENTARY ARTICLES

CONCLUDED AT NEW ECHOTA, GEORGIA, DECEMBER 29, 1835, BETWEEN THE UNITED STATES AND CHEROKEE PEOPLE.

Whereas the undersigned were authorized at the general meeting of the Cherokee people held at New Echota as above stated, to make and assent to such alterations in the preceding treaty as might be thought necessary, and whereas the President of the United States has expressed his determination not to allow any pre-emptions or reservations his desire being that the whole Cherokee people should remove together and establish themselves in the country provided for them west of the Mississippi river.

I

It is therefore agreed that all the pre-emption rights and reservations provided for in articles 12 and 13 shall be and are hereby relinquished and declared void.

II

Whereas the Cherokee people have supposed that the sum of five millions of dollars fixed by the Senate in their resolution of—day of March, 1835, as the value of the Cherokee lands and possessions east of the Mississippi river was not intended to include the amount which may be required to remove them, nor the value of certain claims which may be required to remove against citizens of the United States, which suggestion has been confirmed by the opinion of the War Department by some of the Senators who voted upon the question and whereas the President is willing that this subject should include the objects herein specified that in that case such further provision should be made therefor as might appear to the Senate to be just.

III

It is therefore agreed that the sum of six hundred thousand dollars shall be and the same is hereby allowed to the Cherokee people to include the expense of their removal, and all claims of every nature and description against the Government of the United States not herein otherwise expressly provided for, and to be in lieu of the said reservations and pre-emptions and of the sum of three hundred thousand dollars for spoliations described in the 1st article of the above-mentioned treaty. This sum of six hundred thousand dollars shall be applied and distributed agreeably to the provisions of the said treaty, and any surplus which may remain after removal and payment of the claims so ascertained shall be turned over and belong to the education fund.

But it is expressly understood that the subject of this article is merely referred hereby to the considerations of the Senate and if they shall approve the same then this supplement shall remain part of the treaty.

IV

It is also understood that the provisions in article 16, for the agency reservation is not intended to interfere with the occupant right of any Cherokees should their improvement fall within the same.

It is also understood and agreed, that the one hundred thousand dollars appropriated in article 12 for the poorer class of Cherokees and intended as a set-off to the pre-emption rights shall now be transferred from the funds of the nation and added to the general national fund of four hundred thousand dollars so as to make said fund equal to five hundred thousand dollars.

V

The necessary expenses attending the negotiation of the aforesaid treaty and supplemental and also of such persons of the delegation as may sign the same shall be defrayed by the United States.

In testimony whereof John F. Schermerhorn, commissioner on the part of the United States, and the undersigned delegation have hereunto set their hands seals, this first day of March, in the year one thousand eight hundred and thirty-six.

J.F. SCHMERHORN.

MAJOR RIDGE,	JOHN A BELL,
JAMES FOSTER,	JOS. A FOREMAN,
TAH-YE-SKE,	ROBERT SANDERS,
LONG SHELL TURTLE,	ELIAS BOUDINOUT,
JOHN FIELDS,	JOHNSON ROGERS,
JAMES FIELDS,	JAMES STARR,
GEORGE WELCH,	STAND WATIE,
ANDREW ROSS,	JOHN RIDGE,
WILLIAM ROGERS,	JAMES ROGERS,
JOHN GUNTER,	JOHN SMITH.

WITNESSES

ELBERT HERRING. THOS. GLASCOCK. ALEXANDER H. EVERETT. JNO. GARLAND, MAJR. UNITED STATES OF AMERICA C.A. HARRIS JOHN ROBB. WM. Y. HANSELL. SAML. J. POTTS. JNO. LITLE. S. ROCHWELL.

TREATY WITH THE SIOUX

This treaty between the United States and the various bands of the great Sioux Nation was a product of many years of fighting on the Northern Plains. Although a number of battles had been won by the Indians in the 100 years of fighting the colonists and United States military forces, this was the first time the Indians had won a war and dictated the peace terms. The "peace" established by this treaty, however, only lasted about eight years. As soon as gold was discovered in the sacred Black Hills, all obligations and responsibilities of the federal government were promptly ignored. This breach of the Fort Laramie Treaty brought on the most ferocious fighting yet experienced in the "Indian Wars." It led to a number of historically significant conflicts, the most famous of which was the Battle of Little Big Horn.

Treaty of Fort Laramie
April 29, 1868

ARTICLE I

From this day forward all war between the parties to this agreement shall forever cease. The Government of the United States desires peace, and its honor is hereby pledged to keep it. The Indians desire peace, and they now pledge their honor to maintain it.

If bad men among the whites, or among other people subject to the authority of the United States, shall commit any wrong upon the person or property of the Indians, the United States will, upon proof made to the agent and forwarded to the Commissioner of Indian Affairs at

Washington City, proceed at once to cause the offender to be arrested and punished according to the laws of the United States, and also re-imburse the injured person for the loss sustained.

If bad men among the Indians shall commit a wrong or depredation upon the person or property of any one, white, black, or Indian, subject to the authority of the United States, and at peace with the Indians herein named solemnly agree that they will, upon proof made to their agent that is noticed by him, deliver up the wrong-doer to the United States, to be tried and punished according to the United States, to be tried and punished according to its laws; and in case they wilfully refuse to do so, the person injured shall be re-imbursed for his loss from the annuities or other moneys due to them under this or other treaties made with the United States. And the President, on advising with the Commissioner of Indian Affairs, shall prescribe such rules and regulations for ascertaining damages under the provisions of this article as in his judgement may be proper. But no one sustaining loss while violating the provisions of this treaty or the laws of the United States shall be re-imbursed therefor.

ARTICLE II

The United States agrees that the following district of country to wit, viz: commencing on the east bank of the Missouri River where the forty-sixth parallel of north latitude crosses the same, thence along low-water mark down said east bank to a point opposite where the northern line of the State of Nebraska to the one hundred and fourth degree of longitude west from Greenwich, thence north on said meridian to a point where the forty-sixth parallel of north latitude intercepts the same, thence due east along said parallel to the place of beginning; and in addition thereto, all existing reservations on the east bank of said river shall be, and the same is, set apart for the absolute and undisturbed use and occupation of the Indians herein named, and for such other friendly tribes or individual Indians as from time to time they may be willing, with the consent of the United States now solemnly agrees that no persons except those herein designated and authorized to do so, and except such officers, agents, and employees of the Government as may be authorized to enter upon Indian reservations in discharge of duties enjoined by law, shall ever be permitted to pass over, settle upon, or reside in the territory described in this article, or in such territory as may be added to this reservation for the use of said Indians, and henceforth they will and do hereby relinquish all claims or right in and to any portion of the United States or Territories, except such as is embraced within the limits aforesaid, and except as hereinafter provided.

ARTICLE III

If it should appear from actual survey or other satisfactory examination of said tract of land that it contains less than one hundred and sixty acres of tillable land for each person who, at the time, may be authorized to reside on it under the provisions of this treaty, and a very considerable number of such persons shall be disposed to commence cultivating the soil as farmers, the United States agrees to set apart, for the use of said Indians, as herein provided, such additional quantity of arable land, adjoining to said reservation, or as may be required to provide the necessary amount.

ARTICLE IV

The United States agrees, at its own proper expense, to construct at some place on the Missouri River, near the center of said reservation, where timber and water may be convenient, the following buildings, to wit: a warehouse, a store-room for the use of the agent in storing goods belonging to the Indians, to cost not exceeding twenty-five hundred dollars; also a school-house or mission building, so soon as a sufficient number of children can be induced by the agent to attend school, which shall not cost exceeding five thousand dollars.

The United States agrees further to cause to be erected on said reservation, near the other buildings herein authorized, a good steam circular-saw mill, with a grist-mill and shingle-machine attached to the same, to cost not exceeding eight thousand dollars.

ARTICLE V

The United States agrees that the agent for said Indians shall in the future make his home at the agency-building; that he shall reside among them, and keep an office open at all times for the purpose of prompt and diligent inquiry into such matters of complaint by and against the Indians as may be presented for investigation under the provisions of their treaty stipulations, as also for the faithful discharge of other duties enjoined on him by law. In all cases of depredation on person or property he shall cause the evidence to be taken in writing and forwarded, together with his findings to the Commissioner of Indian Affairs, whose decision, subject to the revision of the Secretary of the Interior, shall be binding on the parties to this treaty.

ARTICLE VI

If any individual belonging to said tribes of Indians, or legally incorporated with them, being the head of a family, shall desire to commence farming, he shall have the privilege of selecting in the presence and with the assistance of the agent then in charge, a tract of land within said reservation, not exceeding three hundred and twenty acres in extent, which tract, when so selected certified and recorded in the "land book" as herein directed shall cease to be held in common, but the same may be occupied and held in the exclusive possession of the person selecting it, and of his family so long as he or they may continue to cultivate it.

Any person over eighteen years of age, not being the head of a family, may in like him or her, for purposes of cultivation, a quantity of land not exceeding eighty acres in extent, and thereupon be entitled to the exclusive possession of the same as above directed.

For each tract of land so selected a certificate, containing a description thereof and the name of the person selecting it, with a certificate endorsed thereon that the same has been recorded, shall be delivered to the party entitled to it, by the agent, after the same shall have been recorded by him in a book to be kept in his office, subject to inspection, which said book shall be known as the "Sioux Land-Book."

The President may, at any time, order a survey of the reservation, and when so surveyed, Congress shall provide for protecting the rights of said settlers in their improvements and may fix the character of the title held by each. The United States may pass such laws on the subject of alienation and descent of property between the Indians and their descendants as may be thought proper. And it is further stipulated that any male Indians, over eighteen years of age of any band or tribe that is or shall hereafter become party to this treaty, who is now or who shall hereafter become a resident or occupant of any reservation or Territory not included in the tract of country designated and described in this treaty for in permanent home of the Indians, which is not mineral land, nor reserved by the United States for special purposes other than Indian occupation, and who shall have made improvements thereon of the value of two hundred dollars or more, and continuously occupied the same as a homestead for the term of three years, shall be entitled to receive from the United States a patent for one hundred and sixty acres of land including his said improvements the same to be in the form of the legal subdivisions of the surveys of the public lands. Upon application in writing sustained by the proof of two disinterested witnesses, and made to the register of the local land office when the land sought to be entered is within a land district, and when the tract sought to be entered is not in any land district then upon said application and proof being made to the Commissioner of the General Land-Office, and the right of such Indian or Indians to enter such tract or tracts of land shall accrue and be perfect from the date of his first improvements, and no longer. And any Indian or Indians receiving a patent for land under the foregoing provisions, shall thereby and from thenceforth become and be a citizen of the United States, and be entitled to all the privileges and immunities of such citizens, and shall, at the same time, retain all his rights to benefits accruing to Indians under this treaty.

ARTICLE VII

In order to insure the civilization of the Indian entering into this treaty, the necessity of education is admitted, especially of such of them as are or may be settled on said agricultural reservations, and they therefore pledge themselves to compel their children, male and female, between the ages of six and sixteen years, to attend school; and it is hereby made the duty of the agent for said Indians to see that this stipulation is strictly complied with; and the United States agrees that for every thirty children between said ages who can be induced or compelled to attend school, a house shall be provided and a teacher competent to teach the elementary branches of an English education shall be furnished, who will reside among said Indians, and faithfully discharge his or her duties as a teacher. The provisions of this article to continue for not less than twenty years.

ARTICLE VIII

When the head of a family or lodge shall have selected lands and received his certificate as above directed and the agent shall be satisfied that he intends in good faith to commence cultivating the soil for a living, he shall be entitled to receive seeds and agricultural implements for the first year, not exceeding in value one hundred dollars, and for each succeeding year he shall continue to farm, for a period of three years or more, he shall be entitled to receive seeds and implements as aforesaid, not exceeding in value of twenty-five dollars.

And it is further stipulated that such persons as commence farming herein provided for, and whenever more than one hundred persons shall enter upon the cultivation of the soil, a second blacksmith shall be provided, with such iron, steel, and other material as may be needed.

ARTICLE IX

At any time after ten years from the making of this treaty, the United States shall have the privilege of withdrawing the physician, farmer, blacksmith, carpenter, engineer, and miller herein provided for, but in case of such withdrawal, an additional sum thereafter of ten thousand dollars per annum shall be devoted to the education of said Indians, and the Commissioner of Indian Affairs shall, upon careful inquiry into their condition, make such rules and regulations for the expenditure of said sum as will best promote the educational and moral improvements of said tribe.

ARTICLE X

In lieu of all sums of money or other annuities provided to be paid to the Indians herein named, under any treaty or treaties heretofore made, the United States agrees to deliver at the agency-house on the reservation therein named, on or before the first day of August of each year, for thirty years, the following articles, to wit:

For each male person over fourteen years of age, a suit of good substantial woolen clothing, consisting of a coat, pantaloons, flannel shirt, hat and a pair of home-made socks.

For each female over twelve years of age, a flannel skirt, or the goods necessary to make it, a pair of woolen hose, twelve yards of calico, and twelve yards of cotton domestics.

For the boys and girls under the ages named, such flannel and cotton goods as may be needed to make each a suit as aforesaid, together with a pair of woolen hose for each.

And in order that the Commissioner of Indian Affairs may be able to estimate properly for the articles herein named, it shall be the duty of the agent each year to forward to him a full and exact census of the Indians, on which the estimate from year to year can be based.

And in addition to the clothing herein named, the sum of ten dollars for each person entitled to the beneficial effects of this treaty shall be annually appropriated for a period of thirty years, while such persons roam and hunt, and twenty dollars for each person who engages in farming, to be used by the Secretary of the Interior in the purchase of such articles as from time to time the condition and necessities of the Indians may indicate to be proper. And if it is within thirty years, at any time, it shall appear that the amount of money needed for clothing under this article can be appropriated to better uses for the Indians named herein, Congress may by law, change the appropriation to other purposes; but in no event shall the amount of this appropriation be withdrawn or discontinued for the period named. And the President shall annually detail an officer of the Army to be present and attest the delivery of all the goods herein named to the Indians and he shall inspect and report on the quantity and quality of the goods and the manner of their delivery. And it is hereby expressly stipulated that each Indian over the age of four years, who shall have removed to and settled permanently upon said reservation and complied with the stipulations of this treaty, shall be entitled to receive from the United States, for the period of four years after he shall have settled upon said reservation, one pound of flour per day, provided the Indians cannot furnish their own subsistence at an earlier date. And it is further stipulated that the United States will furnish and deliver to each lodge of Indians or family of persons legally incorporated with them, who shall remove to the reservations herein described and commence farming, one good American cow, and one well-broken pair of oxen within sixty days after such lodge or family shall have so settled upon said reservation.

ARTICLE XI

In consideration of the advantages and benefits conferred by this treaty, and the many pledges of friendship by the United States, the tribes who are parties to this agreement hereby stipulate that they will relinquish all right to occupancy permanently the territory outside their reservation as herein defined, but yet reserve the right to hunt on any lands north of North Platte, and on the Republican Fork of the Smoky Hill River, so long as the buffalo may range thereon in such numbers as to justify the chase. And they, the said Indians, further expressly agree:

1st. That they will withdraw all opposition to the construction of the railroads now being built on the plains.

2nd. That they will permit the peaceful construction of any railroad not passing over their reservation as herein defined.

3rd. That they will not attack any persons at home, or traveling, nor molest or disturb any wagon-trains, coaches, mules, or cattle belonging to the people of the United States, or to persons friendly therewith.

4th. They will never capture or carry off from the settlements, white women or children.

5th. They will never kill or scalp white men, nor attempt to do them harm.

6th. They withdraw all pretense of opposition to the construction of the railroad now being built along the Platte River and westward to the Pacific Ocean, and they will not in future object to the construction of railroads, wagon roads, mail-stations, or other works of utility or necessity, which may be ordered or permitted by the laws of the United States, but should such roads or other works be constructed on the lands of their reservation, the Government will pay the tribe whatever amount of damage may be assessed by three disinterested commissioners to be appointed by the President for that purpose, one of said commissioners to be a chief or head-man of the tribe.

7th. They agree to withdraw all opposition to the military posts or roads now established south of the North Platte River, or that may be established, not in violation of treaties heretofore made or hereafter to be made with any of the Indian tribes.

ARTICLE XII

No treaty for the cession of any portion or part of the reservation herein described which may be held in common shall be of any validity or force as against the said Indians, unless executed and signed by at least three-fourths of all the adult male Indians, occupying or interested in the same; and no cession by the tribe shall be understood or construed in such manner as to deprive, without his consent, any individual member of the tribe of his rights to any tract of land selected by him, as provided in article 6 of this treaty.

ARTICLE XIII

The United States hereby agrees to furnish annually to the Indians the physician, teachers, carpenter, miller, engineer, farmer, and blacksmiths as herein contemplated, and that such appropriations shall be made from time to time, on the estimated of the Secretary of the Interior, as will be sufficient to employ such persons.

ARTICLE XIV

It is agreed that the sum of five hundred dollars annually, for three years from date, shall be expended in presents to the ten persons of said tribe who in the judgement of the agent may grow in the most valuable crops for the respective year.

ARTICLE XV

The Indians herein named agree that when the agency-house or other buildings shall be constructed on the reservation named, they will regard said reservation their permanent home, and they will make no permanent settlement elsewhere; but they shall have the right, subject to the conditions and modifications of this treaty, to hunt, as stipulated in Article 11 hereof.

ARTICLE XVI

The United States hereby agrees and stipulates that the country north of the North Platte River and east of the summits of the Big Horn Mountains shall be held and considered to be unceded Indian territory, and also stipulated and agrees that no white person or persons shall be permitted to settle upon or occupy any portion of the same; or without the consent of the Indians first had and obtained, to pass through the same, and it is further agreed by the United States that within ninety days after the conclusion of peace with all the bands of the Sioux Nation, the military posts now established in the territory in this article named shall be abandoned and that the road leading to them and by them to the settlements of the Territory of Montana shall be closed.

ARTICLE XVII

It is hereby expressly understood and agreed by and between the respective parties to this treaty that the execution of this treaty and that ratification by the United States Senate shall have the effect, and shall be construed as abrogating and annulling all treaties and agreements heretofore entered into between the respective parties hereto, so far as such treaties and agreements obligate the United States to furnish and provide money, clothing, or other articles of property to such Indians and bands of Indians as become parties to this treaty, but no further.

In testimony of all which, we, the said commissioners, and we, the chiefs and headmen of the Brule band of the Sioux nation, have hereunto set our hands and seals at Fort Laramie, Dakota Territory, this twenty-ninth day of April, in the year one thousand eight hundred and sixty-eight.

N. G. Taylor,
W. T. Sherman, Lieutenant-General
Wm. S. Harney, Brevet Major-General U.S. Army,
John Sanborn,
S. F. Tappan,
C. C. Augur, Brevet Major-General
Alfred H. Terry, Brevet Major-General U. S. Army.

Executed on the part of the Brule band of Sioux, by the Ogallahlah band of Sioux, by Minneconjon band of Sioux, by the Uncpapa band of Sioux, by the Blackfeet band of Sioux, by the chiefs and headmen, they being thereunto duly authorized, at Fort Laramie, D. T., the twenty-ninth day of April, in the year A. D. 1868.

TREATY WITH THE NAVAJO

With the outbreak of the Civil War, the Navajo began to increase their raiding. With no U.S. troops to contain them, they wreaked havoc on the white settlers and stepped up their sorties into the Pueblos. General James H. Carleton, military commander of the New Mexico Territory, sent Kit Carson, who was serving as a colonel in the territorial militia, to subdue the Navajo.

As the U.S. troops began harassing the Navajo, they withdrew to Canyon de Chelley, where they were impossible to dislodge by military deployment. Carson burned the Navajo crops and destroyed their orchards. He finally starved the Indians into surrender and marched them to Fort Sumner, where they were held prisoner for four years.

The Navajo finally were permitted to return home under the provisions of a treaty.

Treaty with the Navajo
Fort Sumner, New Mexico Territory
June 1, 1868

ARTICLE I

FROM THIS DAY forward all war between the parties to this agreement shall forever cease. The Government of the United States desires peace, and its honor is hereby pledged to keep it. The Indians desire peace, and they now pledge their honor to keep it.

If bad men among the whites, or among other people subject to the authority of the United States, shall commit any wrong upon the person or property of the Indians, the United States will, upon proof made to the agent and forwarded to the Commissioner of Indian Affairs at Washington City, proceed at once to cause the offender to be arrested and punished according to the laws of the United States, and also to reimburse the injured persons for the loss sustained.

If bad men among the Indians shall commit a wrong or depredation upon the person or property of any one, white, black, or Indian, subject to the authority of the United States, and at peace therewith, the Navajo tribe agree that they will, on proof made to their agent, and on notice by him, deliver up the wrongdoer to the United States, to be tried and punished according to its laws; and in case they wilfully refuse to do so, the person injured shall be reimbursed for his loss from the annuities of other moneys due or to become due them under this treaty, or any others that may be made with the United States. And the President may prescribe such rules and regulations for ascertaining damages under this article as in his judgement may be proper; but no such damage shall be adjusted and paid until examined and passed upon by the Commissioner of Indian Affairs, and no one sustaining loss whilst violating, or because of his violating, the provisions of this treaty or the laws of the United States shall be reimbursed therefor.

ARTICLE II

The United States agrees that the following district of country to wit: bounded on the north by the 37th degree of north latitude, south by an east and west line passing through the site of old Fort Defiance, in Canon Bonito, east by the parallel of longitude which if prolonged south, would pass through old Fort Lyon, or the Ojo-de-oso, Bear Spring, and west by a parallel of longitude about 109 30 west of Greenwich, provided it embraces the outlet of the Canon-de-Chelly, which canon is to be all included in this reservation, shall be, and the same is hereby, set apart for the use and occupation of the Navajo tribe of Indians, and for such other friendly tribes or individual Indians as from time to time they may be willing, with the consent of the United States, to admit among them; and the United States agrees that no persons except those herein so authorized to do, and except such officers, soldiers, agents, and employes of the Government, or of the Indians, as may be authorized to enter upon Indian reservations in discharge of duties imposed by law, or the orders of the President, shall ever be permitted to pass over, settle upon, or reside in, the territory described in this article.

ARTICLE III

The United States agrees to cause to be built, at some point within said reservation, where timber and water may be convenient, the following buildings; a warehouse, to cost not exceeding twenty-five hundred dollars; an agency building for the residence of the agent, not to cost exceeding three thousand dollars each; a carpenter shop and a blacksmith shop, not to cost exceeding one thousand dollars each; and a schoolhouse and chapel, so soon as sufficient number of children can be induced to attend school, which shall not cost to exceed five thousand dollars.

ARTICLE IV

The United States agrees that the agent for the Navajos shall make his home at the agency building; that he shall reside among them, and shall keep an office open at all times for the purpose of prompt and diligent inquiry into such matters of complaint by or against the Indians as may be presented for investigation, as also for the faithful discharge of other duties enjoined by law. In all cases of depredation on person or property he shall cause the evidence to be taken in writing and forwarded together with his finding, to the Commissioner of Indian Affairs, whose decision shall be binding on the parties to this treaty.

ARTICLE V

If any individual belonging to said tribe, or legally incorporated with it, being the head of a family, shall desire to commence farming with the privilege to select, in the presence and with the assistance of the agent then in charge, a tract of land within said reservation, not exceeding one hundred and sixty acres in extent, which tract, when so selected, certified, and recorded in the "land-book" as herein described, shall cease to be held in common, but the same may be occupied and held in the exclusive possession of the person selecting it, and of his family, so long as he or they may continue to cultivate it.

Any person over eighteen years of age, not being head of a family may in like manner select and cause to be certified to him or her for purposes of cultivation, a quantity of land, not exceeding eighty acres in extent, and thereupon be entitled to the exclusive possession of the same as above directed.

For each tract of land so selected a certificate containing a description thereof, and the name of the person selecting it, with a certificate endorsed thereon, that the same has been recorded, shall be delivered to the party entitled to it by the agent, after the same shall have been recorded by him in a book to be kept in his office, subject to inspection, which said book shall be known as the "Navajo Land-Book."

The President may at any time order a survey of the reservation, and when so surveyed, Congress shall provide for protecting the rights of said settlers in their improvements, and may fix the character of the title held by each.

The United States may pass such laws on the subject of alienation and descent of property between the Indians and their descendants as may be thought proper.

ARTICLE VI

In order to insure the civilization of the Indians entering into this treaty, the necessity of education is admitted, especially of such of them as may be settled on said agricultural parts of this reservation, and they therefore pledge themselves to compel their children, male and female, between the ages of six and sixteen years, to attend school; and it is hereby made the duty of the agent for said Indians to see that this stipulation is strictly complied with; and the United States agrees that, for every thirty children between the ages who can be induced or compelled to attend school, a house shall be provided and a teacher competent to teach the elementary branches of English education shall be furnished who will reside among said Indians, and faithfully discharge his or her teaching duties.

The provision of this article to continue for not less than ten years.

ARTICLE VII

When the head of a family shall have selected lands and received his certificate of above directed, and the agent shall be satisfied that he intends in good faith to commence cultivating the soil for a living, he shall be entitled to receive seeds and agricultural implements for the first year, not exceeding value one hundred dollars, and for each succeeding year he shall continue to farm, for a period of two years, he shall be entitled to receive seeds and implements to the value of twenty-five dollars.

ARTICLE VIII

In lieu of all sums of money or other annuities provided to be paid to the Indians herein named under any treaty or treaties heretofore made, the United States herein named under the agreement to deliver at the agency-house on the reservation herein named, on the first day of September of each year for ten years, the following articles, to wit:

Such articles of clothing, goods, or raw materials in lieu thereof, as the agent may make his estimate for not exceeding in value of five dollars per Indian—each Indian being encouraged to manufacture their own clothing, blankets, &c; to be furnished with no article which they can manufacture themselves. And, in order that the Commissioner of Indian Affairs may be able to estimate properly for the articles herein named, it shall be the duty of the agent each year to forward to him full and exact census of the Indians on which estimate from year to year can be based.

And in addition to the articles herein named, the sum of ten dollars for each person entitled to the beneficial effects of this treaty shall be annually appropriated for a period of ten years, for each person who engages in farming or mechanical pursuits, to be used by the Commissioner of Indian Affairs in the purchase of such articles as from time to time the condition and necessities of the Indians may indicate to be proper and if within the ten years at any time it shall appear that the amount of money needed for clothing, under the article can be appropriated to better uses for the Indians named herein, the Commissioner of Indian Affairs may change the appropriation to other purposes, but in no event shall the amount of this appropriation be withdrawn or discontinued for the period named, provided they remain at peace. And the President shall annually detail an officer of the Army to be present and attest the delivery of all the goods herein named to the Indians, and he shall inspect and report on the quantity and quality of the goods and the manner of their delivery.

ARTICLE IX

In consideration of the advantages and benefits conferred by this treaty, and the many pledges of friendship by the United States, the tribes who are parties to this agreement hereby stipulate that they will relinquish all right to occupy any territory outside their reservations, as herein defined, but retain the right to hunt on any unoccupied lands contiguous to their reservation, so long as the large game may range thereon in such numbers as to justify the chase; and they, the said Indians, further expressly agree:

1st. That they will make no opposition to the construction of any railroads now being built or hereafter to be built across the continent.

2nd. That they will not interfere with the peaceful construction of any railroad not passing over their reservation as herein defined.

3d. That they will not attack any persons at home or traveling nor molest or disturb any wagon-trains, coaches, mules, or cattle belonging to the people of the United States, or to persons friendly therewith.

4th. That they will never capture or carry off from the settlements women or children.

5th. They will never kill or scalp white men, nor attempt to do them harm.

6th. They will not in future oppose the construction of railroads, wagonroads, mail stations, or other works of utility or necessity which may be ordered or permitted by the laws of the United States; but should such roads or other works be constructed on the lands of their reservation, the Government will pay the tribe whatever amount of damage may be assessed by three disinterested commissioners to be appointed by the President for that purpose, one of said commissioners to be a chief or head-man of the tribe.

7th. They will make no opposition to the military posts or roads now established, or that may be established, not in violation of treaties heretofore made or hereafter to be made with any of the Indian tribes.

ARTICLE X

No future treaty for the cession of any portion or part of the reservation herein described, which may be held in common, shall be of any validity or force against said Indians unless agreed to and executed by at least three-fourths of all the adult male Indians occupying or interested in the same; and no cession by the tribe shall be understood or construed in such manner as to deprive, without his consent, any individual member of the tribe of his rights to any tract of land selected by him as provided in article V of this treaty.

ARTICLE XI

The Navajos also hereby agree that at any time after the signing of these presents they will proceed in such manner as may be required of them by the agent, or by the officer in charge with their removal, to the reservation herein provided for, the United States paying for their subsistence en route, and providing a reasonable amount of transportation for the sick and feeble.

ARTICLE XII

It is further agreed by and between the parties to this agreement that the sum of one hundred and fifty thousand dollars appropriated or to be appropriated shall be disbursed as follows, subject to any condition provided in the law to wit:

1st. The actual cost of the removal of the tribe from the Bosque Redondo reservation to the reservation, say fifty thousand dollars.

2nd. The purchase of fifteen thousand sheep and goats, at a cost not to exceed thirty thousand dollars.

3rd. The purchase of five hundred beef cattle and a million pounds of corn, to be collected and held at the military post nearest the reservation, subject to the orders of the agent, for the relief of the needy during the coming winter.

4th. The balance, if any, of the appropriation to be invested for the maintenance of the Indians pending their removal, in such manner as the agent who is with them may determine.

5. The removal of this tribe to be made under the supreme control and direction of the military commander of the Territory of New Mexico, and when completed, the management of the tribe to revert to the proper agent.

ARTICLE XIII

The tribe herein named, by their representatives, parties to this treaty, agree to make the reservation herein described their permanent home, and they will not as a tribe make any permanent settlement elsewhere, reserving the right to hunt on the lands adjoining the said reservation formerly called theirs, subject to the modifications named in this treaty and the orders of the commander of the department in which said reservation may be for the time being, and it is further agreed and understood by the parties to this treaty, that if any Navajo Indian or Indians shall leave the reservation herein described to settle elsewhere, he or they shall forfeit all the rights, further agreed by the parties to this treaty, that they will do all they can to induce Indians now away from the reservations set apart for the exclusive use and occupation of the Indians, leading a nomadic life, or engaged in war against the people of the United States, to abandon such a life and settle permanently in one of the territorial reservations set apart for the exclusive use and occupation of the Indians.

In testimony of all which the said parties have hereunto, on this the first day of June, one thousand eight hundred and sixty-eight, at Fort Sumner, in the Territory of New Mexico, set their hands and seals.

W.T. SHERMAN,
LIEUTENANT–GENERAL, INDIAN PEACE COMMISSIONER.

BORBONCITO, CHIEF, HIS X MARK.
ARMIJO, HIS X MARK.
DELGADO.
MANUELITO, HIS X MARK.
LARGO, HIS X MARK.
HERRERO, HIS X MARK.
CHIQUETO, HIS X MARK.
MUERTO DE HOMBRE, HIS X MARK.
HOMBRO, HIS X MARK.
NORBONO, HIS X MARK.
NORBONO SEGUNDO, HIS X MARK.
GANADO MUCHO, HIS X MARK.
COUNCIL:
RIQUO, HIS X MARK.
JUAN MARTIN, HIS X MARK.

SERGINTO, HIS X MARK.
GRANDE, HIS X MARK.
INOETENITO, HIS X MARK.
MUCHACHOS MUCHO, HIS X MARK.
CHIQUETO SEGUNDO, HIS X MARK.
CABELLO AMARILLO, HIS X MARK.
FRANCISCO, HIS X MARK.
TORIVIO, HIS X MARK.
DESCENDADO, HIS X MARK.
JUAN, HIS X MARK.
GUERO, HIS X MARK.
GUGADORE, HIS X MARK.
GABASON, HIS X MARK.
BARBON SEGUNDO, HIS X MARK.
CABARES CABARES COLORADOS, HIS X MARK.

ATTEST:
GEO W.F. FETTY, COLONEL THIRTY-SEVENTH INFANTRY, BREVET MAJOR GENERAL U.S. ARMY. B.S. ROBERTS, BREVET BRIGADIER–GENERAL U.S. ARMY, LIEUTENANT–COLONEL THIRD CALVARY. J. COOPER MCKEE, BREVET LIEUTENANT–COLONEL, SURGEON U.S. ARMY. THEO. H. DODD, UNITED STATES INDIAN AGENT FOR NAVAJOS. CHAS. MCCLURE, BREVET MAJOR AND COMMISSARY OF SUBSISTENCE, US ARMY. JAMES F. WEEDS, BREVET MAJOR AND ASSISTANT SURGEON, U.S. ARMY. J.S. SUTHERLAND, INTERPRETER. WILLIAM VAUX, CHAPLAIN U.S. ARMY.

Index

277